Also by Paul Spike

Bad News

PHOTOGRAPHS
OF MY FATHER

PHOTOGRAPHS
OF MY FATHER

PAUL SPIKE

New York / ALFRED A. KNOPF / 1973

Library of Congress Cataloging in Publication Data
Spike, Paul, (date).
Photographs of my father.
Autobiographical.
1. Spike, Robert Warren. 2. Spike, Paul.
I. Title.
BX7260.S72A33 1973   323.4′092′4 [B]   72-11042
ISBN 0-394-47334-5

Manufactured in the United States of America

First Edition

Photographs on pages 23, 25, 59, 75, 79, 95, 140, 189, 200, 218, 219, 221, courtesy of Ken Thompson; page 73, courtesy of Religious News Service; page 216, courtesy of Wide World Photos; page 253, courtesy of Richard Howard.

Quotations on pages 35, 76, 94, from *The Freedom Revolution and the Churches* by Robert W. Spike, New York, 1965, © Association Press; on pages 183–4, 188, 229, 231, from *To Be a Man* by Robert W. Spike, New York, 1961, © Association Press—both by permission of Association Press. The passages on pages 5–8, 20–1, 24–5, 58–60, 77–80 are from a pamphlet, *Civil Rights Involvement, Model for Mission,* by Robert W. Spike, Detroit Industrial Mission, Detroit, Michigan, 1965.

Here. A photograph of a young man in ecstasy. It is my father. Handsome and skinny, twenty-three years old, he is holding me in his arms. Now twenty-three years have passed since the camera caught our image and froze it on the black film.

Try to grow up when everything is starting to fall down. A difficult thing to try.

But some things are easy. The arithmetic of father and son: addition, subtraction, addition. I was born. My father was murdered. I grew up.

A biography should be written about my father's life. That is not this book. I could never hope to give an "objective" picture of Rev. Dr. Robert W. Spike. Even his full title is difficult for me to put on paper. This book is a collection of pictures, family pictures, taken from years which stick in America's back like daggers. This book is an album of photographs: developed in his blood, printed on my flesh.

—1

HIGH SCHOOL

I am on my way to college. It is 1965, hot August, and I arrive in America. I have graduated from high school three months ago and spent the summer bumming around Europe. Nervous, I walk through the windowless halls of U.S. Customs wearing sandals, jeans and long hair. Each person's name is looked up against the names in a large book. Perhaps they will find "Spike" and suddenly whisk me off behind these concrete walls. I have done nothing wrong so of course I am safe. Looking forward to the long taxi ride into the heart of the city, through the shambles of Queens to the Triborough Bridge which lifts you up above the lizard's tongue of Manhattan, ablaze in fumes of soot. I don't trust these officials, my fellow Americans, in their gray shirts, polished chrome badges, stale coffee on their breaths, with their "duties" stamped right on the foggy plastic of their irises. I feel vulnerable in official territory.

There is a long wait in line before a stall, similar to a

check-out counter in a supermarket, where I will be checked into my country. A man with white hair and black-framed glasses opens my rucksack with a jerk and begins to poke around in my dirty clothes. I have nothing to declare except a bottle of whiskey. I am dismissed, gather up my sack and step into the free zone.

"Put your luggage on the cart and follow me," says a man in a muddled green sportcoat. He is heavy and blunt, a plainclothes cop. His partner pushes a metal shopping cart. Is this the A & P supermarket? No, I follow them along the wall to a blank door, inside to a blank office.

"Personal inspection, kid. Empty everything in your pockets on the . . . Oh, yeah. Did you maybe *forget* to declare anything just now?"

"No." Did I forget? My mind races.

"Okay. Empty your pockets on the desk." I pull out keys, change, a wallet stuffed with scraps of paper, an address book, some antibiotics for a fever I had during my last ten days in Spain. The silent partner begins to make a list. This is just like prison movies. Will they hand me a striped uniform and take me away? The talking cop picks up the pills and gives them a shake. "What's *this?*"

"Medicine. I got those in Spain. Antibiotics."

"You ill, kid?"

"I had a bad fever for a couple of days. Went to a doctor. He gave me these."

"So what kind of 'antibiotics' are they?"

"Chloromycetin."

"Jesus Christ! That's the strongest antibiotics you can get. Chloromycetin!"

"Well, my parents were there. My father actually went to the drugstore and bought them. So . . ."

The cop shakes his head. "Do you know what I would do if a doctor ever gave these pills to my kid? Punch him right in his mouth! Punch his *mouth!* Your father ought to know these are the strongest antibiotics you can get."

"I was really sick."

"Boy, so was this doctor." He laughs. His partner smiles and finishes the list. I am in a zone between jet and taxi. I have landed, but on a different planet. The planet of official territory. These beings speak English out of manufactured gadgets stuck down inside their synthetic throats. They are the U.S. Customs.

"Put your hands over your head. Lean up against that wall." The cop gives me a real television detective search. He finds nothing and I can drop my hands. He goes to my rucksack, empties it on the floor, and pokes around with his toe. Nothing there either. So he goes back and sits on the top of the desk. "Tell me, kid, you see a lot of pot in Europe?"

Can you be arrested for having smoked pot in a foreign country? "No. I didn't see any."

"You smoke pot, kid?"

"No."

"You're as full of shit as a Christmas turkey!" He picks up the pills. "What are you doing with these antibiotics?"

"I told you." He shakes his head, tosses them up and down in his hand. Then he starts to stare at me as if he is running a movie in his mind of punching me in the face. He stares very hard.

"Okay. Get your stuff and get out of here." He tosses the pills. I catch them on the rebound off my chest. Turns his back and says to his partner, "What kind of a father has this kid got?"

I'll let my father's own words introduce him:

In the last week of May, 1963, I attended a meeting in the Harlem YMCA that lasted most of the night. This was a week following the occasion when James Baldwin, Harry Belafonte, Kenneth Clark, and a number of other Negro leaders from vari-

ous professions and jobs met with Attorney General Robert
Kennedy—and both the Attorney General and this group came
out of the meeting filled with dismay. The Attorney General was
dumbfounded to discover the depth of hostility in that group,
particularly on the part of some who said that if the government
of the United States would not protect them in Mississippi,
then they had no intention of ever trying to protect the government of the United States in Cuba or anywhere else. The Attorney General was very upset by this. On the other hand, the
group that met with him was dismayed and disheartened by
what seemed to them to be a complete lack of appreciation for
the intensity of feeling that existed in the Negro community at
that time. This was just at the end of the Birmingham demonstrations when hundreds of people had gone to jail.

A week later, this same group of people, largely gathered
around James Baldwin, met with a group of us who were leaders
of various denominations and ecumenical agencies, to see what
kind of communication might possibly exist with that group of
people. They had been so really disheartened by their conversation with the Attorney General that they were now beginning to
explore what other segments of the Establishment in this country really were feeling during this period. Through some mutual
friends we arranged the meeting.

Nearly all the people in the room that night have been in
positions of leadership in various denominations and in the
National Council of Churches, some for a number of years and
some only recently. All of us who were there felt that we were
clean as far as our lack of prejudice was concerned. We had
good records on race relations; we had fought for the right
resolutions in church assemblies; we were against evil in this
area. But somehow it had never come to us quite the way it
came on that night. We left there about 3:00 in the morning,
after the most intense kind of conversation that you can imagine, with a feeling that we had been on the other end of Na-
than's finger—that is, that Baldwin and others had said to us

for the first time, 'You are the man!' We felt a sense of personal guilt, of personal responsibility for the denial of full justice to Negro citizens, resulting in the deterioration of relationships between the races to the place it was in the spring of 1963.

Those of us who left that place that night decided that we had to do something. Individual ministers had gone on Freedom Rides and had been involved in all kinds of other things—but this was of a different nature. We had to begin somehow to mobilize what there was of power and strength in the Protestant community, and direct that power toward positive action.

As it happened, the General Board of the National Council of Churches was meeting the following week, so we immediately took this concern to the president of the Council, Mr. Irwin Miller, a distinguished Disciples layman from Indiana. He appointed a special committee which came up with a resolution to establish a special commission with power for *direct action*. This went to the Council's General Board and was adopted on the 7th of June, thus establishing the Commission on Religion and Race. The Commission, to be appointed by the president of the Council, was charged with the responsibility of moving directly into the heart of the civil rights struggle, to take risks if necessary, to move ahead of the constituency if necessary, to involve the power and resources and personnel of the member churches in a twofold ministry: a ministry of reconciliation, and a ministry of action on the side of achieving justice.

A staff was gathered and I was asked to be the director of the Commission. We set about to try and develop an action agency tied to a body accustomed to planning and consultation rather than action.

We did not know where to begin, so we decided to start at points of most stress and tragedy in the life of the nation. Three days after the Commission was established, Medgar Evers was shot in the back. The first act of the Commission was to send a representative group of Protestant leaders to Medgar Evers' funeral. And at that funeral came the first invitation—no, that is too mild a word—entreaty from Negro Christians in Mississippi, in the name of God, to come into that situation where there was the kind of terror symbolized by Medgar Evers' murder.

I am lying down in the suburbs. My room is on the top floor of our split-level house. Just outside my window a maple tree is shooting green sprouts. Spring has come to Tenafly, New Jersey. With it comes a slow tug. The season makes me unhappy. I am fifteen in 1963. My father and mother, my younger brother and I have been living in this small, upper-middle-class town, a few minutes from Manhattan, for only two years. We live on the West Hill, the "wrong" hill. Across the little valley, on the back slopes of the Palisades, is the exclusive, wealthy East Hill of Tenafly. The East Hill is a mixture of doctors and businessmen, stately mansions and hundred-thousand-dollar homes. For example, almost two hundred psychiatrists live in Tenafly. We live in an almost-new, comfortable (but modest by East Hill standards) house which my parents bought at a bargain price. (The original owner sold suddenly—soon after the first Negro family in Tenafly's history moved in across the street in an almost identical house.

Why am I unhappy this spring? Perhaps because I am in love with a Tenafly girl who doesn't pay much attention. Or, more likely, perhaps because I am doing poorly in the high school. Since seventh grade I have been stuck in brick and glass corridors lined with metal lockers, days divided into seven or eight "periods" by electric buzzers, life a series of special forms that must be completed before one can leave for the bathroom, gym class, health class, drivers' and sex education; I have been working my way up through the grades of junior and senior high school. We moved from Teaneck, a nearby suburb, to Tenafly but nothing much changed. The teachers in both school systems are still a mixture of old and young graduates of state "teachers' colleges," taught how to teach before they learn what they are teaching. I do not mesh with suburban public schools. My family is too open and free. I am encouraged to read books at home that they won't let me bring to school. I have been raised in a liberal tradition while the public schools are outfitted in a phony progressivism. New math, student council, sex education: it all adds up to the same rigid day, sliced into seven "periods," punctuated by the same electric buzzer they use when they open the cages in prison.

Besides, kids at school turn me off. There is a "crowd" which I could join. But I am not a great athlete; my parents aren't rich; my looks are average; and I refuse to adopt the blandness necessary to make the grade as a "good guy" among a rash of "good guys." Instead, I hang around on the edge of the "crowd" with a couple of other self-styled teen-age "outsiders."

My room is my refuge from Tenafly. The walls are lined with books. I am trying to read everything at once. From cheap novels like *Battle Cry* to a paperback edition of *The Myth of Sisyphus* which I buy after one of my friend's sisters tells him it is "cool." It is very cool. But besides Camus, who does blast my thinking out of the corridors of junior high school, my favorites are Beat writers. I have a special shelf with my collection of their works. Kerouac, Ginsberg, Corso. *On the Road* and *Howl,* of course, but also *Junkie* and John Clellon Holmes's novel *Go,* plus a complete set of early *Evergreen Reviews* (my father subscribes) and rare copies of *Big Table,* where portions of *Naked Lunch* were first printed. I even have a copy of Kerouac's first novel, *The Town and the City,* which I stole out of the Teaneck library.

Lying on my bed in the suburbs, surrounded by all this literature of protest, I try and daydream up a memory of when we lived in Greenwich Village. For that is where we lived before we came out to New Jersey. My father was minister of the Judson Memorial Church on Washington Square. He actually knew Ginsberg and Corso and some of the early "Beats." My father used to drink in the San Remo and the Cedar Street bars. I lie on my bed and think about one afternoon when he took me to visit a wild friend of his named John Mitchell. Mitchell was standing in a foot of brown water, digging out a basement on Macdougal Street to turn it into the Gaslight Cafe where the first cafe poetry readings and folk sessions were to be held in New York.

Bob Dylan sings on the phonograph in the corner of my room, his early voice like a jar of razor blades shaking in the amplifier. All I listen to this spring is Dylan. His song "Blowing in the Wind" is becoming popular through a version sung in saccharine style by a group called Peter, Paul and Mary. Dylan got started in the Gaslight Cafe. And I am stuck out in the suburbs, on my way to college, inevitably, two years more struggling upstream like a salmon toward whatever lies on top of that waterfall called "college admissions." Why bother? I don't know. Perhaps because from way back, even before junior high school, teachers were pouring their propaganda about "college," especially a "good college," into my head. "This is your permanent record," they told me. "Everything you do in school: your grades, your behavior, your personality records, all these go into this permanent record which goes to the colleges." And at home it is the same. Even in my house, there are no exceptions. Study hard, be good, cut your buddy's throat to get into a "first choice college." Higher education has become a religion. I kneel before the altar of College.

In Dylan, in his voice and in his music, you can hear an undercurrent. "Fuck them! Fuck college! Fuck high school and junior high school, drivers' education and sex education. Run away. Fight. Be a hobo, a bum, a Blind Boy Grunt. What do they know anyway? Didn't they build the bomb? Didn't they kill Medgar Evers? All the answers are up for grabs, blowing in the wind."

In the other corner, my desk sits with my portable type-writer on top. A Christmas present from two years ago. In the desk drawers, hundreds of poems written over these last years are stuffed in envelopes. I am going to be a writer. Just last week, I finished a short story I call "Max, An American." It is a satire about growing up, getting a job and getting married. It is quite vulgar, and funny. When I show it to friends they are shocked. Both by the story and by the fact that I was able to write it. This afternoon I have sent the story and a covering letter (mentioning, of course, that I am fifteen) to *Evergreen Review*. There is a chance, slim but real, they might even accept it. What a thrill that would be. Published at fifteen.

I am thinking about my small envelope of pot. Down-stairs, my mother is cooking supper. My brother is watching television. He is eleven. Four years separate us. Now I reach back behind my shelf of Beat writing and locate the enve-lope. I have no papers so I take a Lucky Strike and slowly grind almost all the tobacco into an ashtray. My parents allow me to smoke. Not like a lot of my friends who have to sneak out to the garage every time they want a few drags of tobacco. But my parents have no idea about the pot. I suck the weed out of the envelope up through the empty cigarette until it is full again, full of finely shredded green material. One twist seals the end, lick the whole joint, and light up. The drug tastes delicious. Too bad tobacco doesn't taste this good. In a few minutes, I am lying back in delicate trem-ors. My stomach is slightly chilled, my mouth dry, my mus-cles relaxed. Thoughts wander in zigzags.

I wonder what next year will be like. My parents are sending me away to school, to "prep" school. Getting into "prep" school is good preparation for getting into college: all the visits, applications, interviews, transcripts, even spe-cial "high school board exams" and then finally the Wait. I apply to five schools. All but one reject me. I am going to my "safety" school, an academy in Pennsylvania named The

Keaton School. What will it be like in "prep" school? I wonder if I should bring my pot.

I am lying in my room in the suburbs, stoned out of my
mind. I long for "freedom." Yet I live one of the most
comfortable lives imaginable. I have a room stuffed with
hi-fi, radio, expensive clothes, books, paintings. I am fifteen.
But I don't feel happy, don't feel free. What is wrong with
me? My guts sometimes quake with rebellion but I wouldn't
know where to start. Against my parents? Not likely, I love
them very much, am always open with them about almost
everything (pot's an exception). They are my greatest allies.
Rebel against school? Yes, but . . . I still feel this longing to
go to a "good college" inside me. Yet I already think of
dropping out. I have read an article in the newspaper about
how Harvard encourages students to take a year, even two,
off before coming to the university. I would love a year off;
dream of bumming around Europe and America for a year.
Harvard! That is the heart pounding in the center of my
darkest possibilities. I would love to go to Harvard. My
parents would be in ecstasy. To go to Harvard would be
revenge on all the lousy teachers, all the "guidance counsel-
ors" who have held sway over me for these past years. Harvard. It sounds like the biggest coup anybody could possibly
pull at my age, in this country. It is 1963. I have two hard
years of study ahead of me if I am to keep this dream alive.

Great South Beach stretches along the coast of Martha's
Vineyard for miles without a soul. In the marsh behind the
beach, we are standing waist-deep in a clear stream holding
screwdrivers. Steve, Ray and me. Steve is my best friend
from Tenafly. He has already fled from public high school to
a private school in Massachusetts called Stockbridge School.
Ray teaches woodworking at Stockbridge, is a sculptor, and
much older than us. He stands in the stream with a fully

developed man's body, deep tan, a full beard of chestnut whiskers streaked with silver. We are visiting Ray and Alice. They are running the Youth Hostel on the Vineyard this summer.

Ray shows us how to pry the oysters off the submerged rocks. They look just like part of the mossy stone until you feel their sharp edges under the slime. Then you dig with the tip of your screwdriver, trying to keep your hand from slipping and getting cut. We wear sneakers and bathing suits. I trip on a rock and bash my ankle against the jagged shells. When I move into shallower water I see wisps of blood trailing off, feel a little fish nuzzle his nose in the sore. The hot sun beats on our backs. But Ray makes this great fun, treats us with respect even though we are just kids.

When three buckets are full of the sloppy wet oysters, Ray says we have enough. We climb out of the water, hoist the buckets, and walk through the marsh to where we have hidden Ray's battered and scratched old car. This is private property and we don't want to get busted for poaching oysters.

The Hostel is only ten minutes away. A two-story wooden house in the center of a clearing, bicycle racks line the front lawn, out back is a huge stump which Ray spends hours hacking and chiseling. Alice is talking to Mercy in the kitchen.

"Surprise!" says Ray, dropping his bucket on the table.

"You got them," beams Alice.

"Oh, Ray. This will be delicious," says Mercy, a tall, willowy blonde who also goes to Stockbridge. Her father is a musician and she is a year older than us. Mercy has come to visit with Bill, another Stockbridge student. He is a skinny, quiet guy who acts tough a lot, talks about motorcycles when he talks, and sleeps with Mercy. There are only three private rooms in the Hostel. Ray and Alice have the biggest. Mercy and Bill share another. And Steve and I take the third. There are two enormous dormitories, boys and girls, where the hostelers sleep. These are young people on bike trips from Boston, Hartford, New Haven and New York. They come through for a couple of days with their adult leaders, sleep in the dormitories, cook their own meals. Ray and Alice just maintain the place. They don't care much for the hostelers.

Alice is dark and small, with long hair over her shoulders, wears glasses most of the time, but without them she is beautiful. She is in her twenties and quite a bit younger than Ray. Alice gives Steve, Rick and me a kind of combination mothering-sistering-cockteasing which is nice. She loves to cook and makes huge, tasty meals.

There are tons of oysters, fried in crispy batter. When you break into them they melt into gobs of succulent shellfish in your mouth. The beer is icy and bitter. For dessert (Alice is too much!) there is strawberry shortcake with homemade whipped cream.

We are all going into town after supper. Jack Elliot, a cowboy singer from Brooklyn and an old pal of Woody Guthrie's, is singing at a folk music cafe. Ray and Alice have never seen him. But Steve knows him. Arlo Guthrie, Woody's son, goes to Stockbridge and is a friend of Steve's, of everybody here except me.

Half the Stockbridge School students play the guitar and sing, and the other half are learning how. Steve is very serious about music. He writes his own songs and plays a big Gibson guitar with real finesse. He also, just like everybody at Stockbridge it seems, holds Arlo in a little bit of awe.

On the way into town, we get Ray to stop by a liquor store. While we wait in the car, Bill, who looks old with a scruffy beard though really only sixteen, goes inside and purchases booze. His choice turns out to be a quart of premixed screwdrivers, vodka and orange, which goes down like sticky-sweet soda. By the time we arrive at the club, we have chugged it all. Heads spin in a "high" which is still new enough to marvel at.

Jack Elliot is about Ray's age. Short and stocky with a weatherbeaten face, cowboy jeans and boots, a cowboy stetson on his head. He sings with alternating humor and seriousness, lots of gusto, makes reticent little jokes between songs, songs like "Diamond Joe" and "Sowing on the Mountain." When he finishes his first set, the little club goes haywire with enthusiasm, he grins and doffs his hat, then sneaks out to find a drink. They only serve coffee and coke in this cafe.

Sharing the bill with Jack Elliot is a jug band called The Charles River Valley Boys. In a couple of years they will become famous under the name of the Jim Kweskin Jug Band. Now we listen, stomachs full of oysters, salad, strawberries and screwdrivers, to the guitar, mandolin, and thumping washtub bass. Somebody sticks a kazoo in his mouth and soon the audience is banging on tables and singing.

On the way back to the Hostel along the midnight roads of the island, Steve has a stomachache from the screwdrivers. Ray is raving about Jack, what a great guy he seems like, so much fun, so relaxed. Alice is talking about Fritz, the tall, spaced-out-looking cat who played the washtub bass. Ray gets a little jealous at this. But then Steve starts singing, and we all join in:

> Sowing on the mountain,
> Reaping in the valley.
> You've got to reap
> Just what you sow.

We keep singing this chorus, with Steve and Alice alternating on the verses, like:

> God gave Noah
> The rainbow sign,
> God gave Noah
> The rainbow sign,

No more water.
The fire next time.

Before we know it, Ray is pulling up outside the dark Hostel. We tiptoe past the dormitories full of snoring hostelers and upstairs to our rooms. Steve goes out in a second but I linger in my thoughts, unable to sleep. Suddenly, a noise. Strange noise, like a cry but muffled and quick. Mercy's cry. She and Bill are making love on the other side of the thin wall. I am a virgin. I have a crush on Mercy. The noise again, the undertone of moving bedsprings. Steve mumbles sleeptalk into his pillow. Lord, I want her. Downstairs, the bicyclists snore in rows of cots. I want some girl to sleep with all night, to love, to make that noise.

We only stay at Alice's "restaurant" for ten days. Steve goes straight from the Vineyard to Fire Island, where his parents have a summer house. I go back to Tenafly. But after a couple of miserable days, flee again. Steve has invited me to spend August at his house.

Ocean Beach is one of fifteen or so towns strung like beads on the thin strand of the island. It is a "family community" where mother and kids spend the summer and Daddy commutes on the weekends. There are no cars, so people go shopping with children's wagons. The ferry slip on Friday night is a madhouse of red wagons, harried and lonely wives, and restless five-year-olds waiting for Daddy to step off the boat in his suit and soaked shirt, having rushed early from the office to catch the 4:30 train from Pennsylvania Station.

Steve hangs around with a slightly older crowd. We have long hair, wear white sailing jackets, jeans and bare feet. At night we smoke a little pot and sit around the main square. Sometimes we sneak into one of the bars and order a few drinks. During the afternoons we lie on the beach, mess around in town, or take out one of his cousins' boats. They live on the bay, while Steve's house is by the ocean.

After a week, I find a girlfriend named Liza. She is tall with olive skin and black hair, large breasts that stun me when I catch their full weight in my palms under her sweatshirt. We lie in the moist sand of the night beach and duck under the probing headlights of dune taxis. Liza is my age and lives in the city. She goes to Stuyvesant High School, is Jewish and very smart and we don't talk much. Our routine is to meet around nine o'clock in the main square, then walk around the darker paths holding hands, exchanging bits of non-information about our day. Until the time comes to veer suddenly onto the beach. I am a little surprised that Liza seems to want this detour as much as I do. And more surprised when I meet no resistance as my hand fiddles with her bra. But grateful when her fingers touch me on my tight jeans. If I try to go below her waist, she grabs my hand and locks it like a vise to her belly. As soon as I sigh defeat, she lets me return to where I belong, polishing the rubies on her breasts.

August passes slowly. Fine with me, I'm in no hurry to discover what The Keaton School will turn out to be. One morning the phone rings and then Steve's mother is standing in the doorway, It is very hot in the beach house. "Your father's on the phone," she says. I stretch naked under the thin sheet. His mother was once the top model in America. There are framed magazine covers all over the house, covers full of his mother's face, blonde hair, elegant figure. Now she stands in a yellow jersey and white shorts looking down at my bed. She and Steve's father are separating. She told this to Steve three days ago. "Okay," I say. She leaves and I jump into a bathing suit and go out to answer the telephone.

"How is everything? Having a good time?" he asks.

"Sure."

"Listen, do you remember I told you about this demonstration in Washington? The march which we're helping to sponsor."

"Yeah. I wanted to go."

"Do you still want to go? How about Steve?"

"We both want to go, Dad."

"Great. You guys can carry the banner for us then."

"What does it say?"

"Just 'National Council of Churches.'"

"How are we going to get down to Washington?"

"You can fly down with me the day before."

A week later in the airport, some guy in sunglasses, with a seersucker jacket slung over one shoulder, asks the ticket clerk in front of us, "Where can a man get a can of beer around here?" The clerk sends him to the airport bar. "Did you see that guy?" my father asks.

"You mean the asshole with the beer can?" I say, in my true cynical style.

"That was Paul Newman."

"The movie guy?"

"That's right. He must be going to the March too." It dawns on me for the first time that this March is going to be something big. Even movie stars are going to it.

Reporters and photographers wait at the foot of the gangplank. They go straight to my father, Paul Newman and a woman who turns out to be Marian Anderson and take them aside. Flashbulbs explode; in the morning, the picture is on the front page of the Washington papers.

We are staying in the Mayflower Hotel. It is big and impersonal and my father says it is probably the best hotel in Washington when I ask him, "What's the best hotel in Washington?"

Steve and I are impressed. My father has a suite. This is really an adventure. We both feel very adult as we look around the rooms of our "suite." Immediately, people start to arrive. The phone starts to ring. And work for my father begins. Members of the staff of the Commission on Religion and Race crowd inside. They are mostly in their thirties, ministers and lawyers, friendly to me and Steve but when they look at my father it is with an almost passionate respect. He is sitting casually in an armchair, his jacket off, tie loose, feet resting on top of a coffee table. He looks very young, relaxed, optimistic.

"Did they get those sandwiches all packed?" somebody asks. The National Council is donating a hundred thousand sandwiches to the March on Washington. At the last minute it occurred to people that the thousands of marchers were going to get hungry. Earlier this afternoon we had stood in my father's office and looked at them loading the rented trucks with peanut butter and jelly sandwiches out on West 120th Street. The Commission offices are in the Interchurch Center at 475 Riverside Drive. Nicknamed the "God box," this building houses national offices of many of the Protestant denominations in the country.

"What a mess," laughs my father.

"That's what June said on the phone." June is his secretary.

"I want to have a staff meeting tonight. Not just about tomorrow, but to talk about the whole fall program." He is getting serious but his face loses none of its glow. "I guess we might as well eat dinner from room service. Paul, see if you can find a menu around." Dinner is full of jokes. About four other staff, my father, Steve and I. We drink wine, then linger over coffee as the rest of the staff gradually arrive.

It is very interesting for me to watch my father and the staff work together in these meetings. They do most of the talking while he listens, occasionally filling in with a few words when his own thoughts run as fast or faster than the speaker's, but directing the conversation too. He will suddenly cut off talk on one subject and it will be like a chapter closing in a book: neat, and logical. On to the next chapter.

Obviously, he is not just my father. He is the father, in varying degrees, of everybody in the room. He is thirty-nine years old but looks younger than most of the staff. And it is plain that for them, just as for me, there is magic in the man who sits with his chair tilted back, one finger alongside his sharp nose, listening, thinking, directing the conversation as naturally as a valley directs a river through its middle. He is *our* father. Something in him that gives him this incredible "fatherness" which touches so many. I don't feel jealous. Perhaps some of the staff do, just a bit. He really *is* my father. His blood is my blood. It makes me glad.

The first big event involving the Commission was the March on Washington. Part of the mandate which the General Board itself passed in setting up the Commission was a call to a national meeting of Christians in Washington to symbolize the concern of the whole nation. This was before there were any crystallized plans for a March. Then we began hearing about Phillip Randolph's plans and some other plans that Martin Luther King had, so we all put together our efforts and established the March on Washington Committee. Ten sponsoring organizations participated. The major civil rights organizations, organized labor (at least one part of it), and three religious groups— the Catholic Interracial Council, the Synagogue Council of America, and our Commission on Religion and Race of the National Council of Churches. It was our deep feeling that there had to be an affirmative, positive, committed kind of demonstration involving many parts of the population of this country on behalf of civil rights in the summer of 1963. That was our only hope to prevent an open outbreak of hostility, so deep and intense was the feeling. So we set out to reach a simple goal: to get 30,000 white people into that March. And we got slightly over 40,000 out of about 250,000 to 300,000 people who marched that day.

That was our first entree, really, into what one could call

the civil rights establishment in this country, that is, the NAACP, CORE, SCLC, and civil libertarian groups working with them. It is difficult to report how suspicious and how reluctant they were, how little expectation they had from the church in this whole thing. There was an unbelievable kind of cold shoulder at the beginning, because we had made so many protestations, we were so involved in pious platitudes in race relations, and we were so guilty.

In the morning, we eat breakfast at a banquet for the National Council of Churches leaders who have come to march. Afterwards, we take an elevator back upstairs to the suite. My father has an appointment with a man who is now ambassador to a small African country. A white man from the west, he is an active layman in the Congregational Church. He was appointed by John F. Kennedy after having helped elect him in the 1960 campaign.

"I had breakfast with Him," says the ambassador. He is short and highly groomed. His blue suit must be custom-tailored and his haircut looks about an hour old. He crosses one leg over the other gingerly.

"What are they thinking about over there in the White House this morning?" asks my father. He likes to tilt back in chairs, but his eyes are brutally alert to every nuance of gesture.

"Well, Bob, I was talking to the Big Boy about that. He's quite concerned. Quite concerned. I would say they are, ah . . . praying for a peaceful day. Not much else they can do until the day is over."

"The leadership of the March Committee is with him right now."

"Yes, I believe so, Bob." Later a picture will come out of a smiling, tense President surrounded by civil rights lead-

ers. Beside Kennedy, with an expression of calm foreknowl-
edge, is King. He must have the speech tucked in his breast
pocket. He knows the day will be his.

"Do you think they are willing to work with us on getting a strong bill through Congress?" my father asks.

"He's having problems with this Congress. You know
that. In any case, today is the day. It all depends on what
he sees. If there is a bloodbath in the streets of the capital
during his administration . . . you've probably thought of
that. If there's violence, you're going to have some tough
times on this bill."

"At least," says my father, "he's going to be paying
attention to today. I don't think there's going to be violence." After a few more minutes of conversation, my father
walks the ambassador out to the elevators. When he comes
back, he shakes his head and grins a wry grin. "Big Boy?
That may be a pretty accurate description of Kennedy. I
hope not." Then adds, "Come on. We have to get downstairs and form the line. You guys have to lead us."

Steve and I stay eight feet apart so the banner will not
sag. We move at the head of the ministers. It suddenly hits
me that Steve is Jewish. He can't have thought much about
it as he wrestles with the bamboo pole to keep "National
Council of Churches" stretched out.

We are insignificant particles in a chain reaction that
floods the streets. Everywhere signs bob amidst black and
white faces. It is impossible to keep together. Some groups,
mostly white, try to sing freedom songs. But the songs do not
catch at all. The crowd is mostly black and moves with stiff
dignity. The difference between the whites and blacks in the
March is so plain and predictable it almost makes one cry.
The difference which makes the March necessary in the first
place. The whites are off on an adventure. With a few exceptions, these 40,000 liberals are having a mixture of catharsis

and outing. For months they have watched television news full of civil rights demonstrations in the South. They have heard the strains of "We Shall Overcome" on Huntley-Brinkley reports while eating supper in their suburban living rooms. Now, they come to Washington to share in the struggle by listening to black leaders, singing black songs, getting a contact high off black nightmares. At the end of the day, they will drive back North to white Chevy Chase, white Forest Hills, white Tenafly.

Steve (right) and I carry the banner at the March on Washington, 1963. My father and Bishop Julian Smith in the lead.

I am just as guilty as any of them. I am on an adventure. I have come to be with my father, to carry a banner for him. I would follow him on a hike into the Arctic Circle in support of free ice cream if that was what he wanted.

The black crowd has not come to sing. They don't want to perform for America this afternoon in a national "civil rights" minstrel show. This is not a Jerry Lewis telethon for

"Freedom," even though television cameras hang out of the treetops and down into the marchers' faces like prehistoric reptiles, bringing it all back home.

Steve and I sit down in front of the Lincoln Memorial. There are two moments this afternoon. The blacks in the crowd burst out in waves of thunder when Mahalia Jackson sings "Buked and Scorned" with tears pouring down her face. She turns the city of Washington into a hot Baptist church on a dusty Sunday street in Niggertown, Mississippi. It is almost enough. But Martin Luther King will take the day and make it his, his gift to the crowd. His Dream reaches down inside each listener's ear, a silver lance of language piercing not only the head but into the guts, touching that invisible envelope, whatever it looks like, soul. Men weep around me. Women grab their hair and shake. Steve looks lost and we move from one foot to another, our voices shouted away.

". . . let Freedom ring." He closes each mirage with this command, which is also a warning, which is also a prayer. " . . . let Freedom ring."

I have never seen Martin Luther King before. I have not been prepared. He picks me up and shakes me as if a black Andalusian bull had got his horns into my guts and was tossing me above his head. Then drops me on my feet. I am not bleeding. But I have been gored, I am open in front. The March passes away slowly, like the approaching autumn of 1963, the hundreds of thousands drifting back through the trees to buses and cars.

I remember the March as one of the great events of my life. When we stepped off the curb onto Constitution Avenue and started toward the Lincoln Memorial, I glanced around me and saw under the banner of the National Council of Churches 200 of the leaders of Protestantism—Ralph Sockman right behind

On the steps of the Lincoln Memorial.

me — and every name off the cover of the *Christian Century* for the last two decades. As we got into the middle of that crowd and started down Constitution Avenue, I felt for the first time in my ministry that the church was where it belonged, in the middle of the street. There was an eschatological feeling about the whole day; it was very unreal, because everyone knew this was an affirmation of determination. By this event we were inescapably committed to move beyond acquiescence in present conditions.

I get out of bed on a Sunday morning not long after the March. It is past noon. Downstairs I can hear my father's voice. He must be talking on the telephone. His voice sounds angry. I know Sunday mornings in this house in Tenafly and something is going on out of the ordinary today.

"Yes. I already talked to somebody at the Justice Department," he says into the phone. I walk past him to get some orange juice out of the refrigerator. He is still in his pajamas and robe, sitting on the edge of the formica table. "Sure, a telegram is okay. And we have to get a large delegation down there for the funeral. But I want federal protection there. Yes, I have the number of somebody closer to Bobby. . . ."

I walk into the living room. I have rarely seen my father so upset. The fat package of *New York Times* sits untouched on the seat of our red armchair. The television is running, with the sound turned down. One of those interview shows with some government official and three reporters. My father hangs up in the kitchen.

"What's happening, Dad?"

"They bombed a church in Birmingham, Alabama, this morning. Killed four little girls in the Sunday school."

"What?"

"It's unbelievable, isn't it? I called the Justice Department this morning and told them if we can protect three-quarters of the world from communism, we ought to be able to protect a Sunday school from being bombed in Alabama."

"Have they caught anyone?"

"No. And they won't. There is a riot going on down there now. God only knows how many are going to die today. The President has got to step in. They have to put more FBI from the North down there. The FBI in the South are racists like anybody else."

"Four little girls? That's incredible."

"Isn't it sickening?" He sits down. "I don't know if I should go down or send someone else and organize. King will be going there. Right now we have to build a national coalition of all the local churches. When something like this happens, we have to be right there to put pressure on the government. Otherwise nothing is going to change."

On the television, there is suddenly a special news bulletin. "Turn it up," my father says. Then a series of still photographs of the bombed-out church, the frantic congregation being fired on by the Birmingham police, the bodies being hauled on stretchers past wailing women, police chasing a black man up the street with his shirt ripped and their clubs raised high over their heads. The newscaster says another Negro has died, killed by a shotgun blast from the police. My stomach is knotted; I am disgusted and furious. I look at my father and remember the night of the March. There was a celebration thrown in the Mayflower suite for many of the leaders. I was introduced to Floyd McKissick, who spoke for CORE at the March. "This is Bob Spike's son."

"You Bob Spike's son?" he asked, leaning toward me, obviously a little high and full of the afterglow from that afternoon.

"Yes."

"I hope you know you got a great daddy. Your daddy is a great man. If it weren't for him, hardly none of these white folks would have marched today."

My father is looking at a photograph of a Birmingham cop slugging a young black in the neck with his truncheon. He lets the air out of his mouth in a hiss. "Would you look at that son of a bitch!"

"I'd like to kill that cop," I say. My father says nothing. I have never seen him so disturbed.

"I'm going to call the Justice Department again," he says and gets up.

"What are you going to say?"

"I don't know." The sound of his finger dialing. Then he says, "I'm going to tell them the Protestant churches in this country are finished ignoring the lynchings and bombings in the South. If they don't do something about them, the Protestant churches are going to find somebody who *will* in the next election."

My father was a gentle man who filled people with strength. His early biography might be something out of Horatio Alger.

He was born in 1923 and grew up on a farm in upstate New York in that stretch of harsh terrain and gravel-bottomed lakes which runs from Rochester to Buffalo. From

My father (middle row center) in one-room school-
house in upstate New York.

the beginning, he was an exceptional child, especially in school. His high school record was flawless, after having skipped two grades in elementary school. In his senior year, he set a record on the New York Regents' Exams and won a scholarship to Denison University in Ohio. Besides being a top student, he was regarded as one of the most remarkable and promising young men ever to have passed through his local Baptist church.

His mother, Lucy Spike, was a former schoolteacher and a loyal Baptist. She began taking her son Bob to church from infancy. Lucy did not allow or approve of smoking, drinking or cards. She was a little round woman in spectacles who could be sweeter than honey to a grandchild, and I remember the summers that I spent in her Rochester house as the best of my childhood. As soon as I arrived, she would take down a huge jar of pennies which she had been saving all year and we would roll them up. Then take them to the bank and exchange them for spending cash. The best part came after we got off the bus in downtown Rochester. I was free to go through the toy departments of all the local stores and spend every last penny on whatever toys caught my eye. It was almost better than Christmas. But a grandchild's memories are not a child's. I know my father lived his childhood under her strong influence and then spent years breaking away from it. And, from what I have heard, my grandfather spent much of his life pushing his wife away.

Warren Spike was gassed in the trenches of France during World War I. He returned alive, but with his face a red map of exposed veins and capillaries. The German gas gave him an incurable skin condition and blood disease which while it wasn't fatal, left him looking flushed and furious for the rest of his life. Sad, for the rest of his life would too often justify his angry face.

My grandfather moved from disappointment to disappointment, failure to failure. He began as a farmer and ended as a salesman for furniture with built-in massage vibrators. He kept his failures stored inside and they dissolved into a bitter acid which rarely leaked out, for he was not a talkative man. On those summers when I visited Rochester, when he touched me, I felt the uneasiness and confusion in his fingers. He would tenderly show me his beautiful garden and suddenly, in the middle of a row of flowers, walk away and into the house without a word. He loved to hunt and fish and care for his dogs. He treated each dog he ever owned like a son.

One afternoon in her kitchen, my grandmother turned from her baking and began to tell me about how my grandfather had beaten my father when he was a boy. I was six on this afternoon. I remember she told me in vivid detail of how Grandpa had stripped off my father's pants and whipped him with a special leather strap until the blood poured down his naked legs. She told me she screamed and pleaded with him to stop. "Your father was a good boy. But if he was just a little naughty, Grandpa would whip him."

My father told his best friend, who later told me, that when he was about two years old, he suddenly felt his father stop loving him. He could remember the feeling clearly. Utterly, completely, the love was taken away. What failure or disappointment in Warren Spike's life made him withdraw his love from his oldest son, I do not know. But my father grew up without a father's love, knowing that nothing he could do would win it back.

Lucy Spike had enough love and enough visions to shelter him, to keep him alive, to drive him to straight A's and Denison. Her real vision was of her son Bob in the pulpit. He majored in philosophy in college, joined a fraternity, acted in college plays, and kept active in the Baptist Church. When he graduated, Phi Beta Kappa, the whole bundle of college honors, he decided to return to upstate New York and the Colgate-Rochester Divinity School. He was ordained in 1945 and shortly afterwards he married my mother.

They had met at Denison. She was from Arlington, Virginia, the daughter of a government scientist and a schoolteacher mother. My mother was not what my grandmother probably saw in her visions of a wife for Bob. She was outspoken, vivacious, very bright and independent, with a zany sense of humor. She smoked, drank and played bridge. She wanted children but she wanted her own life, to be more than a "minister's wife" serving coffee to the church women's society and ironing his clerical collars. Marrying my mother was probably my father's first step toward total independence. It was a rejection of his mother not only in classical Freudian terms, but in terms of the basic facts of the situation. In college, my father's thought had already moved far beyond the Baptist theology of his childhood. By the time he was ordained and out of seminary, he had developed his own kind of pragmatic Christian existentialism, very much directed at the sociological mission of the Christian church, based heavily on his understanding of Niebuhr, Tillich, Barth and Kierkegaard. Many years later at the March he would feel, "for the first time in my ministry . . . the church was where it belonged, in the middle of the street."

His ministry is best seen in four chronological parts. He was minister of the Judson Memorial Church in Greenwich Village from the late forties until 1955. He left this pulpit to become a "church executive" for the Congregationalist Church, now the United Church of Christ. There he served for eight years before going to direct the Commission on Religion and Race in the summer of 1963.

The final section of his career began in 1966 when he went to the University of Chicago as a professor and administrator.

Written above, the four parts of his ministry lie upon the page like four spoons on a bare table. But each was full of substance, each was electric.

His beginning, at the Judson Church, was crucial. Here he changed himself, as he changed Judson, from a conservative Baptist into a modern pioneer in the wilderness of postwar American society. I think it was at Judson that he felt for the first time the injustice deeply engrained in our society and felt his own nature respond to it with an urgent need for change. He became a rebel, on his way to becoming a revolutionary. He was one of the most radical ministers in the American church and he was blessed with not only radical ideas and imagination, but a sense of *how* to change things.

Judson had once been the most fashionable church in New York, back in the days when Henry James was writing about Washington Square. But by the late 1940's the huge Stanford White–designed brick building was a relic without congregation or program, a dead property in the midst of an Italian ghetto sprawling with life. At the time of his arrival, one of the biggest problems in the Village, as in every part of New York City, was the teenage gangs that were making war on one another and anyone who happened to wander into the middle of their "turf." This was one of the two chief annoyances for the neighborhood Italians, who liked to run their lives in quiet, secretive order. The other was the presence of some of the most unhappy but brilliant men and women in the country. These were the artists and writers, the would-be artists, and the self-proclaimed bohemians who lived in the cheap tenements and drank in the local bars. When my father arrived at Judson, he looked around the community to see where his congregation would come from and where his ministry must go. For the most part, it was a question of the ministry going outside the church, because his congregation, he felt, consisted of the gangs and the bohemians. Along with a small but active group of young people recently out of college who were drifting around on the fringes of the Village. These people weren't sure if they believed in God, but they came to believe in the Judson Church.

There were several "youth programs" connected to other churches in the Village, but they all barred any gang members or troublemakers from entering. The people who most needed a place to get off the street were the last ones to find a place. In the basement of Judson was a large gymnasium, several locker rooms, and about seven meeting rooms.

These were turned into the "Judson Center" and thrown open to any kids in the neighborhood who wanted to come. In a few weeks, the toughest kids in the Village, all of them Italian and Roman Catholic, were members of the "Center." They called him "Spike" and they gradually came to trust him with everything. We, my mother, brother and I, lived behind the church on Thompson Street. I remember many mornings when my father would dress in his clerical collar, usually worn only on Sunday mornings, and I would ask him why he was getting dressed up.

"I have to go to court. Vinnie is going on trial today." It could be Vinnie, Tony, Al, or Rocco. It got so his clerical collar stopped meaning Sunday morning to me but, instead, meant he was on his way to court. Eventually he was such a familiar face in the youth courts, they asked him if he would be interested in serving as Protestant Chaplain of "Youth House." This is the prison for New York boys awaiting trial or sentencing. For the next several years, he got up early every Sunday morning and went to hold a service and talk individually with kids in Youth House. As Protestant Chaplain, most of the boys he dealt with were black. For the gangs of Harlem and Brooklyn were made up of black Baptists and other Protestant boys who gave themselves names like "The Deacons" or "Chaplains" or "Bishops." My father had already spent one summer living and working in Harlem during seminary. He formed friendships with some of the toughest leaders of these gangs and, though he was white, they often asked him to go into court with them. Later on in the fifties, when gangs suddenly became a kind of national craze for a few years thanks to movies like *The Wild Ones* and *Blackboard Jungle, Life* Magazine ran a series of memoirs by a warlord of one of the Harlem gangs named "Churchy." My father happened to look over my shoulder as I was devouring this piece with great interest.

"I knew him," he said.

"You did? Do you want to read this?"

"I don't think so. I think I know too much about it already."

The other day, I heard my father's voice for the first time in six years. It was only a tape but suddenly I felt my own strength shift inside me at the sound. He lived in his words and spent most of his life talking to people. That was chiefly how he "ministered" to them. After he left Judson and went to the office of the Congregationalist Church, he began to travel all over the country, preach in hundreds of churches, talk to thousands of ministers, laymen, people on airplanes, everyone. His congregation became a group of men and women stretched across America who had only him in common. After he died, hundreds of letters came to our house saying, "Bob Spike was my minister. He changed my life." Writing this is almost embarrassing. It sounds like schmaltz and my father detested sentimental eulogizing. Knee deep in confusion in America, it seems almost impossible to write about a man like my father. He does not seem like a modern hero but someone out of a book written in the early part of the century. On the other hand, when the total story of his life is recalled, he is as typical of the sixties as any man was. Impossible as it sounds, my father could heal people just by talking to them. He was a man who believed in his own "soul," who helped other people believe in theirs: government people in Washington, students in Harlem, people who worked in the White House and people who worked in the White Tower hamburger stand; there were hundreds of members in his congregation.

In his calm voice, he would lay out reasonable views of the world in such crystal-clear visions that you couldn't help feeling hopeful. Even though some of his visions were highly critical, almost despairing, of the future of this country, and the church's place. He never talked as a "minister" or "church leader" or even "father." It was as Bob Spike, a man who combined all three roles but made them his own. He would lend you his faith in things as things *were.* He didn't paint heavenly pictures in the air but pinned down reality in each moment, "in the middle of the street."

He liked to laugh at himself and to sit over a drink and trade stories. Dirty jokes were okay and so was profanity. I never saw my father shocked by language, and by only one movie — *The Ten Commandments.* What did shock him was cruelty and injustice, hypocrisy and betrayal.

As I grew up, I often asked him questions about religion and the Bible, which I loved to read. But he never forced any religion on either me or my brother. We both were baptized and confirmed. But he trained me himself at home for the latter and I was confirmed at Judson Church in the Village, though we were living, by then, in Tenafly. We rarely went to church in the suburbs. There weren't any that he really felt comfortable in near our house. Most Sundays, anyway, he was off preaching somewhere around the country. I began to wonder if I was an atheist when I was about eleven. I asked my father why he believed in God.

"When things get hectic or very troubled, I have this thing I feel. I suppose I call this 'God.' It is just a feeling, very mysterious but I get it, which I can rest inside, feel safe inside. I rest in this feeling of 'God.'"

In his book *The Freedom Revolution and the Churches,* he wrote:

> The whole human race is encamped once again by the Red Sea. Will it be engulfed by the terrible forces that the clever shamans have let loose — destructive hydrogen bombs, or mechanically clever devices to enslave the whole race to idleness? The human spirit is aching with anxiety about the future. And, in addition, some parts of the human family are still kept in slavery because of their color. I believe that the God of our Fathers will deliver us.

So do I. At least, I believe the God of *my* father will.

My father delivers me to Keaton in late September. When he drives away in his little cream-colored Morris Minor, I stand on the curb and wave good-bye like a good scout. In fact, I am curious about what will happen next. In hours, I find that I have jumped right into a combination New England prep school (with all the pretensions but none of the quali- ties) and West Point military academy (with both the preten- sions and the qualities). As a new boy, I have to spend two ridiculous weeks under "New Boy Rules," which are a kind of martial law administered by the senior class. I must doff my blue and gold beanie at all the seniors, always wear one blue and one gold sock, a blue and gold bowtie, and recite cheers and fight songs for any upper classmen who request it. I have come to accomplish one thing: get the grades to get into Harvard. But I quickly see that Keaton is in business not just to educate but to "mold character." I like mine the way it is, and so do my parents, but that is hardly relevant. The next year becomes a struggle to shut up and study.

Built around a grassy "quad," the brick buildings of Keaton are square and plain, not ugly but not attractive. Most monstrous of them all is "Smyth Hall," an enormous building in which about half the four hundred students are housed, along with the vast dining hall and the "butt lounge," which is the only area where boys sixteen and over, with parents' permission, are allowed to smoke. The rest of the campus is built on a thin crust of dry land floating over the marshes of eastern Pennsylvania. There is a mudhole called "Tom's Lake" and a nine-hole golf course used by the golf team, faculty, and God only knows who else. It is off-limits to most of the students. The focal point of the campus, at the south end of the quad, is the Baptist chapel with its white steeple and new, redbrick walls.

True, I love to read the Bible. But not for the religion in it. I read it like a novel, especially the Gospels, and look at Christ as a rebel-hero to identify with, to weep over at his Crucifixion, but not to worship. Any kind of worship leaves me feeling self-conscious and uncomfortable. I know my father may be leading the prayer, all heads are bowed, yet I stare around the room looking at people for my own interests. Whose lips are moving? Who else doesn't close his eyes? Now at Keaton we go into the chapel five times a week for worship. Four days during the school week we have "chapel," in which local ministers, from fundamentalists to liberals, come and deliver short homilies to the boys. There is Convocation one Sunday a month. Other Sundays we go to local churches in Coaltown. Worship abounds. Yet nobody, not the teachers or the students, seems to take it seriously. In fact, Keaton is no more Christian than the most public of public schools.

Keaton is run by bells, not God. A bell wakes me up. A bell orders me to sleep. The first step is learning to cheat the bells.

When the "wake-up" sounds shortly before seven, I burrow my head under the pillow and continue sleeping. Not until the warning bell for breakfast do I jump up, dive into my clothes, and run across a hundred yards of quad, trying to tie my tie as I sprint. Up the stairs, getting the knot to my throat just in time to melt through the door with the last bit of crowd and into the dining hall. Nothing can adequately describe the sinking feeling, the depression, which hits you in the face as you enter this vast warehouse for eating first thing in the morning. Like a prison or an army camp, the tables are lined up across the wide interior for hundreds of boys to stand and wait through Grace so that they can explode into a thunder of scraping chairs. Then wait for the "master"—as every teacher must be called—to pass out the tubs of soggy cereal and greasy eggs.

I try to think of nothing. Not the day that is just beginning. Not the day passed. Not the night nor the weekend nor the next vacation. One tries to survive by blanking out all thoughts which do not go with the bells.

In public high school in the suburbs, I felt a hidden

fascism underneath all the glittering new equipment, the student council elections, and the bullshit about "democracy" and "school spirit." At prep school, I have to admit, I finally have found overt conditions that beg, absolutely beg to be rebelled against. Yet the joke is on me, for I have come to Keaton of my own free will. In fact, I have asked my parents to send me away and they are paying several thousand dollars for the right to experience a totalitarian education where nothing is subtle or hidden, everything as overt as the greenish brack that floats atop Tom's Lake.

The school is run on an ingenious foundation called the Credit and Demerit System. Every possible instance of misbehavior that could occur, from missing the first two minutes of breakfast to being caught drunk and in your skivvies on the roof of the chapel, has already been assigned a value in "credits" and "demerits." Each boy is given one hundred credits. If he is late to a class, he can lose five. If he is caught smoking in his room, he can lose a considerable bit more. Losing credits is called a "sting."

"I'm going to sting you ten for that."

Or, "Consider yourself stung." Keaton is a hive of stinging Wasps. The "masters" rely on a group of student turnkeys known as "monitors" to do most of the "stinging." Each morning a "sting sheet" is posted outside the Dean's office with yesterday's "stings" listed on it. In the basement, one's "credit rating" is posted every week. If it dips below seventy, you are put "on campus." This means the loss of all privileges, including the right to take a stroll around the dingy streets of Coaltown with its several gas stations, one diner, one stationery store and two groceries.

In any case, with all this "stinging" going on, it would be absolutely unlivable if it were not for that great institution known as The Bribe. The "monitors" (not all but a good many of them) will accept money in return for turning the other way should you want to buy your way out of a week of breakfasts, a month of work programs. The "masters" must know about all this, but free enterprise prevails.

I, through some luck and some fast talking, end up as a junior in one of the smaller dorms reserved for seniors. I have a small, single room with a window that looks out on Tom's Lake. There is also a fireplace which it is completely forbidden to use, but up which I blow the smoke from my illegal cigarettes in the winter.

I must teach myself how to study. I have never really studied since my first year in junior high school. At Keaton, there is five times the amount of homework as in the suburbs. And it becomes quickly clear that most of this "study" means old-fashioned memorization. The more I memorize, the better grades I receive. That is how life goes, like a jackhammer, a continual series of "stings" and "grades," facts and bells, a routine as mechanical as possible.

My problem is, however, glaringly obvious to the "masters." While I am a good student and do not get in disciplinary trouble, it is clear that I have "the wrong attitude." So long as my grades and "credit rating" are kept up, they will tolerate me at Keaton. But should I slip, should I lose a little control in either area, they will waste no time in sending me home, expelled, tuition nonrefundable. Keaton expels a huge quantity of boys each term.

But in its harsh way, the school is fair. At public school, I often found my grades much lower than I had expected because of some mysterious thing called "class participation" upon which a teacher could base anything and grade you off for it. Here, if a teacher doesn't like you, your grades will not suffer. You get what you deserve. He will take out his displeasure in other ways, on the "sting sheet" or by making your life generally miserable.

All this talk of "grades"! But that is Keaton's most important product. Parents pay money so their boys will get "good grades" and eventually barter them for an admission to a "good college." Life is simple. Life is preparing to live. Perhaps once in college, life will cease being a preparation and begin being a life.

We are sitting in Zeke's room. It is mid-morning and we are both cutting chapel, having bribed our way out. We sit and smoke. "I would really like the rest of the day off. I'm tired from staying up all night writing that report," I say.

"I know," he nods. Zeke is my best friend at Keaton. He is built like a bear and lumbers across the lawn. With his brown hair messy and his spectacles sitting on a pug nose, he makes quite a sight in the bib overalls and wool shirt he wears when it is "free time" and he can climb out of the regulation jacket and tie.

Zeke is sitting on his bed leaning against the wall, and picking a guitar. He sings cowboy songs like Jack Elliot but doesn't really want to be a folksinger like my friend Steve. Zeke wants to be a painter. "Zeke" is not his real name, either. He gave it to himself as a kind of present when he arrived at Keaton.

"Your father's going to speak next weekend, isn't he?" he says.

"Yeah."

"You're lucky, Spike."

"Why?"

"Your father. My father is messed up." Lucky? I don't say anything. I know it's true. Keaton is driving into winter. Already the snow has fallen over the brick dormitories like wads of boiled notebook paper. Zeke is going to get thrown out of Keaton.

He is very smart. There are even rumors floating around about how his I.Q. is the highest in the school. But each day he performs an act. Zeke plays the role of a country hick somehow enrolled in a "sophisticated" Eastern prep school.

He is unable to understand more than the most perfunctory instructions. He refuses to study. On the weekends, parents and visitors look aghast at this young "farmer" who wanders around the campus in his overalls. The rest of the preppies either ignore or else try to bait or abuse him. He is too spaced out to pay any attention. At night, just before "lights out," he takes off his farmer's outfit and gets back into his tweed sportcoat and khaki slacks. Then knots his rep tie, turns off the light, and falls on his bed. That is how he sleeps, using the prep school uniform for his pajamas. So that in the morning when he comes into the huge dining hall rubbing his eyes, on the verge of being late, it is obvious that he has just gotten out of bed. His jacket and tie are incredibly rumpled and creased. He is like a 6 foot 2 inch Charlie Chaplin stumbling into breakfast.

"Did you do the assignment for Turner?"

"Bullshit," he says.

"You want to copy mine?"

"Okay." I give it to him; he takes out his notebook, filled with sketches and cartoons, and finds a clean page. Turner is an ex-Marine who teaches us history, though in different sections, and who absolutely hates Zeke.

"You know," he says to me, "you ought to tell your old man about Wechsler's speech."

"I already did. On the phone." Wechsler is the master in charge of Zeke's floor. He claims to be a graduate of Yale and Annapolis, a world traveler, a bon vivant from Vermont who now teaches at Keaton. The March on Washington and the Birmingham bombings have not won America over to civil rights just like that. The fall of 1963 sees the invention of the "white backlash." Throughout the country, not only in the South, resentment against black demonstrators is growing like a malignant disease. Some of it is the raw sewage of hatred. Other kinds are more careful and "respectable." Wechsler requested from the administration a special assembly one afternoon (during a time period reserved for such rare occasions) in which he wanted to present some other "aspects" of the civil rights problem. Nobody quite knew what to expect and Wechsler had blown himself up to be quite a scholar so we all were required to attend. Whereupon, Mr. Wechsler pulls out a speech that is the result of his own private "research" and clippings, "proving" he claims, the genetic inferiority of Negroes. Unreal. It leaves most of the four hundred Keaton students bored. Who listens to assembly speakers anyway? A few of the younger faculty are appalled. And the five or six Negro students sit with dazed expressions. As if they have been beaten with pillows. One can only imagine what worm of hatred feeds on Wechsler's speech in their minds.

"Wechsler blew it with that speech," I say.

"A complete prick."

"Total racist. Those statistics were as phony as a three dollar bill."

"Introduce your father to him," says Zeke.

"I hope I get the chance." I pick up the guitar and take a few token strums on it.

"What do you think would happen if I introduced your father and my father?" I ask Zeke.

He looks up. "Jeez, are you kidding? They'd both get so uptight they'd pop their skulls."

"I guess so." His father is a highly successful businessman with a huge company.

"My father told me he wants to be a millionaire in five years. That's what he said. Can you imagine that?"

"Being a millionaire wouldn't be so bad," I say. I am thinking that in five minutes I will have to get up and run to class. "Christ, I feel like cutting the rest of the day."

"Maybe we should try the Infirmary," he says.

"I've never been in there yet."

"Good. A point in your favor. I was there in the beginning."

"What's it like?"

"Boring. But you can sleep all you want. And the food is a little better. We could tell them . . . or *you* could tell them you have the runs. That would get you in for a day. Especially if you work up a little fever."

"What about you? I don't feel like going to the Infirmary by myself."

"I'll tell them I have pains in my back."

"Not bad." I smile.

"Out of sight: they'll never go for it but it's definitely worth a try." He stands up and reaches for his sadly abused gray tweed hanging off the doorknob.

"If they do, a little vacation wouldn't hurt. I could dig about twenty-four hours of total sleep."

"Okay. I'll try first."

I wish him luck. In a few minutes, I see him through the window trudging out of Smyth Hall in the direction of the Infirmary. A couple of times he rubs his back. Already putting on a show, in case the nurse may be staring out the window with nothing to do this morning. Suddenly, Zeke falls down on the concrete path and begins to writhe. Both hands clutch at the small of his back as if there was a small animal biting him. For a minute of pure craziness, Zeke rolls around on the ground alone, acting, but not acting. I can see that the act has taken possession of him and he is lost in a seizure of mad energy. I'm sure the nurse is missing this. Good thing, she would probably send him straight to a psychiatrist. Only I am watching his performance, his fit of Keaton Spirit. They are always talking about the "Keaton Spirit." Now here is a boy who really has it.

Far away beyond the row of chestnut trees, big columns of the main classroom building obscure the little Infirmary. Zeke is up and on his feet again, moving toward this target. He mounts the three steps and disappears. I look at my watch. If he is inside for twenty-five minutes, then I will get up and leave his room and go launch my own act. This is tricky, for chapel is almost over. If I wait twenty-five minutes, I will definitely have to go to the Infirmary or else be accused of cutting my English class without an excuse. The Infirmary will write down exactly what time I arrived. So there will be about fifteen minutes of unaccounted time. I will say I was in the bathroom. Nine minutes have now gone by.

The bearlike figure in the rumpled clothes appears on top of the steps of the Infirmary. He walks down, then breaks into a trot back to the dormitory just as the bell rings from the top of the chapel. No luck this morning.

There are two classes after lunch. Zeke has his American history with Turner and I have geometry. Math is my weakest subject and I doze while formulas are run. The bell rings, I yawn and hoist my books.

A strange buzz in the hallways. I leave the building and head toward the library across the quad. History is in a classroom on the second floor. Zeke and I usually pass each other going in opposite directions. On the lawn someone says, "Kennedy was shot."

"What?"

Several people turn and look at the boy. He keeps walking. Another instance of "Keaton Spirit," I think. Every day there is a new rumor, a new secret expression or a new way of giving the finger to the "masters" behind their backs. "That's what I heard too in Higgins's class," says another.

"The President was shot?" There are about sixty boys crisscrossing on the lawn. At the south end, to my left, the chapel pokes its white needle into the afternoon sky. Looks like an advertisement for prep school, I think. The sky is full of mashed potato clouds and royal blue gravy. The sun blinks in and out of the cumulus. Here comes Zeke making an end run around a line of football players. They laugh at him when he passes. His ragged notebook drips out of one hand and the other is buried in his pocket. He looks sad.

"How was the drill sergeant?" I ask.

"Off the wall. As usual." We stop for a second.

"You going to gym?"

"No. She gave me a gym excuse at the Infirmary."

"So at least you got that."

"We better hurry. The bell is about to ring." I nod and run. I am thinking about this rumor as I hurry into the classroom. The big blond conference table is full. But Turner is not in his seat. I sit down and get my notebook arranged. There is a good possibility of a surprise quiz today, I think. Everyone is chattering.

"O'Brien came into our room and asked Mr. Hurst if he had heard about it."

" . . . Dallas."

"What a piece of bullshit."

"Got to be a rumor, Santini. No way."

Turner steps in the door. "All right, everybody shut up! Are you all talking about this rumor? Does anybody have any *facts* besides this scuttlebutt?"

Roy Sanders raises his hand and Turner nods. "Sir, Mr. O'Brien came into our class and said it was true."

"What was true?"

"The President was shot, sir." This is a Keaton fact. If another master has openly stated something, it cannot be quickly dismissed without an investigation.

"I frankly don't believe it," says Turner. "Mr. Wechsler and I were just told the same by a couple of students. If this is a rumor, a perverted mind thought it up. I don't know about you guys."

"Sir? Why don't you send somebody upstairs to turn on the television?" It is Rick Hiller, a star on the lacrosse team which Turner coaches.

"What's the matter, Rick? You missing your favorite cartoons?"

"I just thought if the President was shot . . . it would be on the tube. That's all sir." Turner stares at him and mulls this idea over.

"Maybe so. Okay, Rick. Let's everybody go up and turn on the television in the lecture hall. Bring your notebooks. If this rumor isn't true, you can all take your quiz upstairs." He twists the word "quiz" like a dull knife. Half the class, the half which didn't do last night's assignment, moans. "Quiz?"

Upstairs, he switches on the lights in the back of the room. Rick turns on the television.

"Nice idea Rick, you prick!"

"Way to go, Ricky boy." They blame him for the quiz.

"Why don't you get *Captain Kangaroo,* your favorite show, you stupid cunt!"

"Fuck off, you guys," says Rick. The television begins to hum. Still no light on the mud-colored screen.

"Turner really eats the bird," a guy on my right whispers.

"Everybody shut up!" shouts Turner from the back. The hum of the electronic gear in the console jells into a voice. A frantic voice in Dallas. It nails the confusion of the boys. Everybody shuts up. Turner catches the tone and walks to the front to stand beside the television with his arms limp. I can see a tiny edge of sweat below the line of his crewcut bristles. The screen fills with an unrecognizable picture. Much later I know this is Dealey Plaza, empty. The room is cold and quiet. Only the flickering box has any heat. Wechsler appears at the door and leads his class silently into the room. Several boys sit with looks of relief on their faces. Thank God, they think. The President was shot. No quiz today.

———————————

I talk to my mother on the phone. "Where's Dad?"

"He's in Washington. He called this afternoon."

"They might let us all go home."

"When?" she asks.

"They probably won't. What's wrong with this country? It's going crazy."

"I know it," says my mother.

On Saturday night at Keaton, there is no place to go except the "butt lounge," the little snackbar or the lousy movie.

In keeping with its religious tradition, anyone caught drinking is liable for expulsion on the spot. If you go out for lunch with your parents on a "day leave" and have a sip of your father's martini and a master smells alcohol on your breath when you return, it's all over. I think they like to expel people. It keeps the budget balanced.

Zeke and I discover the pleasures of a bottle of thick cough medicine gulped on an empty stomach. Half-drunk, half-drugged, you tend to fall down a lot and mostly want to lie on your bed and listen to music. Then Zeke and I read about people who are getting high on morning glory seeds. I remember my grandfather showing me his morning glories in the Rochester garden. We go to the local hardware store and find they have stocked just the kind that makes you high: "heavenly blue." I decide I don't want to "trip." I am afraid to lose control. I have fitted my mind into harness and the fit is tight, the harness weak. I still want to go to a "good college" and to get out in June, not in the middle of a term. I am a robot in tweed and necktie.

Zeke grinds up packets of morning glory seeds and washes down the foul-tasting powder with orange juice. In an hour, he is hallucinating. He lies on his bed and watches the gyrating flame of a small candle which he has put inside one of his wire sculptures. This throws eerie shadows on the walls of the room. I have drunk some cough medicine.

Later that night, I am awakened at four o'clock when a flashlight zaps me in my sleeping face. It combs the room.

"Is Zeke here?"

"No."

"He's out of his room. We're looking for him." The master closes the door and I listen to him walk down the steps and outside my dorm.

I am worried. Tom's Lake sits outside in the darkness. Last year a boy, the most sensitive boy in the school, who wrote poetry and was into drugs, was found floating face down in Tom's Lake. His blood was choked with barbiturates. I don't want them to find Zeke floating in four inches of water. A few more months and we can be out of this place. We can be friends in a world without bells. I love Zeke. I have never had a friend I felt so close to before, whom I could talk to so easily, who understood me, both my strengths and my weaknesses.

Most everyone at school despises him. More seem to like me. Very strange, for Zeke is quiet and gentle and never says a hostile word to anybody. But I am continually blasting, bitching and moaning, possessed of a nasty cynical streak. I cut people down to their face, behind their backs, from left and right. I never let up the flow of insults hurled at Keaton. If I must be here, and I know I must for I have put myself here, I will fight it tooth and nail, while trying to ride it out for a year and the "grades."

One afternoon after one of my caustic tirades against the school, Zeke looks up and says, "I want to teach you how to be nice." He stares at me through his glasses, not angry but with seriousness. I know exactly what he means and for a moment, I feel tears building.

Four hundred boys stuck together in this school and everyone is afraid of being queer. There is a lot of talk about it. Who do you think on the faculty is queer? Who among the students? And each boy wondering, "Am I queer?" I know I love Zeke. And I worry. Yet I have no desire to touch him sexually. No fantasies about his cock or anything of the sort. Yet I know that there are nights I would just like to lie in bed beside him, not even hugging. Just to sleep next to my friend all night would be enough. This is the first year I have ever lived away from home and I am very lonely . . . No good thinking of that. Must make my mind a blank and get those grades . . .

The next morning, I find Zeke before breakfast. "Where were you?"

"Walking around. I was having a great time on the seeds. Couldn't stay in this room. Went out to walk. Wechsler came into my room about five minutes after I got back. They went to your room, huh?"

"What's going to happen?" I ask.

"What do you think?"

"Mr. Wechsler, I'd like to introduce you to my father." They shake hands. Almost at once, Wechsler himself brings up the speech he has given. He knows my father works in the civil rights movement. The lounge is filled with mothers and fathers down for Parents' Day. A table is covered with cookies and punch, big red bowls of the same stuff we drink with meals and call "bug juice." Now they have slices of fruit floating in it. The walls and ceiling are festooned with blue and gold decorations. Wechsler is here with his girlfriend. A tall girl with long hair and long legs, she looks like a Vassar or Wellesley caricature. Each weekend he has her down. Nobody among the students is yet sure if they sleep together all night in his dorm apartment. Many investigations have been launched to garner this information, but so far he has evaded them all.

"Dr. Spike, take for example this law about segregated

bathrooms in the South. People are making such a big protest about this. They want to make this illegal with the Civil Rights Bill."

"Yes?" says my father. A faint smile flickers just beneath the surface of my father's face.

"You're a learned man, Dr. Spike. You have to respect the statistics. And the statistics show the necessity for segregated bathrooms." Wechsler is smoking a cigarette in a very pompous way. His girlfriend is watching him carefully, with big eyes. My mother looks as if she wants to punch him. And I am waiting for my father's move. I hope he gets Wechsler, I really do.

"Which statistics are those?" he asks.

"Statistics about venereal disease in this country. The rate among Negroes is at least three times as high as among white people." Wechsler can hardly resist a big grin. He probably has the clippings with this statistic upstairs in a manila envelope labeled "Negroes." He senses he is on the verge of triumph. At last! The chance to put one of these civil rights liberals straight.

"You're also a learned man, Mr. Wechsler," says my father. "I guess you've been around quite a bit too." Wechsler nods. Is my father conceding, surrendering?

"Yes," says Wechsler.

"Don't you know where you get venereal disease?"

"What do you mean?"

"Not on toilet seats, Mr. Wechsler." This hits the mark to bring a red blush over Wechsler's face. He doesn't know what to say. His girl is watching him. My father smiles. I am thinking, "You racist, you got what you deserve." The conversation dies right there and the "master" and his girl melt away to the far side of the room.

"Thanks, Dad."

———————

They expel Zeke. The final straw comes at dinner one evening. A master named Mr. Fendler has the job of saying grace before meals. Fendler is an obnoxious little man. He hangs around the wrestlers and most everyone agrees he is a queer. Fendler likes to write very elaborate, original graces. They begin with openings like "Lord, Almighty God, watch over this room full of young lions as they prepare to break bread . . ." He imposes this on a room full of starving people for five or six minutes at a clip. Finally one night he has a Grace which is based on his feeling that things have been getting out of hand lately around the school. Several seniors have just been caught drinking, some others have been caught stealing exams. Fendler's Grace begins: "Lord, most Almighty God in Heaven and on earth, you have given these boys a sack of gold. Now they turn around and treat it like a bag full of bent pennies. . . ." His masterpiece goes on for eight minutes. At its conclusion, everyone groans and sits down in a din to eat supper. Except Zeke. He remains on his feet and gives Fendler one minute of standing ovation for his "Grace."

The next afternoon the Dean comes to his table in the middle of tunafish salad lunch. Zeke follows him out. His father is waiting outside in the empty hall.

"Dad?"

"Let's just get your stuff," says his father. For an instant, Zeke thinks his father has come to rescue him. But the Dean's bloated expression tells him the truth.

We ride a bus through the early evening traffic on the thruway to a small city. The school is on top of a little hill in a residential area. I ask someone, "What are they like at Plum Hill?"

"You mean Prostitute Hill?"

"Cherry Hill," corrects somebody else. "Mostly pigs. One girl last year looked pretty hot. Carson was supposed to have planked her in the bathroom." Maybe you *can* get venereal disease on a toilet seat? "I had a boss chick last year," says a guy in front. Seems to be a group of dance regulars. Maybe fifteen guys. They fancy themselves studs. The rest have less experience. This is my first prep school dance.

It is being held in the library. Everything has been done to disguise the books and make this place pulse with "Christmas cheer." Red and green everywhere. The girls cling together, party dresses and high heels for all. Tons of make-up. "Check the one by the globe, in the corner," says a guy I know named Jim. I locate the girl. She *is* cute, a gumdrop face, soft brown hair cupping a dazed, expressionless stare. She is a dormitory fantasy, a Keaton antidote.

"She's pretty."

"You can have her friend," he says. The friend is weasel-faced with a figure like a stalk of celery.

"You're pretty generous, Jim."

"Don't mention it. Why do they always travel like that? Beauty and the beast."

"Symbiotic relationship," I say. I have been reading about symbiotic relationships in some book recently. A girl suddenly comes out of the librarian's office holding a handful of white cards. The girls stir with excitement as if she was holding the results of a million dollar lottery. These are the "dance cards." On the front of each some girl has carefully drawn a little bunch of candy canes lying on top of a holly leaf. Inside each card, five names are listed. These are supposed to be the first five girls you dance with. "Why do they have these things?" I ask Jim.

"To make sure all the ugly girls get a crack at some handsome boys."

"So my first dance is with this name here . . . Diane Nuccaroni?"

"That's right." I go over to the girl who has just handed out our cards.

"Who is Diane Nuccaroni?" She looks around the room.

"Don't see her right now."

"Is she pretty?"

"You'll like her." I get a funny look from her. In a couple of minutes, the records start, mostly rock and roll "oldies." The segregated groups of Keaton boys and Plum Hill girls slowly join on the floor, holding their cards up in front of them, searching for partners. Jim and I lean against the wall. "Let them find us," he says.

Immediately, the little gumdrop girl is floating on the arms of a handsome halfback named Wells. The two stars have located each other already. Might as well forget about her for the rest of the night. "Paul Spike?" A finger jabs my arm. Standing behind me is a girl around my height, with a beehive hairdo, a hard but not unattractive face. She looks a little older than most of the others.

"I'm Diane."

"Nuccaroni?"

"Yes. How are ya?" she asks, cute as a Christmas cookie.

"Okay. You want to dance?" We move onto the floor and fortunately it is a slow record. I don't feel like "twisting" or "frugging" because, frankly, I don't do it very well. Her breasts poke through my jacket like hard cones. She must be wearing an aluminum bra. Her cheek rests on mine without hesitation and I catch a thunderbolt of tutti-frutti perfume. On my back, her hand begins to rub implications. She wants me closer. At once, she responds with a grind on my upper leg. This is amazing, the first dance. I get a hardon immediately. My brain doesn't hesitate but hands me a fantasy sandwich: "I am going to get laid tonight." What a thought! This girl has already taken her hand out of mine and is dancing with both arms around my neck. The grinding moves over from my thigh onto my zipper. I move my hand down and press the top of her ass. Underneath, I feel something smooth and slick in contrast to the wool of her skirt. A girdle! Diane seems to be wearing a set of armor. Who cares? The grind goes on.

"What are the chances of sneaking out of here?" I ask after two more dances.

"See that woman over by the door? She's our head-mistress. She's guarding the door. Anybody caught outside will be expelled." One good thing about Keaton, they have never expelled any of their boys for sneaking out of a dance at a girls' school. Only at Keaton. The double standard.

"Do you like Keaton?" Diane asks.

"Can we talk about something else?" I am considering the possibilities of making this fantasy sandwich come true. "What's upstairs?"

"The language lab." I flash a room full of cubicles and headphones. Hardly a room in the Holiday Inn but I would lie down in a pool of slush to make love to this girl. I am a virgin. Weeks of midnight masturbation alone in my dormitory. Six weeks of seclusion at Keaton since my last visa to Tenafly. The grinding armor of Diane Nuccaroni has set me on fire.

"Let's sneak upstairs. They won't throw you out for that."

"Do you think . . . I guess we could."

"Sure. Where are the stairs?"

"Follow me."

I am searching for a match to light her cigarette. The lights are off in the language lab. When I get it, the dim shadows grow blindingly familiar. About ten stalls with headphones hanging from hooks and dials built on the countertops. I wish this was the Infirmary or a teacher's lounge. Something with a bed or couch to lie down on. Her hand slips into mine. Language labs are supposed to improve your pronunciation. I used to fall asleep with my head on the edge of the table, sitting in the chair. The time has come to kiss her.

Just in time to catch a face full of exhaled smoke. Her hands embrace me very hard, the grind is going again. This is fantastic, I think. Who cares if you are leaning up against the partition in a dark language laboratory with a girl you find moderately attractive who doesn't know how to kiss. Maybe you will get laid! I try for second base, shoot under her arm to cup one tightly wrapped breast. So many nights in the dormitories jacking off to fantasies of this. Now real! Stay there, Experience! I want to memorize you like the date of Teddy Roosevelt's inauguration or the formula for determining the circumference of a circle. I'm going to be needing you soon, Experience. Tomorrow night in Coaltown.

Grind and rub. Knees poke knees. I feel the volume controls of the language stall crunching against my thigh. I try to pull her down on the floor. "My dress . . ." she whispers. Then drops her cigarette on the floor and searches with her shoe to stomp it out. I had not realized it was still burning. She sticks her tongue in my ear and gives me an agonizing rake job of delicious noise. Time for skin.

She senses what I am doing and pushes me away. But it is only so she can unzip the back of her dress, pop the brassiere and then pull her arms out of the sleeves. So cooperative, I pray that her headmistress will not suddenly pop in the door on a casual inspection of the language lab. I gently remove her bra and lower my face between the two headphones on her chest. Her nipples have a terrific pronunciation. What is that they are whispering to me? I think I hear a special message . . .

"That stays!"

"Come on . . ."

"I mean it!" I remove my fingers from the girdle. Immediately, the grind of her pelvis begins again. I shrug and kiss her breast but something occurs to me. Maybe there is a misunderstanding. I want to make everything clear. So I say, "I want to stick my cock in you."

"You must be kidding!"

Downstairs, a convention of honeymooners has replaced the previous shy group of students. Everyone is dancing in deep embrace, eyes closed, hands rubbing intricate messages around the fringes of each other's zones. Jim comes over holding a girl's hand, a cute girl, but he lets go and takes me aside for a second.

"Where did you go? Outside?"

"Upstairs. The language laboratory."

"You bastard. Did you screw? She really looks hot."

"I've got a hot set of blue balls."

"You mean you didn't screw?"

"Lend me a blowtorch so I can take off her girdle." He punches me in the shoulder.

"Tough luck, buddy. You can't win 'em all."

"Go fuck yourself," I tell him.

"I would if I could, believe me."

At the bus, the scene is definitely out of a 1940's war movie. Sweethearts kiss their soldier boyfriends good-bye on the dock, off to the war in the Pacific. Only now it is outside the Trailways bus hired for the evening to take us off to prep school. Practically in tears, they tug and tear at each other on the dark sidewalk. "I'll write you."

"Call me tomorrow."

"So long. Be sure to write." All the Keaton guys want letters. It is a big thing to take a letter out of your mailbox in the crowd before lunch and sniff it. Pass it around. "Man, smell the perfume on this one!" Mailbox Romeos. They even caught a guy who was perfuming and mailing letters to himself.

"This is crazy. Look at these jerks," says Jim, as we wade through the crowd of young lovers making their final adieus. Jim and I go to the back of the bus and he takes the window seat. The master in charge of the bus goes to the door and shouts, "Everybody has thirty seconds to finish saying good-bye and then we're leaving without you." There is a last frenzied farewell outside.

"These idiots act like they're leaving their wives or something," says Jim. He is in a bad temper and this scene is bugging him for some reason. The driver starts the engine. This is the last signal and now the final lovers leap aboard. The girls line up outside the bus and wave good-bye from the curb.

"Good-bye, my love," shouts Jim sarcastically. "Farewell sweet dreamer! Good-bye, good-bye." He is arching his ass off the seat. I had not seen him unzip. But now he has the end of his cock in his fingers and stretches it out like a pink sausage, plainly visible to the girls outside the bus.

A few see him exposing himself! Confusion, and then a kind of terror. The driver pops the clutch and we move off the curb. Twenty-five girls get a quick flash of Jim stretching his prick in their faces. It is insane. Nobody on the bus has seen him except me. Everybody stares at us curious to know why we laugh so hard as the bus rumbles us back to the dorms. Why I am laughing so hard is a mystery to me too. Keaton is a daily excursion through madness. It lies down the dark road waiting for us, completely isolated yet continually devoured by the darker madness of the whole country. Keaton takes the sixteenth year of my life.

While I sit in the seclusion of Keaton, far away from worldly struggles, except the one to keep my behavior mechanical and my head running like a computer till June, my father takes the air shuttle back and forth to Washington several times a week. The Commission is building a lobbying effort in Congress, based on the enormous resources of people and money in the Protestant Church. The effort has only one goal: passage of the bill. My father writes about this in some detail:

While all this was going on in the area of community action, we had other staff members helping to form what developed into a national bipartisan consensus in behalf of the strongest civil rights legislation that has ever passed the Congress of the United States. Early in this effort we decided that a major responsibility of the Commission was a regional one—not in the south but in the midwest—because the key votes for the passage really resided in those states in the midwest where the intensity of the racial crisis was less severely felt. There was a kind of irony that the fate of the legislation was held in the hands of the white, Anglo-Saxon, largely Protestant constituency of the midwest. We set out to try and inform that part of the country about the issue, beginning with a big meeting in Lincoln, Nebraska, in September, 1963, to which we brought people from councils of churches throughout the area. Then we sent out traveling teams of people, both Negro and white, some of whom had participated in the struggle in the south, to carry on a continuous program of informing people and attempting to build a consensus favoring passage of a strong bill.

So central did this issue become in the life of the churches that in December, 1963, when the General Assembly of the National Council of Churches met, it took formal action in respect to a small parliamentary matter that was delaying passage of the civil rights bill through Congress at the time. It was unheard of for a church body to get that involved in details of political process, and it is something I would be steadfastly opposed to on most issues. But in this case, the issue seemed so morally unambiguous, so essential, that the Assembly took action.

Toward the end of April we held a large interreligious assembly of Catholics, Protestants and Jews at Georgetown University gymnasium. Thousands of people came from all over; many could not get into the building. Dr. Blake gave what I consider the greatest address I have ever heard him make. I shall never forget at the end of that address seeing a nun, the

Demonstrating for passage of the Civil Rights Bill
with James Farmer of CORE and John Lewis of
SNCC, Washington, 1964.

first person to her feet, seeming to jump straight up into the air
with approval and applause.

The next morning, we began holding daily services of worship on Capitol Hill with the announced intention that we would
not pronounce benediction for these services until the bill had
been passed. At 9:00 a.m. every morning, six days a week, we
brought into the Lutheran Church of the Reformation, just behind the Capitol, preachers from every communion all over the
country for daily worship. People came from everywhere. Sometimes we'd have seven or eight people; sometimes we'd have
twenty-five; sometimes we would have a hundred. We never
really knew what to expect. Following the service, there would
be a period of briefing in the basement of the church about the

state of the legislation. Then people went to the Hill to talk to
their Senators. This went on for over two months until the bill
was finally passed.

We have some satisfaction in having it said in Washington
that the bill was passed because of what the churches did.
This was said by both our friends and enemies. Hubert Humphrey said so many times, both to me in private and also
publicly. And Senator Russell said "The bill would never have
passed if those damn ministers hadn't got an idea that this was a
moral issue!"

The breakthrough comes when Senator Dirksen of
Illinois, the leader of the Republicans in the Senate, is con-
vinced by his local minister that civil rights is, indeed, a
moral issue. Once Dirksen decides it is not just another political problem to be dealt with in private fashion, the
other Republican senators, with some exceptions, move to
support the Civil Rights Bill.

I sit in the Tenafly kitchen. It is eleven o'clock at night. My
father has just come back from Washington and is upstairs
talking to my mother. I am home from Keaton for a glorious
few days of freedom. I hear him close the door to their
room. He stops in the hall and listens to my brother snoring
lightly in his dark room. Then he comes down the few stairs
and into the bright kitchen. He has taken off his jacket and
tie, wears his dark suit pants and a Brooks Brothers shirt,
striped, with no pocket, which is half unbuttoned. His eyes
are bloodshot and the skin on his face is etched with what
I think are new wrinkles. "You look tired, Dad."

"I had an exhausting two days."

"What's the trouble?"

"These amendments they keep trying to attach to the
bill."

"Why?"

"Each amendment delays everything. You have to go around and talk to everyone all over again. It's just a stalling tactic. Like the filibuster."

"Is it going to pass?"

"Johnson is putting a lot of pressure on his old Senate pals. It will pass. But how strong it ends up is another problem."

"You home for a while now?"

"No. Tomorrow I have to fly to Des Moines. Then to Chicago. Be gone for three days."

"What's happening in Chicago?" I ask just to keep the conversation going.

"Meetings." It was the wrong question. Ever since he left Judson Church and went to become the Secretary for Evangelism at the Congregational Church, this word "meetings" has been in our house. He flies across the country hundreds of times a year to these "meetings." They pursue him seven days a week, all twelve months. He takes few vacations. Only when my mother puts her foot down and demands that he take a rest, will he stop for a week of recuperation. After seven days of sleep and some sunshine, he looks young again and is eager to be back in "meetings."

Late at night is when he and I talk. After I come home from a friend's house and he is sitting up reading in the living room. Or just returned from a trip.

He can't fall asleep for hours on some of these nights. He tosses and turns and goes downstairs and lies on the couch in the darkness. I get up to go to the bathroom. It is 3:00 a.m.

"Paul?" he asks from the dark living room. "You okay?"

"Sure. How about you?"

"I couldn't sleep. My head is racing."

"You have gas pains?" He complains often of severe pain in his stomach. The tension ties it into knots and when he tries to unwind, it is a painful, slow process.

"A little," he concedes.

"I haven't been able to sleep either." I sit down in the armchair across from where he lies wrapped in a blanket on the couch. It is not so much a feeling of father and son when we talk. It is more like brothers. Or even very close, special friends. But it is father and son, there is never any confusion in the end. I feel very close to him in everything. He knows all there is to know about me. Sometimes I get a funny feeling about this. I want to know everything about him.

"What were you thinking about?" he asks.

"About the story. I feel very happy." *Evergreen Review,* after months of nothing, has just sent me a letter. They want to publish my story "Max, An American." I feel so incredibly full of myself. I have been lying in bed with my head full of visions of my future. I told myself I wanted to be "published" before I turned eighteen. I have sent close to twenty poems away to various little magazines and received twenty printed rejection slips in return. Now my story has suddenly slammed me into a different world. I am going to be *published!* I know there are two quite different universes of writers. One is full of "unpublished" ones and the other of "published." I feel that now I am suddenly going to jump from one to the other.

The truth is two and a half years away in the sad future. When I am eighteen and a freshman at college, I will get a brief note from Fred Jordan, the managing editor of *Evergreen.* They are no longer able to "use" my "piece." No explanation, no apology. But this night when I am sixteen, I am full of amazement at my own accomplishment. I feel that, truly, I am one day going to be what I want more than anything to be: a "writer." Before this, it was only a dream. Now it is a warm glow inside. In a way, it could have nothing to do with being a "writer." It could just as easily be a jet pilot, a physicist or a (but no!) minister. For what gives me the rushing exultation is the feeling of my own power. Suddenly, it works. Suddenly, I have done something in the *world,* not just the *school.* I have been given a success that is not part of preparing for college but is alive, is Life. The meat of this nut is sweeter than any I ever tasted before. Better than two years of straight A's. My first success. I cannot wait to see my words on the printed page. I cannot wait so hard I am about to stop writing for the next three years. Success floods my mouth with sweetness but rushes into my body like polio. I am paralyzed by it.

"Paul, I am terrifically proud . . . of you." Whenever my father says something full of love directly to me, it is almost too much for both of us. There is so much love. His voice almost breaks. I feel like crying. This relationship is rooted far back in his own relationship with his father. I sense this.

In certain ways, my father encourages me to be a rebel. He wants me to be independent and free; at the same time, he hopes I will play the games, work within the system, get into college. He is a rebel in his theology, in his lack of dogmatism, in his visions of the revolution which he believes is happening all over America. It is not just a civil rights struggle. He sees civil rights as only one part of a vast social, technological, sexual and moral revolution. In this way, he raises me to be a revolutionary, he hopes, equipped to work within the system as well as outside it. Just as he works within the church and the government. It also has to do, just a little bit, I think, with the image he has of a "minister's son." Such a boy should be rebellious, reject the strict religious upbringing of his childhood. Such a boy my father probably wishes, in certain ways, he himself had been. Instead of so dependent on the unconditional but conservative support of his mother. He likes this image of the "minister's son." I can feel that. And to a certain extent I try to model myself on it. The irony is that I am far closer to my father, the "minister," than any other friend of mine is with his own father. They are lawyers, businessmen, film makers, advertising executives. And their sons all relate to them in a far more "minister's son" manner than I do.

At the same time as my father makes me the son he wishes he had been, *he* tries to be the father he never had. His father withdrew his love and his support. My father gives endless unconditional love and support.

"I want to be a great writer when I grow up," I tell him.

"Paul," he speaks slowly. "I've thought about it a lot the last few days since your mother told me about *Evergreen* on the phone. I know you have talent . . . a hell of a talent. You *must* have, otherwise this wouldn't have happened. I really believe there is a chance you could become a great writer someday.

"But I worry about you. I hope you don't go too fast. This story is fine. But really only a start. If you are going to become a writer, it will take years of very hard work."

"Oh, I know that," I say quickly, defensively.

"You just have to write and write. Keep writing."

"That's true. I can feel my writing get better the more I do."

"It's the only way to learn. The thing I worry about with you, Paul, is discipline. You know writers have to discipline themselves. Nobody tells you to sit down and do it. No boss, except yourself. You have to build your own discipline into your life. Keep writing all the time. That's the only way you can make it."

His advice annoys me. It is not what I want to hear, stewing in my sweet success. Much later I recall this advice and realize I have written virtually nothing for three years. I have been waiting, paralyzed, to see my words in print.

"I guess you're right, Dad."

"I know a lot of you is having adventures and experiences. You say you want to travel. All that's part of being a good writer, I suppose. But you have to combine them with a personal discipline." He laughs. "Right now I feel like I'm completely dominated by my own discipline. I can't seem to control it any more."

"You work much too hard, Dad."

"I know." He admits it without wanting to do so.

Suddenly, I think about him. He has been absorbed into the civil rights struggle, into the Commission, and into the country. His life seems to have merged with History. I have never before known anyone who has done this. These people are the ones you see only on television. Now when we watch the news, we know, oftentimes, more than they tell us. The stories are merely the tiny tip, polished and refined, of the reality underneath. When my father comes home, he brings us an education. He talks about what is really happening in the South and in Washington. My father has been to Alabama and Mississippi. He has been to the Oval Office.

The pride flows back and forth between us. The love is steady but the pride moves in flashes. One thing is certain, his love is my anchor to myself. And I know it.

Spring takes an unusually long time to blossom at Keaton. Weeks pass when there is nothing to do but sit in my room looking out the window at a cold rain. The campus soaks up the water and becomes more swamplike every day. If you step off the concrete paths, you sink up to your ankles in grass soup.

When Zeke is gone, I feel friendless. But almost immediately I find the Toomans. Ron Tooman is a tall man in his late twenties who is master in charge of a dorm full of fourteen-year-olds. He teaches English. Viv, his wife, is a petite Chinese girl and one of the two pretty faculty wives at Keaton. They have a son almost three named Craig. Zeke got to be friends with Viv because she was showing him how to do Chinese brush painting. Sometimes I would tag along when he went for a lesson and we would find Viv in her kitchen painting exquisite bamboo and mountains with quick little flips of the traditional Chinese brush. Ron Tooman walks around the campus with a straight expression, almost a scowl.

Now I discover Ron's slightly sour face is a bluff for the retention of his job. He can smile! And burst into rich laughter. He keeps his eyes open, watches everything at Keaton and stores it. We sit in his kitchen, Ron having telephoned my "master" and told him I am "babysitting for Craig," and we laugh for hours at the billion absurdities of Keaton. Ron also has great stories about his days in the army and as a welfare worker in New York. He is from Wisconsin and loves basketball, which he coaches for Keaton. In certain ways, he reminds me of John Updike's hero Rabbit Angstrom. Only Ron is smarter.

He gives me a copy of *In Our Time* by Hemingway. I had always thought of Hemingway as one of those authors they assign you to read in high school because he is simple and noncontroversial. This is because they only gave us *The Old Man and the Sea* plus some of the more innocuous stories. But in this book, his first collected short stories, I discover Hemingway for the first time. The book overpowers me with its skill. The way the sentences are honed to such sharpness, you don't feel them until they have cut right through. One story especially clicks with my mood. This is "Soldier's Home," about a young man returned to the Midwestern home of his parents after World War I. The mood of this story matches my own alienation at Keaton. My favorite sentence comes when the hero's mother asks him to pray with her on their knees beside the breakfast table: "Krebs looked at the bacon fat hardening on his plate." Yes, I know, the fat can take days, months to harden. Especially at The Keaton School.

Afternoons spent in the Toomans' apartment are like medicine. After talking to Ron and Viv, playing with little Craig on the rug, I can go back to my dormitory for five hours of memorization and feel fresh. Ron and I are equally uncomfortable at Keaton. But for him, just as for me, it is a "system" he must work within in order to do what he loves, that is, work with kids. The boys at Keaton who study with him, who come to know him, feel the same affection as I do for the guy. Only I am luckier than most and become his friend. Ron and I talk about how most Keaton boys are sons of middle-class businessmen, lumberyard owners or something, who have survived a depression and a world war. Now they want to give their kids all the "breaks." They can afford to ensure their son's entrance to college. Everybody *has* to go to college. My father calls the B.A. degree a "union card for our society." These parents will guarantee their son's entrance by sending him to "prep school." He will be packaged and pushed, "prepared" and passed, like a Coca-Cola, out the Keaton gate and into college.

I get an unusual assignment from Mr. Gewirtz, my English teacher. We are free to write a paper on any topic we fancy. I ask after class if I may write a short story instead of an essay. Sure, go to it, he says. That night I write a three-page story entitled (I have to wince, though I remember I chose the title as a joke): "Monday Morning Rhythms." The story is based on fact. One Monday morning in New York City waiting to catch a train back to Keaton, I called up Liza, my girlfriend from Fire Island. It was a school day at Stuyvesant but I was sitting in my father's office, the telephone staring at me, and I dialed the number for the hell of it. She answered, she was home with a slight sore throat. Both her parents were at work. Did I want to come over? I found her in blue jeans and black turtleneck. My first question was why had she refused to come down and visit me at a dance Keaton had sponsored several months before. I had written asking her, explaining that the girls would be put up in a special dorm vacated for that night. But she had written back that her parents would not let her. Now she said, "My parents don't want me going out with you."

"Why not?"

"You're not Jewish." This was the first time I had ever been the object of racial prejudice and it felt strange. Because I was a Wasp, her parents wanted nothing to do with me. I was unclean, gentile, not fit to date Liza.

"Who knows if I'm Christian? I don't know what I am," I said.

"You're a gentile." She looked very sad about it. "I don't agree with them at all. But there's nothing I can do. I love my parents." There was a magnificent view of Central Park from her windows and a couch to lie on instead of a damp beach. We eventually got on this and spent two hours dialing orgasms on each other. I wanted to make love to her completely. But she would not allow it, even though she was ready and seemed to want it. I thought perhaps she would be disgusted by the act of being penetrated by my gentile penis. It was very frustrating and I felt confused. Should I be angry and indignant? Or should I ignore it? Eventually, I left to catch the train. That was the last time I ever saw Liza.

I write a short story about this in which I concentrate on the music of the words describing that afternoon of sex. In fact, in the story I imply that I actually made love to her. Wishful thinking.

The repercussions of "Monday Morning Rhythms" build to an absurd crescendo. First, my English teacher thinks it is great! He gives me an "82" on it. Mr. Gewirtz is proud of his reputation as a tough marker. But later in the evening he comes around to my dormitory. "I've been thinking about that grade all day. It's ridiculous. That story was the best I've ever gotten from a student. Let me change it." He comes in and takes out his pen, draws a line through the old number and writes a "90" on top. Big deal. But then he asks, "Could I borrow this overnight to make some copies?" He wants to give it, he says, to Mr. Underwood, the adviser to the Keaton literary magazine this year, and to a committee of the English Department which awards prizes. There is a Prize Day in the spring and one of them is fifty bucks for the student author of the best piece of "creative writing."

In about three weeks, Mr. Gewirtz tells me I have won this prize, called something like "The Charles Ludlow Graham Writing Award." I mention this to my parents. Unexpectedly they show up on Prize Day. It is a Saturday afternoon and spring has finally taken control with plenty of blue sky and sunshine. The big hall is packed with proud parents and young prizewinners. My parents and I sit down. I pick up a program and open it to scan the list of prizes. Strange, there is no listing this year for "The Charles Ludlow Graham Writing Award." I know they gave it last year to the boy they later found floating face downwards in Tom's Lake. He wrote strange, excellent poems. But no prize is going to be given for "creative writing" this year because, evidently, I am the one to whom it would go. Either the administration detests me or they find the story objectionable. A little of both. They know I have the "wrong attitude" and they used to tell me when Zeke was still at school, "You have the wrong friends, Spike." Mr. Keller, Zeke's most bitter enemy on the faculty, walked up to me the day after his expulsion and said, "One false move, Spike, and *you're* going too."

My father is furious. He has come expecting to see me get this prize. I explain the situation. "What is this, Russia?" he asks.

In a few days, I find even more trouble coming along because of this story. The administration finds it completely objectionable. The "administration" in this case is an old man who has been at Keaton longer than anyone else. He has a grand title and a large office and little to do except keep traditions alive and censor all Keaton literature. He returns the manuscripts for this year's literary magazine to Mr. Underwood. They are fine, except for this story "Monday Morning Rhythms." That has to be cut. Mr. Underwood is a young guy, he plays guitar, and he thinks he wants to be a writer himself. This is his first year at Keaton. We are friends. So are he and the Toomans. His first name is "Lee" and he insists that's what we call him. Lee is a very idealistic guy and, at times, this irritates me. But right now it only amazes me and makes me feel a little ashamed for ever having been irritated. He refuses to cut my story. He says he will prevent any literary magazine from coming out unless my story is in it. For there is no doubt my story is the best in the bunch of rather mediocre stuff.

Mr. Underwood is opposed to censorship of any kind. He makes his stand clear to the Baptist elders of Keaton. They immediately fire him.

This is the church at the other extreme. This is the church of my grandmother Lucy. And the church in which my father is a rebel at the same time as a "church bureaucrat," the label he gives himself sarcastically.

Not only is Underwood fired. I am summoned to stand trial before the dreaded "DC"! This is the nickname for the Discipline Committee of Keaton. Most of the conservative, old-fashioned masters sit on this DC, along with the Dean and the chaplain. A trip to the DC is a prelude to expulsion. The whole school knows whenever people go to their meeting with it, usually late in the afternoon while everyone else is at sports. You never know if you will walk out of the room still a Keaton boy or a stranger who has to get off campus before nightfall.

I take two Miltowns out of a small jar I have swiped from my home just in case of an emergency like this. A couple of other glum boys wait in the hall outside the faculty lounge where the DC meets. They pace back and forth. One of them knows he is definitely being expelled. This DC is just a last bit of torture. He grins at me a little nuttily. He was caught stealing money from another boy's dresser. I look away from him.

I have done nothing but write a story. It didn't have either dirty words or explicit sex. Only the clear knowledge that it was *about* sex, not the details. Am I going to be expelled? *Is* this Russia?

Finally, I am summoned into the room. The thief has gone before and spent only two minutes inside. When he comes out he says, "Nothing to it." They have expelled him. Another boy goes in for a long time. I wonder what his offense is. The grapevine has not carried any news of it.

There is a ritual in the DC well known by all the boys. You go in and face eight or nine masters staring at you like a convention of hanging judges. "Stand up against the wall. Your back should touch it. Straight. Don't lean on it. Hands out of pockets. Stand tall!" They literally put you right up against the wall.

"Do you know why you're here, Mr. Spike?" asks Keller in an effeminate voice. He is the most horrible master at Keaton, himself a graduate of the school; after Princeton he came straight back to teach. He is the only boy in the school's history who never lost *one single credit* during four years! Now he teaches Spanish and patrols the campus like a crab.

"No, sir."

"You must not try our patience. Or our credulity. You know we are considering your role in this story situation."

"Yes, sir."

"I don't know what sick fantasies drove you to write such trash . . ." he continues. The Miltowns have relaxed me wonderfully, I have to stifle a yawn. Meanwhile, all the "masters" look at me with hot glares. If I get expelled, all my days at Keaton, all the study, the enforced loneliness, go right out the window. I will have to repeat my junior year at another high school. I will have to forget all about my dream of Harvard.

"You understand why we can't allow it to be printed in a

school-financed literary magazine, Paul?" the chaplain inter-
rupts Keller to ask.

"Not really."

"The magazine goes to the parents of all the boys." He
speaks with a "reasonable" voice which sounds extremely
patronizing, though he doesn't know it. He is a young man. I
have studied the New Testament with him in a required
Bible class. We studied the writings of Paul. Irony there
somewhere. "Some parents would be very upset if they
found this story in a Keaton magazine."

"*Especially* the parents of the junior school boys," hisses
Keller.

"Underwood has acted in a completely unethical way.
You understand that, don't you?" says another old master.

"Not completely, sir."

"What?"

"Sir, I thought it was the students' literary magazine and
the students ought to choose what went into it. Not the
teachers. Or the administration."

"It is not the students' magazine. Whatever gave you
that idea?" rasps Keller. "It is *owned* by the school. The
Keaton School.

"I want to make it clear to you that everyone in this
room has a good picture of your attitude. Inside you is a very
stubborn, rebellious young boy. You and your friend have
caused a great deal of trouble with the morale here this
year."

The Dean clears his throat. Big and gray like an old
moose, he has a reputation for fairness. "Paul. Are you
happy at Keaton?"

"Yes, sir." The biggest lie I have ever told.

"Because we don't want boys here who are unhappy.
We want Keaton boys to be happy boys."

I spend the last weeks of spring studying for exams. No disciplinary action is taken against me for the story. Mr. Underwood is also allowed to finish out the year. On a hot afternoon full of June happiness, my father's car drives up the long Keaton approach road. I am sitting on the lawn with Lee Underwood and the Toomans. I jump up and do a little dance of joy. Next year I will go to a new school. My fourth school in four years of high school. But right now my father has come to redeliver me back to Tenafly. To use the phrase of the moment, I am free at last.

My father returns from his first meeting with President Johnson astounded. It is 1964. This summer America is pregnant with her election. When Kennedy was killed, the illusion of the sixties as a kind of Florentine Renaissance, led by

President Johnson meets National Council of Churches leaders to discuss civil rights. Bishop Smith, Father, Dr. Eugene Carson Blake (standing); Irwin Miller and Bishop Reuben H. Mueller (seated).

our own New England Medicis, was quickly ditched. Now we have a cowboy in the White House. My father tries to joke about it. But he is disturbed enough to say to my mother and me at supper, "The man is an egomaniac."

With a group of black and white church leaders, my father has gone to the White House to talk about the passage of as strong a Civil Rights Bill as possible. They emphasize the need for a good public accommodations section. Johnson says he agrees. He even has a little anecdote, presumably to convince the ministers of his firm belief in equal use of public accommodations. My father reports him saying, "We have had a woman work for us in the Johnson household for many years. A Negro woman. She has become a regular member of our family. She is a real close friend of mine and of my wife, and our two daughters.

"Do you think I would want this woman to go out and squat down on a rocky hillside? No sir. This woman does her business on the same toilet seat as the President of the United States!"

It is easy to blame all our troubles on the South in 1964. The news from the region is grotesque. Pictures of lard-bellied deputies lashing out with clubs, gas, dogs, electric prods. The nightmare of Mississippi where every tree may once have been festooned with a black corpse. These sleepy little towns with their apple-pie American names: Hattiesburg, McComb, Jackson. The Southern drawl comes to reek. It is the South that is ruining America's image around the world. If we could only amputate it, float it out to sea, perhaps ram Cuba and solve two problems at once . . . so goes the Northern view. Of course, plenty of "guilt" is trucked around in the North. Cocktail parties to raise money for the Southern struggle where thirty or forty white Northern suburbanites sip and nibble with a couple of overalled blacks

John Lewis and my father lead a group of Northern
ministers in a Mississippi demonstration.

wearing buttons that read "NOW!" But the media focuses on
the South almost exclusively. That is, until the end of the
summer of 1964, the first of the "long, hot summers." In the
last part of that summer, New York, Philadelphia and Rochester explode into riot. This suddenly brings the pressure too
close to home for a large group of Northern whites. The

backlash that had begun in 1963, by the end of 1964 is more of a flogging.

The summer begins in the South. My father commutes between New York, Washington and Mississippi. Several times he has "close calls" with nightriders on back roads of the Southern state. My father never talks about any of these occasions at home, for my mother is already anxious about his trips to Mississippi. But he writes about one such encounter experienced by his friend Ed King:

Nightriders became even bolder in stopping people. On one such occasion, the chaplain of Tougaloo, the Rev. Ed King, a white man who has been prominently identified with civil rights causes, was stopped en route from Canton to Jackson. His carload included his wife, some Tougaloo faculty people, and a visiting professor from India. For over an hour, they were held prisoners in their car, while the Protectors of the White Race debated whether to kill them or not. Only the presence of the foreign guest finally deterred the nightriders. When the visitors were released, they drove the thirty miles into Jackson still followed by their attackers. They drove directly to the Governor's mansion, where they were shunted aside, as they were also when the incident was reported to the police.

Whenever they fly into Jackson, the license plate numbers of the cars they rent at the airport are quickly passed out to a network of racists throughout the state. It gets so bad they begin flying into Memphis instead. Within a week, this racist subscription service has found an informer in the Memphis airport to phone the plate numbers to Mississippi. The danger is real but my father never talks about it. My mother pleads with him to be careful. She gets furious, too, at his taking these chances. But he just shrugs and acts like it is utterly ridiculous to think there is any danger. His act fools me. Not until much later when I talk to staff members of the Commission do I hear about any "close calls" in which he has been involved.

Here is his brief description of the 1964 Summer Project in Mississippi:

But through most of that first winter we tried to stay particularly close to the movement in Mississippi because here was located a concentration of the most militant, most capable, most competent of the young Negro leadership in the civil rights movement. These are people who are really outside the pale as far as white Mississippi is concerned. For our association with them, we are branded as dangerous radical communists. The leader of the movement in Mississippi was Bob Moses, a young Negro, a graduate of Hamilton College with a Master's degree from Harvard. For three years, he was the leader of a growing committed civil rights movement in Mississippi.

It became apparent early in 1964 that we were not immediately going to be able to put into operation a long-range ministry of community work and literacy training and remedial education. We were not going to be able to get this mounted by spring or even by the summer. And so the civil rights organizations in Mississippi—the Council of Federated Organizations—decided to go ahead with what they called their Summer Project. This was to be a student program of working in local freedom schools established to do remedial work, and also to work in voter registration. It was apparent by January that their intention to get 1000 students to come into Mississippi was going to materialize.

Those of us in the Commission who had worked in Mississippi the summer before were genuinely alarmed by the prospect of what would happen if 1000 students were let loose in Mississippi without any kind of preparation or orientation. COFO had no money to do any training. Their leaders lived under continuous threat to their lives, terribly overworked. So the Commission decided to offer to train and orient the students going south that summer. After some consideration, this offer was accepted by COFO and we set out to devise such a program and, in the process, to help stabilize the summer program itself through the structure of the training. We brought all the field workers out of Mississippi on a couple of occasions to meet with educators and psychologists and community organization people to try to set up the program. We then looked for a college campus where we might train the students going south. That was not an easy job, because colleges are not notoriously braver at things that might offend public sensibilities than are the churches! Finally, Western College for Women in Oxford, Ohio, offered its facilities for the last two weeks in June.

There were three areas in which training was done. First, the students were given straight factual information about Mississippi and the particular communities where they were going. We divided students into the groups they would be working with for the rest of the summer. Their supervisors met with these groups so that all the training was done as a unit, whether they were going to teach in freedom schools or work in voter registration. This training included information about the communities, what they could expect from the white majority, from the police, what their legal rights were, and related matters. The second area was skill training; that is, going over what they were to teach in the schools and the procedures in voter registration.

The third area was training in nonviolent response to a hostile situation. This was very careful, very detailed suggestions about what you do if you are stopped by a policeman, what you do if he gets out of his car and hits you over the head, what you do if a whole lot of people are arrested, what you do if a bunch of hoodlums attack you, what you do if people spit on you, and so on. This aspect of the training was picked up by the southern press, who said this proved that the people were coming to cause trouble—because they were being told all these terrible things that might happen to them so they would be enraged. Every single example used in training, however, came out of the experience of people who *had* worked in Mississippi.

At the end of the first week of the training, three of the men who had been in Oxford went to Mississippi. On their first weekend there they went up to visit a bombed-out church near

Philadelphia in Neshoba County—and disappeared. This had an enormous effect on the people at Oxford in the second week of training. And yet very few decided to go home. This incident intensified the dedication and commitment of those who went to Mississippi, and I suspect increased the pattern of discipline that we tried to help them see was necessary.

With students about to leave for "Freedom Summer" in Mississippi.

We didn't schedule any worship into this conference. We decided that we were running this as a training program; it was not a campus religious community. And yet, on the night that the burned-out car was discovered in Mississippi, I happened to be at Oxford and there was a demand from the students that we discuss the religious issues involved. About 200 of them gathered and they asked me if I would talk about my theological understanding of why we were involved. Afterwards, they came at us with all kinds of reactions—some assent, some attack, some suspicion. And then there was worship—genuine worship. That is, for the first time, these students faced their own mortality. This was not imposed on them but it was the most genuine worship in which I have participated in a long time.

I ask my parents to send me to Mississippi with the thousand students. My father refuses. "These are college students. Nineteen to twenty-three or -four at least. You are only sixteen."

"One member of the family in Mississippi this summer is enough!" says my mother. She refuses to hear any further discussion.

Instead, I am to get a summer job. Colleges look carefully at the "summer employment" section on your application. "You should support yourself this summer," says my father. "When I was sixteen I was working on the railroad around Buffalo repairing track. Saving money for my college."

"When I was your age!" I mock him. But I do it. The only job I can find is as a clerk-typist in an accounting department in New York City. Then my friend Steve calls up and says his mother is going to be out on Fire Island all summer. He will be working for his father. Would I like to live with him at his mother's place on Madison Avenue?

What an American summer! Held together by a fantastic glue of irony. My father is running back and forth between Mississippi and Washington, trying to improve the lot of rural Southern blacks. I am working at a mindless clerical job for eighty dollars a week. Good money in Mississippi. And living in a palace of an apartment with my sixteen-year-old buddy. Steve's mother has arranged a charge account for us at Gristede's. Each day after work I stop and charge a steak or pork chops and some beer. We blow pot in Steve's room and watch television. My father calls up from Jackson.

I go into the kitchen and fix a midnight snack. In the morning, I ride to work on the Fifth Avenue bus. I work with about a dozen ladies from the Bronx and Queens who are all working to help support their families. I am on summer vacation.

The plain truth is I do not really want to go to Mississippi. I am relieved when they say No. I have asked, I suppose, because I feel I should. Perhaps to impress them. Perhaps to scare them. But I have no real social conscience. What I have, at this point, is a social sympathy. I can feel anger and compassion about what is happening in the South. I can watch atrocities on television and say, "I'd like to kill that cop," who is beating up a seventy-year-old woman with his riot club. But it is really just a television response. I am watching a movie called the "news." What I really mean is not that I would "kill" this person I see on the screen. I mean, "That's the bad guy." A response produced by hundreds of hours before the television.

To sit and watch television: how does a white face look in the process of torturing a black face? How does the black face look as it endures the torture? These questions evoke strong but unreal responses. Television, no matter where you put the dial, is a form of Entertainment.

I don't mean that television is always entertaining. Nobody, not the least critical, would claim everything he sees on television is entertaining. But it is *always* Entertainment. It passes the time. And there is a great need these days in America to pass the time.

When millions of Americans suddenly become aware of the struggle for equal rights in the South, it is because they tune it in. Like a new program. Racism becomes Entertainment. Discussed in some homes, while next door they discuss different shows, *Gunsmoke* or *The Beverly Hillbillies,* those lovable, millionaire rednecks.

One of the few ways to reach through this media distortion and get people to respond to their *own* stake in these rights and this fight to end racial prejudice is church. Church is one of the few places where Americans go any more. Movies? The tube brings movies home. News? The tube brings it. The tube brings America to its people. It is like a country that exists only in airwaves. The actual land, the countryside of forests, rivers, mountains, deserts, is all homogenized and leveled, turned into one long asphalt strip from coast to coast, with the same signs, restaurants, stores, gas stations, everything the same in each town. The real America is in my living room, in that little box.

But a lot of Americans still have this habit called "going to church." Even though churches have come to look identical: A-frame, motel-modern buildings surrounded by parking lots and trimmed, suburban lawn. Still, my father hopes to reach people so they will respond like human beings, not like an audience of viewers. He hopes to do this . . .

What about me, his son? I am trapped between his influence and my own childhood before the tube, watching "America" in a little box. I have known very few Negroes in my life. I cannot feel racism. Nor can I love all Negroes. I cannot give myself to this cause.

How could I? I cannot love *myself*. Do not yet know who "myself" is. I live the life of an "image." This is a popular device for those of us in high school in the early sixties.

"I don't like my image. I think I'll change it," says a guy in front of the Dairy Queen in Tenafly.

"Why? Your image seems okay to me."

"Well, I want to be stronger. I'd like bigger arms. Think I'll start lifting weights again."

The "image" is what television carries to us, children of the electrical age. The "image" is what carried the Kennedys into power. What hurt Nixon in 1960. What won for him later.

My own "image" is half-real and half-created.

I live the life of a millionaire. Spending my father's money, I do not care. I am sixteen. I have survived the suburbs, I think, and Keaton too. One year of high school left. My "image" is designed to carry me through all sorts of social predicaments, Baptist prep school to filthy crash pad. My long hair flows carefully wild over the collar of my Brooks Brothers shirt which is tucked into faded blue Levis which cover the tops of my scuffed boots. I look for girls, try to "pick them up" whenever my nerve holds, but mostly I look for them, dream about them, my days filled with dozens of instantaneous "crushes." I dream of finding a girl who will really understand me. In fact, I need somebody's interpretation fast, in lieu of one of my own. For each visit to the mirror is less an act of vanity than a kind of safari to the murky headwaters of my life. I stare at my face. Who is this? Who am I?

My father has come completely into his own. Working to free black Americans, he has become free. Enormous stores of energy open inside him. He is working, writing, preaching, administering with wisdom and love. He is now the man he was born to be. It is beautiful to see him like this. Our little family is run on pride for him. He is our nuclear engine, keeping us all going. For the moment, we even know *where* we are going, unlike so many millions of television Americans. We are going with *him*. That seems to be enough.

The people in the church more and more regard my father as one of their most important leaders. The church has been drying up, going sterile. Once, a Main Street church was *the* social center of every little American town and neighborhood. Now it is a ritual motel. The congregation drives in for an hour Sunday mornings, sleeps through a sermon, coughs up some dollars, and drives away. The civil rights struggle gives the church a new chance to act in a "Christian" way without that implying narrow-minded or prudish behavior. It may even be the last chance for the Protestant Church in America.

My father believes there is a revolution beginning in

the country, of vast and, perhaps, terrible proportions. He sees the rate of change flipping through traditional American life like a hand flipping through all thirteen channels on a New York television dial. Everything is up for grabs. How do you raise a son in this world? How do you prepare him to live in chaos?

I get as much freedom as he can possibly give. No pat answers, no religious dogma. I think it is just as accurate a reflection of his own beliefs about our home when he writes, "We didn't schedule any worship into this conference. We decided that we were running this as a training program; it was not a campus religious community." I have worshipped with my father. And I have discussed the theological implications of things. I have stood on the porch on a snowy Christmas Eve and watched an especially bright star suddenly appear through a hole in the clouds.

"Do you think that is the same star they saw in Bethlehem?" I asked him. I was about ten.

"It could be. It probably is," he said. My father seems never to forget that I am a person, with all my own rights, who has not chosen to live in this family. But been born to it. Rather than seeing me as his "product," he respects me like a stranger whom he loves. And knows.

An "identity crisis" brews inside me like hot water whistling in a kettle. But he doesn't give gobs of advice or instruction. What he gives is continual support.

There is a struggle in the family. My mother is more traditional. She and my father often quarrel over whether I should be allowed to do this or that. My mother is full of very strong love, but very different from his. My father's love wants to set you free. My mother's love wants to protect and possess. I am in the middle. On the surface, I ask my father to help me fight these battles against all the little rules and restrictions one passes through between childhood and becoming a man. Battles are fought over whether I can stay up late and read a book. Whether I can go see a friend. What time I should be home. My mother wants to enforce these rules because she believes it's her duty. It is part of the way she *feels*. She is a mother. My father looks at each little hassle as a conflict which must be negotiated rationally, with all sides reasonably satisfied. The rational approach often collides with my mother's *feeling* of what is right. And I am in the middle.

The hospital in Atlantic City is near the south end of town, two blocks off the beach, an ugly modern tower of gray brick and glass.

Zeke and I go into the lobby and I head for the desk. "What room is Robert Spike in? What's his condition?"

"Serious condition," says the young black receptionist. We take the elevator to a high floor, full of private rooms. Then a small fight to get past the nurse at the floor desk. She stares in horror at two scruffy boys invading this expensive silence. "Where do you two think you are going?"

"To see my father."

Several people from the Commission on Religion and Race hover inside his room. I see a nurse's uniform bent over the bed. Then I see him. His face stranded in an avalanche of bedclothes. Yellow, eyes dull, unshaven jaw, my father spots me and tries to work a smile. His arm lies on a pillow. Five inches of steel "pin" freshly inserted down its length of forearm.

The evening before, while Zeke and I were pulling into a "teen" resort farther down the Jersey shore, my father was moving across Atlantic City from one meeting to another. In the middle of the street, his foot caught the edge of a protruding manhole cover. Running for the curb, suddenly he was flying forward, then sprawling on his belly. The right arm was bent and cracked against the sharp corner of the curb, splintered into three pieces, filling his sleeve with blood, his whole body with pain. They operated to join the arm back together and stuck this steel pin inside to bind it all. The pain is worse this morning. They are giving him shots of a strong painkiller. "How do you feel?"

"Not so good."

"Mom is on her way," I tell him. He nods his head.

"I talked to her on the phone this morning. How did she find you?"

"She called the State Police. They spotted our car at this motel near Ocean City."

"She called the State Police?" He laughs. "Leave it to your mother! How are you, Zeke?"

"Fine. How are *you?*"

"Well, this happened at the worst possible time. The convention starts today."

"How long do you have to stay in this hospital?"

"At least a week."

"You'll get some rest anyway."

"This MFDP challenge is going to be very complicated," he says, referring to the Mississippi Freedom Democratic Party. This is a group of blacks from Mississippi who seek to unseat the regular Democratic delegates from the state to this 1964 Democratic Convention. They base their challenge on the plain fact that all the regular Mississippi delegates were elected in a segregated election. "And I'm going to miss the Platform Committee hearings." My father and others are trying to get the Democrats to take a stronger stand in their platform on civil rights.

"Bob, you should stop worrying about any of that," says one of the staff guys. "We can do all the legwork. Plus you'll be right here in town, with a telephone. We can get it together." The staff has been keeping vigil all night outside the operating room and now by his bed. There is a great deal of work to be done, all of it in the first few days of the convention. The staff looks glad to see me, a member of the family. Now they can get back to work.

There is always an air of dedication about the Commission staff which is quite different from the kind of dedication I am used to finding in ministers or church-connected people. There is not a whole lot of stuffy sanctimoniousness about these guys. Rather, they are full of energy and humor, highly competitive, yet working for not much money or power. Rather, this work gives a satisfaction which is unique. You know your goals—equal rights and freedom—are correct. So you only have to worry about the means which can achieve them. These people do twentieth-century work. Their tools are the telephone, the press release and the "meeting." In the hall one of them says, "It's good you got here. You cheer him up. He was asking about you."

"Thanks for taking care of him last night," I say, though it sounds foolish coming out.

"Listen, Paul, you and your friend might as well stay in your father's room now. The Commission has a floor rented in . . ." he names some rickety fleabag hotel off the beach. Hotel space is scarce in Atlantic City during the convention. And all of it is under the tight control of Lyndon Johnson's advisers. Johnson has spent months preparing this convention. For the first time, he will be nominated for the presidency. Since the nomination is virtually certain, the convention is going to be run as a week-long advertisement on television for the Democratic Party and for Johnson. The only suspense lies in whom Johnson will pick to run on the ticket with him. Who will be the vice-presidential nominee?

My father has been ill before. But I have never seen him like this. The painkiller has taken control and his eyes are closed in a drugged sleep. I stand beside the bed. There is something deeply embarrassing about seeing him like this. I don't understand it. A broken arm, anyway, is not a life or death matter. He will recover in a few days and this incident will be forgotten. But what must be gone through right now is bad. Witness my father in pain. Pain worse as the day goes on. Pain that burns like an electric fire along the length of this steel pin and by evening makes him twice as haggard as in the morning. His flesh does not want this piece of metal. His bones are shattered.

At least he is left-handed. But his left arm is only two-thirds of what it should be. A similar accident happened when he was thirteen. He fell down a flight of basement steps, smashing his left arm in pieces. The doctor in Rochester botched the job. Botched it so badly that when he tried to enlist in the armed services during World War II not one would take him.

"The painkiller needle. Ask them for the painkiller needle," he moans, biting back tears this evening. My mother and brother have arrived. The nurses are late. Have they forgotten his shot? His suffering makes him plead like a child in front of us. I can't stand it. I run from the room to the nurses' desk where a couple of young ladies in white and pink uniforms are having a lazy conversation.

"Where the hell is the shot for my father? He's in pain. Give him something right now!"

"Calm down," says one of the nurses in her professional voice. She rises and casually goes to a clipboard. Her easy movements while he lies reduced to idiocy by pain ignite me further.

"Don't tell me to calm down. Give him a shot of something!" She stares at the clipboard and then looks at her companion. Her expression says she *has* made a mistake. Now she moves to the cabinets and quickly gathers the syringe, alcohol and cotton for his injection. I follow her down the hall. See my mother's grim face. I don't like to watch them give my father needles. But this time I am happy and so is he to see the sharp point enter his arm, full of relief. After the nurse leaves, brushing by me without a glance, I look at him. His eyes stare up without focus waiting for the medicine. But I already feel something very much like relief. Despite the embarrassment and the anger of the previous moments, I have experienced something good. I feel that I have helped my father.

After he falls asleep, we walk out to the parking lot. My mother and brother are going down to a place called Stone Harbor on the Jersey coast where they are renting a house for three weeks. I say good-bye and walk up to the hotel where the Commission is staying. Zeke is sitting with a bunch of staff watching the opening session of the convention on television. Everyone holds a tumbler of whiskey. I pour one myself and sit down. Somebody arrives with bags of sandwiches and we munch away at these, washing them down with Scotch. The Democrats whistle and shout in mammoth Convention Hall, four blocks away. The screen is filled with prancing fat delegates eager for the blowouts to come. On following days they will swarm around the hall waving signs, balloons, noisemakers and straw hats for their "favorite sons." And for Lyndon Baines Johnson, our leader.

About nine, Zeke and I get up to take a hike on the boardwalk. Atlantic City is a mixture of shingled tenements and tall, Martian hotels. The most interesting edifices are the older "grand hotels" built in the days when the city attracted aristocratic New Yorkers and Philadelphians on holiday. These big hotels sit beside the boardwalk in enormous gingerbread fashion, defying one's imagination with their pomposity. The boardwalk is filled with delegates and their families from all over the United States, plus the whole summer crowd of elderly couples, young families, teenagers in sneakers. Plus many police. We stroll toward Convention Hall.

A demonstration is taking place beneath the tall, windowless façade of the hall. About 150 demonstrators are standing in rows. Marshals dressed in the SNCC field workers' costume of overalls and plain blue cotton shirts move through the ranks. This is a "silent vigil" which will go on until the end of the convention. The marshals snap at people who are talking, straighten the rows and maintain a tight discipline.

"Do you want to get in line? Otherwise please move on," says one of them to us. We are standing right beside the demonstrators.

The next hours pass slowly. We are all demonstrating in support of the black Mississippi challenge. Thousands of tourists pass and stare. This is not Selma or Jackson, not even Washington, D.C. There are no rednecks out night-riding on the Atlantic City boardwalk. The police shy away, ordered to avoid confrontations. The demonstration is proudly nonviolent. Occasionally a delegate from some Southern state will break away from his wife and come toward us shouting, "You're all fools! Fools!" His wife will capture him and lead him by the arm, face red and sputtering, probably drunk, toward another nightclub or back to their room in one of the plastic towers.

I spot familiar faces moving around me. Civil rights workers who during the last two years have become "stars" of the nightly television news. There is Stokely Carmichael, tall and regal with his sunken cheeks and piercing eyes. There is James Forman, built stocky with a full Afro, looking like a black lion. And the large, rotund figure of Fanny Lou Hamer. She is the official leader of the Mississippi Freedom Democrats. Finally, someone I have heard the most about from my father, the man in Mississippi he most respects. Small and slight, glasses and nondescript clothes, this man actually does bear a slight resemblance to Gandhi. It is Bob Moses. Though he rarely appears on television and likes to stay far from the headlines. "That's Bob Moses," I say to Zeke. He has also heard my father talk of him. "I'm going to shake his hand."

I break out of line and walk over to where Moses stands on the edge of a little caucus some marshals are holding. I suppose what I really want is not only to meet him, but to see if he says anything about my father. I want to see if he respects my father as much as my father respects him.

"Mr. Moses. I'm Paul Spike. Robert Spike's son. I just wanted to meet you." I stick out my hand. He looks at me and I cannot tell what he thinks. Only takes my hand for an instant, and turns away. I feel put down. Rightly so. I have been celebrity hunting and the man knows it. I get back on line and Zeke says nothing. This "silent vigil" is really only to keep the Democrats on their toes. The real business of the convention takes place not in the hall or on the boardwalk or anywhere near the television cameras but back in the suites of the "grand hotels."

"What time does the hospital close?" I ask Zeke. He doesn't know either. It is past midnight. "I think I'll go check on my father."

It is closed for visitors. I pay no attention, walk past a drowsy nurse, into an elevator and up to his room. Behind the half-closed door, he is watching television through blurry eyes, his arm on the pillow. "How are you feeling?"

"So-so. They just gave me a sleeping pill. How did you get in here?"

"Walked."

"I'm glad you came. Would you pour me some of that juice over there?" I pour him a glass. Watch him drink, reminding me of a sick child. "Thanks." He gives the glass back.

"Anything else I can do, Dad?"

"Turn the television off, please. And that bright light."

"I thought I would stay here tonight. In case you need anything. I can just stretch out on this rug."

"That would be good." I turn off the lights, sit down, take off my boots, and stretch out on the hospital floor. I wonder what the last patient in this room had?

"Take one of my pillows," says my father. He has three, plus the one for his arm. I reach up and take it.

"Zeke and I stood on the vigil tonight. A lot of people were there. Robert Moses was there. What do you really think the chances are to get the MFDP seated?"

"It all depends," he says softly, "on what support we can get for them. If we could get Senator Humphrey to issue a strong statement, it would make a difference."

"Do you think he will?"

"I don't know. Johnson is dangling the vice-presidency in front of him."

"Does he want it?"

"Sure he does. He deserves it." My father and Humphrey have worked closely together on the passage of the Civil Rights Bill. They are friends. Now I hear his breathing deepen slightly as he descends into sleep, the sedative slipping its first tentative grip on his eyelids.

Remember all those times when you were a child and he took care of you? I had pneumonia five times. Several times I was critically ill. I remember lying in an ambulance delirious, my father beside me, stroking my burning forehead as we wheeled through Village streets to St. Vincent's Hospital on Seventh Avenue. I was five.

Whenever I was sick or had nightmares, my father would get up and come to my bed. When I had pneumonia or a bad cold, he would keep a vaporizer going. If I couldn't get my breath, he would lift up my head and hold it in the hot steam rushing out of the boiling device.

Even now when I returned to our Tenafly house after going out on drinking excursions with my buddies in the suburbs. Reeling and nauseated with a green stomach, I would empty myself into the bowl while kneeling, too drunk to stand. Suddenly he would be behind me. He never said anything, sometimes wiped the hair out of my eyes, once even held my head as I vomited since I was more than half-asleep. The next morning, Saturday or Sunday morning, he asked, "Where did you go last night?" I would tell him. "You shouldn't drink so much you get drunk." I would tell him I

knew that. He never punished me or yelled and he never told
my mother about these episodes. She would have been very
upset. A friend of his told me later that during this period
my father once remarked, "Paul is learning how to drink. I
wish he'd hurry up and learn."

My head swimming with memories, I fall asleep sober
on the floor. Full of gladness, not alcohol. Glad I have been
able, at least once, to return the favor of his caring.

Zeke and I stand on the vigil lines for hours the next day. A
crucial day for the MFDP challenge. The marshals are harsh
as they move about. "This is a *silent* demonstration, folks. If
you can't dig it, then get out of it. *No talking!*" We stand at
attention, silently, while all around us a political carnival is
going on as delegates and their families lug souvenirs and
saltwater taffy up and down the boardwalk. Somewhere, the
Platform Committee hearings are taking place. Along with
the committee which will decide whether or not to seat the
MFDP, and unseat the racist delegates. A small marble bust
of John F. Kennedy, killed less than a year ago, has been
quickly erected across the boardwalk from Convention Hall.
The delegates and their families study this in the daytime. At
night, some guys from Princeton sing folk songs around the
base of the pedestal.

I duck out to check on my father several times. He is
better today. Making decisions. About 8:00 p.m., Zeke and I
leave the vigil lines and walk to a cafeteria around the corner
from the hospital. Zeke has discovered they serve tasty
"steak" sandwiches. Actually, thin strips of pressed beef,
broiled, but served with lots of tomato, lettuce and onion.
This supper is perhaps the most exciting thing we have done
all day. With the exception of being spat at by a delegate.

Three staff members are with my father. There is new
tension in the room. They are worried. They are trying to

get Humphrey on the phone so my father can speak to him.

If the Mississippi delegates were unseated, or even just forced into a compromise, it would have powerful impact on politics in the country. It would be both an internal party reform and a declaration that the American political system was taking the challenge of civil rights seriously. The *moral* challenge. However, it would also be highly embarrassing to President Johnson, who is *not* supporting the MFDP challenge. Though he has been strong on civil rights since taking over the presidency, he still wants to maintain his traditional support from the Southern states.

Humphrey's aides keep deflecting the telephone calls. They promise he will call back in a few minutes. And the Mississippi people keep calling up. Has my father spoken to Humphrey yet? Of all the people in the country, my father is perhaps the one best able to mediate between the black leaders and the white Establishment. He is trusted by both. He writes:

> There have been times when it seemed that we had no friends at all, because everyone was quite sure that we were somebody else's agent: The more militant civil rights people were sure we were secret agents of the Department of Justice. The Department of Justice very frequently thought we were trying to push them or trick them into using federal power that they really didn't want to use. The churches of our constituency frequently thought we were committing them to things they didn't feel committed to. Yet we have maintained relationships with all parties, and so far are trusted enough so that we can play an independent role. Despite the accusations that have come from many parts of the country that all the Commission is doing is disrupting things, it is clear that in the total national scene, it has become a reconciling agency.

A vague threat has already been sent to the administration. If the MFDP challenge is not successful through traditional means (these backstage negotiations and the silent vigil on the boardwalk), the SNCC people have threatened to take drastic action. Massive civil disobedience, perhaps, tying the city into knots. Four years before the 1968 riots in Chicago, these threats have the Johnson administration terribly anxious. They want this TV commercial for the Democrats to run smooth and pretty.

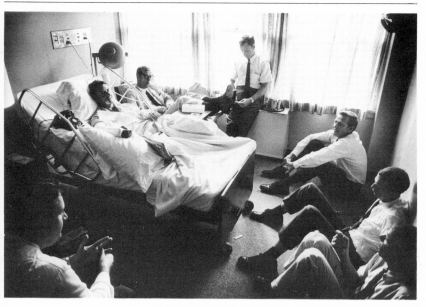

Waiting for Humphrey's call in Atlantic City
Hospital, Democratic Convention, 1964.

The phone rings. It is for my father. He takes it out of an aide's hand and puts it to his ear, lying in his tall hospital bed. During the next ten minutes everyone in the room is silent. My father says little. He says, "I'd like to talk to him," several times.

It was one of Humphrey's top advisers. He has told my father that tonight President Johnson gave Humphrey his terms. If Humphrey wants the vice-presidential nomination, the price he must pay is silence on the Mississippi Freedom

Democratic Party's challenge. If Humphrey strongly supports the MFDP in public, Johnson will choose somebody else from a list of Democrats eager to run on his ticket. This has been made clear to Humphrey.

The aide has been candid with my father. He hopes my father appreciates it. He knows my father realizes Humphrey's true sympathies are with the civil rights struggle. Of course, none of this should ever be made public. When Humphrey is Vice-President, this will mean greater influence for the civil rights movement at the top of the government. Surely my father realizes this.

"Johnson isn't the cleverest politician in the country for nothing," says somebody.

"So Hubert is selling out," says another. We all look at one another. There isn't much else to say.

Later, when the war in Vietnam is being pushed to higher and higher pitch and Johnson is raging at his critics, I think back to this evening in the Atlantic City hospital. People want to know what happened to liberal Hubert Humphrey. Why is he keeping silent during the escalations? Because he is trapped by his role as Vice-President? Or because, somewhere in his history, he has made one political compromise too many and become, forevermore, not a man but a politician?

The rest of Convention Week is spent in the dwindling rows of silent demonstrators, drinking in the Commission suite occasionally, roaring up and down the Jersey shore in an Austin-Healy, and twice meeting girls whom we escort to thickly grassed Jersey dunes for disappointing wrestling matches.

My father is improving slowly. The convention nominates Lyndon Baines Johnson. The day Humphrey is due to be nominated, Zeke suggests we drive back to his house outside Philadelphia. There is something called the Philadelphia Folk Festival scheduled to begin in two days. We leave Atlantic City in the afternoon with a last good-bye to my father, who is really on the mend, and a final "steak" sandwich around the corner from the hospital.

Zeke's home is a sprawling split-level in an expensive Main Line suburb. He lives with his parents and his sister Debbie. Two years younger, she is a brilliant girl. Zeke listens to her talk with a kind of awe. But she worships him right back and follows us around, absorbing our cynical jokes as if they were incredibly witty and perceptive.

On the morning the Philadelphia Folk Festival opens, we wake up to sunshine. His mother yells upstairs. She is making breakfast for us. I come back from the bathroom into Zeke's room and find him with a jar of water and a fist full of brown capsules. He's taking his peyote!

"I wish I had enough for you, Paul," he says.

"I don't mind." I really don't mind at all. Something in my head tells me I don't want to take a trip. There is too much dangerous information I would rather not learn in one flash of drugged "insight." Like a cannon blown off in my face. I would rather learn what stands on the dark platform of my unconscious mind at my own rate, in my own way. Which, indeed, will be just as violent a shock when it comes as this cannon of drug I now want to avoid blowing off in my face.

"Breakfast is ready!" shouts his mother up the stairs. We go piling into the breakfast "nook" which is full of August gilt. What a glorious morning! "I've cooked you kids a special breakfast. Hope you like it," she says.

"I'm not really too hungry," says Zeke. I look at his face. A little strained. The problem with peyote is keeping it down. It has a horrible taste and is very difficult to digest. One has to try to keep it down long enough to give it a chance to pass into the bloodstream.

His mother brings out the special breakfast. It's a feast!

Tumblers of orange juice, fruit salad too. With cream. Followed by pancakes, eggs and thick ham steaks. I am starved. So is Debbie. But Zeke toys with his plate.

"You're not going to waste all this food I made especially for you?" asks his mother. He shakes his head and pushes fruit and pancake down his throat, into his peyote-sick belly. I feel sorry for him and, when his mother isn't looking, help him with his pancakes. Debbie spears one of his eggs and eats it for him fast. We both scramble to clean all three plates before there is an accident.

"Off in such a hurry?" his mother asks. Zeke nods his head. He looks yellow, then white, now green. Out the door, jump in the car and quickly slip down the drive and through the neighborhood. To get to the festival we take a series of country roads to a farm not far from Zeke's house. Cardboard arrows are tacked to trees marking the way. Zeke sits very silent, very nauseated in the rocking, swaying sportscar. We hop through ruts and twist around hairpins. Debbie sits on the transmission hump.

"Stop the car!" he shouts. I pull off onto the grassy shoulder.

We are in a small dell. A stream winds slowly through some trees forty yards away. This is dairy country. Zeke jumps out of the car and runs for the stream, hurdles some barbed wire like an Olympic star, tears to the edge of the water and collapses. On his knees, head down like a dog.

"Isn't it pretty here!" exclaims Debbie as we wait in the car. The sun is pouring through the tops of maple trees. Part of the stream is in shade, while the distant portion is alive with golden light, a dazzle of insects and birds. The ground down to the water is thick green. Beside the stream, a few reeds stand. And the bundle of blue denim amidst it all: Zeke, sick in the water. "I'm almost glad he got sick so we could have a chance to dig this place," says Debbie.

He stays for half an hour. Finally, I climb out of the car

and go toward the stream, duck the wire, shout, "Zeke, you okay?"

He slowly rises. His face turns to me, completely transformed. Not a trace of discomfort, it glows with golden happiness. "Wow, Spike! I started to hallucinate at the same moment I started to puke. It was a rainbow coming out of my mouth."

The pressure sits on the seniors like heavy fallout. After the first marking period, there is no more point in studying. The grades have gone to the colleges. Now computers are chewing them up, along with the results of our college boards, our interviews, our application forms. Nothing to do but put in time. Until April and the results of this national lottery to decide our futures. Till June and the end of high school forever.

Riverdale Country School sits atop a cliff overlooking Westchester County. I am lucky to get in. Only do so because I apply very late and there are some unexpected openings in the senior class. Riverdale is in the Riverdale section of the Bronx. It is called "Country School" but is really inside the limits of New York City. The view from the school, however, is very pretty when you look north. Rolling hillocks of green foliage, beneath which squat invisible communities of Westchester commuters. Only an occasional roof breaks the calm surface of treetops.

Long ago, when Joe Kennedy, Sr., was living in New York City, the Kennedy boys were sent to Riverdale Country School for several years. The school is quite proud of this. But never mentions it. For the place is run with a great deal of taste. The boys who come are still mostly sons of doctors and lawyers, businessmen and diplomats. They are sons of the upper middle class, while Keaton was middle-class right down the center of the barrel. Riverdale has a fleet of red schoolbuses which prowl around Park Avenue every morning picking up students for the journey to the Bronx. There is also a dorm with fifty boys from out of the city. I live here. Happy to have the quiet isolation during the week, and happy because, unlike Keaton, I can go home every weekend. In this dorm, I wage my final assault on the ivy walls of Harvard with a burst of study.

College has become nothing but "Harvard." I am applying to three other schools, but they don't ever enter my thoughts. I am obsessed with this goal of Harvard. Why? I'm not sure. It would please my father a great deal. But there is more to it. In one way, it would also surpass my father. He went to little "Denison University" out in central Ohio. If I could go to Harvard, it would be an accomplishment. Of my own. It would mean I was going to the college in America with . . . with what? Harvard is a great university but there are at least five or six other great universities in America, if not more. What does Harvard have? It is unfortunate I do not understand at the time that what lures me with such a deadly pull toward the walls of Harvard is nothing more than its fabulous "image"!

America, America. You are, in 1965, all locked up in a television set. A selection of "programs" and I am an "image" in search of other "images" with which to bolster my flickering self. Even Harvard has become an "image" to tantalize thousands of the smartest, most ambitious boys in America. What are we but a generation of images? A movement of images across the living rooms of the land.

Still, I sweat it out. Study hard. Study all night. Study all the first term. I end up with honors. Good. Fine. Now comes The Wait.

Each week during the long pause until we hear from the colleges is but a dash in between the weekends. I make new friends at Riverdale and find my "image" going through another transformation. From a folk music "rebel," I drift further into the world of prep school "rebel." Each Friday and Saturday night in New York City contains a new set of adventures where admission is based on what school you attend, what kind of loafers you wear, how your necktie matches your shirt. Once you learn the style and make a few friends, there is a mini-society of parties and bars which caters exclusively to the New York prep school student. I begin to explore this every weekend.

Two bars on the upper East Side are filled on Friday and Saturday nights with boys and girls from Riverdale, Brearly, Horace Mann, Fieldston, Trinity, Dalton, the private schools of the city. On vacations, students from all the other New England preparatory schools flood these places to overflowing. Lines at Christmas vacation stretch for twenty yards outside the bar. There is also a crowd of older people: college kids and would-be socialites. Even some genuine socialites. Several years later I read about one of these who used to hang around Nick's. They find her dead of an overdose of heroin, locked in the trunk of a parked car.

To get served alcohol, it is sometimes necessary to show proof of age. You have to be eighteen in New York. Younger than most states. Those who need them have phony draft cards. In a few months, we will be burning them. Now it is essential to keep our "draft cards" clean and handy in our wallets.

I stand at a bar with a friend from school named Frank. His mother is a psychiatrist. His father he doesn't talk about. We are sipping our third or fourth Scotch and it is hard to converse because of the loud jukebox. In a few moments, we will order another round and soon we won't want to converse any more. Just drift in the sounds and sights of the dark bar, looking at the young women, trying to look handsome and interesting, drunk but not showing it except for an occasional slurred word.

"I go up to Yale for my interview Tuesday," says Frank.

"Yeah? I had my last interview for Harvard this week. At the Harvard Club with about ten old alumni."

"Alumni? What was that like?"

"Not bad. Actually, I think it was the best interview I've had yet."

"I sure hope this Yale interview goes well." It is Frank's first choice. I am certain he doesn't have a chance. Unless he has some great connections. Connections don't hurt at all in the college lottery. But too many Riverdale people with better grades and high scores are applying to Yale. Frank is only at the center of our class. But I can't say this to him. I leave his dream alone and hope he leaves mine the same way.

"Maybe we should go up to Nick's. There aren't any girls in here tonight," I say. Nick's is the other, larger bar about ten blocks uptown.

"Good idea," says Frank. We move off on the chase. To get loaded. Maybe even laid. That is, if she has her own place.

Nick's is larger and much more crowded. It is a famous hangout among prep school students up and down the east coast. Nick is a jovial man who caters to his teenage clientele with plenty of unction. He likes to come up and squeeze your shoulder, beam a huge smile at you and say, "How've you been?" I have seen him do this to friends who are visiting the bar for the first time. He greets them like old buddies. He wants this place to be a little parody of "21." Actually, it functions as a pick-up joint. Not the back room, which is dimly lit and full of young preppies with their dates. Often they come dressed in tuxedos and long gowns, straight from the Plaza debutante parties. To sip sours and Scotch on their parents' money and nuzzle in the reddish glow of the table candles.

Up front is a frenzy. Stag girls looking for handsome, rich boys. Middle-class boys trying to look rich and handsome. On Friday night it is a combination of Mardi Gras, Bastille Day and New Year's Eve in the stuffy place. The jukebox howls with banshee music. Drinks are generous: about two ounces of Scotch for a dollar. By midnight, all the young, well-dressed customers are dead drunk, straining at their bits of sophistication. Meeting a girl is simply a job of wedging through the crowd until you jam up against one and can't move farther. One of the easiest ways to pick her up and to seem interesting is to offer her some pot. This is still rare in middle-class circles in 1964. Many girls are jumping to try it.

One's first impression is of a bar full of young snobs. This is correct, but the crowd is laced with freaks. One girl, obviously from a well-to-do Park Avenue family, has a mania for giving handjobs. The place is jammed. Nobody is paying any attention to very much. Suddenly, I feel her hand fumbling with my zipper. When it is over, she carefully places me back in my pants. She moves off to her next conquest. By the end of the night she must repeat her little service fifteen or twenty times.

The people who hang around Nick's are not "hip." They aren't like the young folk music devotees who trek everywhere with guitar in hand, harmonicas in pocket, decked out in nothing but blue denim work clothes. However, the people in Nick's have started to move in a "hip" direction. The boys are growing their hair longer. The images are melding. And the girls? Anything that looks like a Beatle this year is exciting as hell to the girls.

The year doesn't pass; it sprints. From weekend to weekend, party to party, bar to bar. I have a girlfriend for most of the winter. And find some more serious friends at Riverdale. Besides, there is plenty of studying to be done though it doesn't have the college pressure on it any more. As the spring of 1965 begins, and The Wait gets shorter and shorter, I feel my "image" shiver with anticipation. Will this dream come true?

I am working on my chemistry notebook in my dorm room when there is a knock. "Paul? I just saw your Dad on television," says the school nurse, poking her head in the door.

"What was he doing?"

"He's down in Selma, Alabama, with all the demonstrators. They interviewed him on the news."

"What did he say?" She looks a little confused.

"I don't really remember."

"Okay. Well, thanks a lot for telling me, Mrs. Karsh."

Three days later, I arrive at home for the weekend. My mother is sitting in the living room with a worried look. I go upstairs, dump my clothes, and come back down. "Your father is in Washington."

"I thought he was in Selma."

"He flew to Washington. He's very tired. They've been working him night and day in the White House."

"What are they working on?" I haven't been following the news.

"Voting rights. He wants you to call him at this number," she says, going to the telephone in the kitchen where she has written it down.

He is asleep when I ring his room at the Mayflower Hotel. "Mom says you wanted me to call."

"Right. I've been on the road for a week and only expected to be gone for a day and a half. I didn't pack. Do you think you could bring me some clothes tomorrow?"

"Sure."

"I don't know what your plans are for the weekend.

But I'd like to see you. I've already told your mother what I need."

"Sure, Dad."

"Take the air shuttle."

"You sound very tired."

"I am. We've been working on the President's speech and proposal for this voting rights bill he's going to introduce."

Afterwards, I go sit on the couch. My mother looks grim. "He's going to die before he's forty-five," she says.

"Don't say that, Mom."

"Well, it's true. He's going to have a heart attack. You can't work like he does all the time."

Traveling by myself is satisfying. To go through the ticket buying, airplane rituals, taxis and hotel arrivals always gives me a good feeling, an adult feeling. Now I jump in a taxi holding a suitcase with his fresh clothes.

When I see him, I am a little shocked. His face looks older than I have ever seen it before. "I haven't had much sleep for about four days. Finally last night I took a pill and slept from yesterday until about ten-thirty this morning," he says, opening the suitcase. He has just finished showering and stands still damp, a towel around his middle, his hair slick.

"You look older," I say.

"I feel a lot better. How would you like to go to the White House? Into the Executive wing where all the offices are?"

"I'd like to."

"I'll call them up. Maybe Bill Moyers is still there. I would like to introduce you. I've talked to him about you a little." My father is always talking to people about me. I imagine it is my writing or my wanting to go to Harvard. Always over the years, when I am introduced to people who know him, they say, "Oh, you're Paul. Your father has told me a lot about you." Sometimes they add, "He's very proud of you, you know."

I don't know what to say. Sometimes I say, "I don't know why." But sometimes just "I'm very proud of him, too." Now I ask him, "Will we get a chance to see the President?"

"I doubt it. He doesn't usually pass through the outer offices."

The demonstrations in Selma are the climax of the entire Southern civil rights struggle during the early sixties. Hundreds of demonstrations, sit-ins, freedom rides, marches and more marches have come first. But Selma is *the* demonstration which finally catches the attention of the country.

Martin Luther King has been to Stockholm to accept the Nobel Peace Prize in December. Now in January he flies to Selma to begin a voter registration drive. There are 15,000 blacks in the town, but only 350 are registered to vote. And there are only 14,000 whites, most of whom are registered. The blacks ought to have a 1,000-person majority.

For a time it seems as if everything will be unusually quiet. The city police chief has decided to meet the SCLC drive with restraint, in order to avoid a lot of damaging publicity. But the county sheriff has no intention of showing restraint. A fat man, prone to spittle-soaked cigar butts, Sheriff Jim Clark of Dallas County immediately arrests 100 blacks who have tried to line up to register for the vote. The next day there is a protest march led by King. Sheriff Clark arrests 250 marchers this time. King doesn't put up bail for five days. By the time he leaves jail, the national press has shifted its attention to other things.

But then in a town called Marion, about 30 miles from Selma, a state trooper shoots and kills a young black named Jimmie Lee Jackson without cause. King speaks at his funeral to 4,000 mourners. He proposes a march from Selma to Montgomery, Alabama, in order to lodge a formal complaint with the Governor. The Governor is a man named George C. Wallace. Governor Wallace responds by directing his state troopers to take "whatever steps are necessary" to stop the march. In order to get on the highway that leads the 54 miles north to Montgomery, the marchers must cross Pettus Bridge. Led by SCLC leaders, they number about 550. From the front of a Negro Methodist church, they leave for Montgomery. When they come to the bridge, they run into a solid line of blue uniforms: Alabama state troopers. Major John Cloud of the troopers orders the marchers to disperse. They do not, they stand still. Major Cloud orders his troopers to disperse the crowd. Swinging nightsticks, shooting tear gas grenades, they batter the crowd. Chase them not only off Pettus Bridge, but all the way back to the church. Several photographers are present. By nightfall, the media is full of news from "Bloody Sunday" in Selma.

King calls for a massive repeat of the march on Tuesday. He asks Americans, especially clergymen, to come South and join the demonstration.

The Commission on Religion and Race gets over four hundred clergymen to take the trip to Selma. My father goes down on Monday. Almost immediately, he is at work mediating between the Selma leaders and the White House.

For President Johnson is extremely upset about plans for another march on Tuesday. "Bloody Sunday" has gotten extensive publicity, both in America and all over the world. Now a federal court issues an injunction against the march. The negotiations between SCLC leaders and Washington are very tricky. Eventually, however, an agreement is worked out. Johnson brings pressure on Governor Wallace so that even he is part of the deal.

Tuesday comes. In front of the same Methodist church, there are now 1,500 marchers, my father among them. They move out filling the street from curb to curb for many yards.

Once again, the line of state troopers waits on the far side of Pettus Bridge. When they reach these blue uniforms, Major Cloud orders them to disperse but adds, "You can have your prayer and then return to your church if you so desire." This is the bargain. Everyone kneels in the street and for fifteen minutes, King leads them in prayer.

But that evening, outside a small Negro restaurant, the peaceful day is turned into a shambles. A Unitarian minister, one of the four hundred who came down for the march, Rev. James J. Reeb, is beaten to death by a white man with a baseball bat. The news flashes. Selma is bloody again. It is finally too much for the President. Tuesday night, my father is asked by the White House people to come and help them formulate a response. The world press hovers over the carnage. What will be the President's next move?

None of this is clear on Saturday afternoon as my father and I get out of the taxi in front of the White House. The only clear thing is how hard he has been working. We go into a little white guardhouse. A Marine asks us for our drivers' licenses, checks these against a list of people expected to arrive. He mumbles some confirmation into a telephone and hands us back our papers.

All across the green lawn, I try to find the James Bond devices I'm sure they must have to protect the President. We enter, pass through the press room, and then into the offices themselves. My father asks for someone. It is probably Hays Redman, his chief contact in the White House. Then we go into Moyers's office, empty, and my father and this man talk about things which I have no context to understand. My mind wanders and I look around the office. It is very large, with a big desk, lots of photographs on the wall, a thick carpet and a conference table. About what I would have expected. The only thing unusual is a pigskin football sitting incongruously on top of some official papers. On the side is inscribed something like: "To Bill Moyers, from the Dallas Cowboys of the National Football League." I get a grip on it. These are the most powerful offices in the world. All this power, and yet the absurdity of this football has managed to creep in, past the fences, the Marines, the Secret Service. I am glad to see something absurd in the White House. How about a quick game of touch football? How about a quick nuclear reactive strike, Mr. President? How about a touchdown pass?

The next day I fly back to New York. My father remains in Washington. There is a lot of work left, he says, before the speech.

On Monday evening, President Johnson addresses the American people: "At times history and fate meet at a single time in a single place to shape a turning point in man's unending search for freedom.

"So it was at Lexington and Concord. So it was a century ago at Appomattox. So it was last week in Selma, Alabama."

Johnson closes the speech by drawling, "We *shall* overcome."

It is the strongest civil rights speech ever made by an American President. Somewhere beneath the crust of rhetoric lie my father's words. His words and his ideas of the past week of insomnia, shuffling between White House and hotel. All this I know now. At the time, I am only dimly aware of details. But full of pride. Later people will ask me, "How much of that speech did your father write? What did he have to do with it?" I am not sure. I ask him. He grins and shrugs. He doesn't want to talk about it. But on this Monday evening, he has been invited to sit in the President's box in the balcony of Congress. Johnson is addressing both houses. I am standing in the Riverdale lounge watching it all on television. Now I turn to somebody on my left and say, "My father helped write this speech."

"That's far out," he says.

The day arrives. I climb the stairs in the main school building to Mr. Paige's office. He is our college guidance adviser. By now, late in the afternoon, he has the word by telephone from Cambridge, New Haven, Princeton, Ithaca, Philadelphia, Providence, Hanover and New York City. The seven Ivy League towns.

I do not get accepted by Harvard.

But I do not get the satisfaction of having my dream shattered. It must die a slow death. As if somebody had given it rat poison.

I made the "waiting list." In case enough people whom Harvard has accepted decide to go elsewhere, I will have a second chance. There is light at the end of the tunnel. A dim speck of it.

All my other college choices accept me. Choose one. I don't want to dream any more. I guess I'll spend the next four years in New York City.

II

COLLEGE

Columbia University. Five of us sit in a dormitory room. It is the first evening for us. Freshman Week began this afternoon.

"Vietnam?" says a stocky guy named Phil.

"Vietnam is a *bitch* and you better believe it," says another. His name is Lee.

"I don't understand what's happening in Vietnam," says Phil. "Can you explain it to me?"

"Man! You better do some homework on it." Lee is political. He has already told us, in a half-brag and half-confession, "My parents are Communists." Now he sits on the edge of his bed, legs crossed, arms propped on knees and his lower lip tucked pensively between his teeth. "Vietnam is the worst problem we've got right now."

"I don't know," says Phil. "Black power seems more important to me. Look at our history. What white men have done to Negroes in this country for three hundred years." All five of us are white.

"You ought to see what we did to the Vietnamese people in the last thirty minutes. You ever see a photograph of somebody who has been napalmed?"

"I don't know."

"Flaming jelly. It sucks the air right out of your lungs. You die of suffocation while the jelly fries on your skin."

"Listen," says another boy in the room. "The biggest problem as I see it is how do we screw girls when we can't even bring them in the dormitories?"

I cross Broadway to the campus. My father walks beside me. His offices in the Interchurch Center are only a block from Columbia. This morning I rode into the city with him in his green Triumph. He was going to work and I was going to college.

My father has said nothing, but I can tell he is a little excited. "I'll walk you over," he has said. Columbia is not a new experience for him. He got his doctorate in education at Columbia in the early 1950's.

I carry a small suitcase with clean shirts, another sportcoat, a pair of jeans, some underwear and socks. All new freshmen are required to spend Freshman Week in the dormitories. After this week, about half the class will move back home to live with their parents in the Bronx, Brooklyn or Queens. These are the "commuters." The rest of the freshman class, those who live outside a 50-mile radius, are required to spend the year in the dorms. I live inside the 50-mile limit, across the Hudson in Tenafly, and I have told the college I am going to live at home this year. But that is only a story to circumvent the regulations against freshmen living off campus in their own apartments.

Actually, once I leave the dormitory at the end of Freshman Week, I am going to be living in an apartment on Riverside Drive and West 109th Street. The lease is held by a man who works at the National Council of Churches. I will have my own bedroom and bath and help him with the high rent. An amazing view from the windows of my room should make my freshman year quite different from that of the boys who crowd into the cramped cells of Furnald, Hartley or John Jay Hall.

They will look out on the campus which my father and I are now crossing. On our left is the gray dome of Low Library. It sits atop the whole place like a boil, a volcano filled with smoldering lava, gradually preparing to erupt and spill across the concrete plains, the cobbles of College Walk, the dog grass of South Lawn, right up against the bottoms of these tall, filthy dormitories with their green metal roofs. In the southwest corner, a new and hideous dormitory rises like a square silo into the sunny sky. Not a trace of style ruins the ugly face of Carman Hall. We pass this and up a few stairs and cross the small plaza which fronts enormous Butler Library. On the far side, two tennis courts are tucked into a corner of the lawn in front of John Jay Hall. We thread through the confusing twists of the path, down into a low basin of a quadrangle which runs north to Hamilton Hall. Hamilton is the main building of Columbia College. Most of the classes and the Dean's office are here. But we have to report to the lobby of Hartley Hall, where a tall, pock-marked boy in a blue blazer with a key on the top pocket welcomes me to Columbia with a strained smile. I can tell he has one eye on my father, the "parent."

I sign in, pick up my key, and then am guided by this boy named Bruce back outside and over South Lawn to the reddish silo of the new dormitory. I have apparently been lucky. I will spend this week in Carman Hall. Bruce insists on carrying my suitcase. My father walks beside us, but as we reach the front door to Carman, he stops and says, "I guess I'll leave you here. Why don't you call us in a couple of days."

"Sure." This is a little strange. I am going "away" to

college about a block from my father's office. "I'll call in a couple of days."

"Good. Nice meeting you, Bruce."

"Nice meeting you, sir."

"Have a good time, Paul."

"Don't worry, Dad." He turns and walks back toward Broadway. Bruce guides me quickly to the elevators, up to the room, and is gone. I stand in the middle of a cinderblock room, two beds, two desks, two lamps, two closets, two everything. Boy, am I glad I only have to spend a week in here. This cell is one of two in a "suite" and there is a common bathroom for every four boys.

I go to the window. The lawn is covered with clumps of humanity. Each clump radiates around a blue dot. This is the freshman in his light blue beanie with our class numerals "69" on the front. I have not yet bought my beanie but Bruce has warned me I must. Otherwise, I will not be allowed into any of the official Freshman Week activities. I already have a feeling I will not be attending all that many official activities.

I am familiar with Morningside Heights, the hill in upper Manhattan which Columbia University rules like a little kingdom. I used to come down to this neighborhood last year when I was at Riverdale in the Bronx to use Butler Library and to drink beer in the famous West End Cafe across Broadway from the school. I also had a girlfriend who lived right around here. But down on the lawn now I see a great many confused, gaping faces.

Boys from every state in America are arriving. Many have made the long journey with their parents. To end up here in their brand-new clothes, the jacket not fitted too well, the tie thin, shoes polished with spit last night, and the blue beanie on the top of the head. Class of '69. This first week is going to be a tumbling mixture of "firsts." First meeting with the academic adviser. First ride on the subway. First battery of placement tests in French, Spanish and mathematics. Followed by first meeting with two black kids in sneakers on Amsterdam Avenue. They hold a thin, skeletal blade shakily in front of you as you dip into your pocket for a handful of coins. They look at your silly blue beanie and mockingly say, "Thanks, *man.*"

On the same afternoon you get your first glimpse of the serious faces of the Barnard girls, you see your first dented and black face of a junky woman panhandling the Broadway gate. Hundreds of beanies wander off campus and into busy Broadway. Barely surviving the murderous taxis which come rushing down out of their garages in Harlem, hurrying to the safe zone of midtown.

I leave my room and go downstairs to the campus. Out a back gate, down 114th Street, and cross the street to the West End for a stein of beer. Just as I enter, Bruce exits. We almost bump each other. Only twenty minutes before he had been bowing and scraping and lugging my case of clothes up to my room as a member of Columbia's Blue Key Society. Now I look him in the eyes and say, "Hi." He pretends not to recognize me, turns to his upper-class companion and walks away. My first taste of Columbia warmth.

I am going up on the elevator to my room on the ninth floor of Carman. The rising compartment is jammed with beanies. Everyone eager. Introducing themselves. A mixture of emotions clogs the air. Friendliness, nerves, hostility, doubt, curiosity, competition rising. An elevator full of boys who all know they are "special." High-school editors, politicians, athletes, scholars.

"My name's Bob Helbrandt. North Dakota."

"Hi! Les Remburg. I'm from Queens."

"My name's Jerry . . ."

". . . Walter Rochester . . ."

I say nothing. It occurs to me that all these guys are secretly resenting each other and secretly terrified too. Which one of us is going to be number one in chemistry here? I look around the faces and suddenly stop. There is a face which looks full of the same defensive cynicism that mine must show. It is a thin face, under brown curly hair, with a pair of thick glasses behind which dance large eyes full of expression. The eyes are scowling right now. I nod at them. They nod at me. The ninth floor arrives and I step out. The face steps out too.

"Hi. My name's Paul Spike."

"My name is Paul Bloom."

"You on this floor too, huh?"

"Yeah."

"Where are you from?" I ask.

"Teaneck, New Jersey."

"No kidding. I used to live in Teaneck. Then we moved to Tenafly."

"What junior high did you go to?" asks Bloom.

"Thomas Jefferson."

"Oh. I went to Ben Franklin. Then I went to high school in New York."

"So did I. Where?"

"Fieldston up in Riverdale."

"No kidding. I went to Riverdale Country School."

"Jesus, only a few blocks away."

"I know somebody who went to Fieldston from Tenafly. Tom Ford."

"He was my best friend. Do you know Alice Geller?"

"Wow. Sure. I knew her at Fire Island years ago."

"She's Ford's girlfriend. She told me about you. You're Spike. She said you were going to Columbia. You tried to get into Harvard, didn't you?"

"Yeah."

"So did Ford. He's going to Cornell now."

"It's pretty amazing that we should meet like this. We're on the same floor."

"That elevator was too much," says Bloom.
"Those guys introducing themselves . . ."
"What idiots!"

It seems that at least two-thirds of the freshman class at
Columbia really wanted to go to Harvard. It becomes a joke,
being rejected by the great Cambridge "image." A joke
which elicits a lot of choking, half-felt laughter. I know at
least twenty guys who tell me during this first week that all
they really want to do is get good grades this year so they can
transfer to Harvard. I think about this for perhaps a day.
Then realize I am finished with this crap. Columbia is good
enough for me. My days of preparing for a "good college"
are over. I want to begin living! Right now.

Life at Columbia seems like a dream at first. A boyhood
dream of bursting into total freedom, living in New York
City all on your own, able to subway back and forth between
the various roles of college student, young bohemian, city
sophisticate, man about town.

Supposedly, freshman year is a struggle to bring oneself
academically up to the level of college excellence. But the
high schools have gotten so competitive and so advanced
that I find my Riverdale education makes much of my first
semester at Columbia repetitive and a lark. The famous
"Contemporary Civilization" course which Columbia continues with pride is nothing new to me after my course called
"Humanities" at Riverdale. I have already been introduced
to Plato and Homer and St. Augustine. It's easy to fall into a
pattern of cutting classes and ignoring homework from the
beginning. And many of us do. Except for the great number
of freshmen who have arrived with the intention of becom-

ing doctors. Right here, in their freshman year, comes the moment of true commitment. For a "pre-med program" at Columbia begins with strong, difficult doses of science and math. Many "pre-meds" last only a few weeks. They will end up English majors or in the Department of Sociology.

Actually, few of us have any idea what we want to be after graduation. Bloom has not the faintest idea. Nor do most of the people I know. They change ambitions like socks, every few days, from doctor to English professor to fire ranger to marijuana dealer. I still believe I want to be a writer. Though I am doing no actual writing these days.

Drugs. That is really the theme of many people's freshman year at Columbia. You would think it was a class full of future druggists rather than pre-meds if you overheard the conversations scattered from table to table in the Lion's Den. More pharmacology is studied than Contemporary Civilization. Pot, LSD, mescaline, peyote, psyilocybin, amphetamines, barbiturates, heroin: everything is around and everything is experimented with by someone or other. The restlessness which surfaces on campus during the very first days is amazing. People are bored. People are bitter. We have spent so many years pushing and shoving, hitting the books, cramming for exams, primping for interviews, completing applications, all to get here. Columbia, the Ivy League gem of the ocean. Who owns New York? goes the college fight song. C-O-L-U-M-B-I-A. Now let's get stoned.

The ultimate high seems to be unconsciousness. Bloom and I mix large quantities of pot with booze in order to blot out all cerebral life. My head is a blur when I get stoned like this. Nothing to do but relax and let the music drift through your body as through an empty building.

From the beginning, paranoia is high on campus. Because getting "high" is illegal. "College life" is a drugged life for many of us. The life of a romantic outlaw, an American college student. The avenues to adventure are limited when one is a full-time student. But drugs make adventure happen right there in one's cinderblock dorm cell. Murals of many colors twist and shout on the mind's eye after you drop a tab. Rumors of police and student informers lurk right outside. Occasionally, a kid will freak out and flush his stash down the toilet. Then lie shaking on his bed waiting for the man who never comes.

Columbia deans occasionally discipline students for drugs. But the drug life is far more common than deans like to admit. Columbia is a private university. Bad public relations mean fewer applications which mean more financial problems next year. And Columbia is already in financial trouble. Somewhere in the past, when Harvard and Yale and Princeton and Columbia had to decide where to invest their money, Columbia took the most conservative path. The others invested in the economy. Columbia invested in New York City. The university is one of the two largest landlords in the city. It even owns the land under Rockefeller Center. Now, everything tied up in blocks of concrete, Columbia is hungry for hard cash. At least, so we read in the *Columbia Spectator* every day as we take our poached eggs and coffee in one of the campus luncheonettes. Columbia is always crying financial blues. Nobody in the freshman class pays much attention. What's far more important news is the date of the first mixer up at Sarah Lawrence or the price of the latest shipment of West Coast grass.

As the first weeks become months, I find myself hardly ever thinking of anything but "fun." I am, at last, free. The typical case of reaction to all those years in high school where freedom was a phony ideal tossed around in Citizenship Class.

I cut classes, but my grades are still good. I sleep past noon. Drink and get stoned every night. I shove myself through life like a corkscrew, puncturing each moment as if it were a carnival balloon, each hour a block of dull soap to be drilled through with my freedom. I move like a locomotive. Questions pour out of my head in a thick smoke.

The first thing I notice when I enter the classroom is a skinny kid in the last row. His name is Robert Mawson. I went to Tenafly High School with him. He was supposed to be the brightest boy in the school: a Tenafly genius. He looks at me and blinks. What am I doing here? I was just an average wise guy at Tenafly. He looks embarrassed, too, that I should find him in this ordinary section of Freshman English.

Columbia sends me forms. These always ask questions about my plans after graduation. Multiple choice questions, no less, designed for a computer to collect. I can choose between "law" or "medicine" or "teaching" or "business." But there is never a box for "writing." The closest category is "journalism." I check that, although I know "journalism" is not really what I want to do.

Everyone at Columbia is required to take a year of Freshman English unless you passed a special exam in high school. I was too lazy to take this three-hour exam and, anyway, it is against my "principles" to take a test on my ability to write a good English sentence. The idea seems lopsided, and symptomatic of a lot of what is wrong with education in America. Instead of asking you to write a theme and then reading it, they administer a battery of elaborate, computerized questions. I refuse. And, as a consequence, end up in an ordinary Freshman English class taught by a young preceptor named Richard Fadem.

Mawson is a quiet guy. Harmless. The kind of guy who will one day design a more deadly nuclear warhead for the government, a physics whiz. Seeing him reminds me of suburban life again . . .

I am a wise guy. Fadem enters the classroom, young and neat, with an expression on his face that says, "I've got a surprise for you." I figure he will try and frighten us all. It is common for people to go through high school getting tremendous grades on their papers only to end up with an "F" on their first couple of themes for Freshman English. A kind of deliberate academic boot camp experience. I want to beat this little ritual.

"I'm going to let you choose any topic you wish for this first paper. I want five hundred words. Five hundred of your best words," says Fadem.

I have instantly decided I will write once more on the topic of television advertising. A typical exercise in Freshman Cynicism, but I have written several satirical papers on this in high school and so have a number of routines already worked up and ready to go. I want an "A" on this first theme. Fadem lets us go early, and as I leave Butler Library where the class is held, my head is putting together the first sentences. I work on this for the next two nights, polishing and polishing. Stuffed with metaphors and acerbic little insights, it is finally finished. The morning before class I type a last draft on the big IBM electric machine in my father's office. It looks grand.

A week passes. It is hard to keep my mind off that stupid five-hundred-word paper. At last, the big hour. Fadem enters the classroom with our papers folded neatly and tucked under his arm. I am rigid with anticipation. He begins passing them down the rows. Finally, I reach out for mine, rip it open, find no grade. Look at all that red ink! On the back of the last page, my grade: "B+." I am furious. So close to an "A," yet the guy wouldn't give it to me. A "B+" is the second most infuriating grade you can get, after a "C+," which is really a drag. I look around the room. Mawson's eyes are watering. Most heads are nailed to the desktops. A ceiling of gloom lowers slowly down on us. From what I can spy over shoulders, the grades Fadem has given are hideously low. My "B+" is spotted by a guy on my right and quickly the word spreads. The class turns. I have the highest grade in the class. I am utterly dejected. I want an "A," for

without one, I will not be able to build a case to get out of
Freshman English. I would like to skip it and begin immedi-
ately studying literature with the big guns in Columbia's
English Department: Lionel Trilling, Quentin Anderson,
Steven Marcus, Eric Bentley, Andrew Chiappe and Kenneth
Koch.

Just in case, I go to Fadem's office later in the day. In
humble but rational (I think) tones, I make my case. If I can
write well enough to get a "B+" on my first theme, what is
the point in having to take more Freshman English? Obviously, I already know how to write. Fadem takes it grace-
fully. He knows what I am up to, he's a young guy, and soon
we will be friends. But now he counters with, "Look, your
B+ is good. But don't you want to write truly *exceptional*
prose? Develop your own style? The kind of writing worth
an A+."

I can say nothing. My first game of academic checkers,
and Fadem has clearly won.

. . . Sputnik!

The trouble all started when the Russians launched
their ball of gadgets into orbit. The entire country freaked
out.

What was wrong with the U.S.A.? The Russians beat us
into Space! Panic spread, magazines ran features, politicians
pointed fingers, a scapegoat was needed at once.

It finally came down to this: Russia must have better
schools than us. The onus was on the kids. A thousand new
articles appeared comparing Soviet and American education
and condemning the latter. It was Sputnik Madness!

Across the country, Sputnik Madness caused an enormous surge in new school construction. Each school was
competing with its neighbors. Who would have the fanciest
equipment, the most expensive laboratories, the latest in

academic machinery? Who would do the most in our latest Cold War offensive against the Russians? Ike was still President and it was not long after the McCarthy days in Washington. Because of Sputnik, too, the new emphasis in American education was entirely on science.

I rode the crest of this Sputnik Madness right into the seventh grade. All of us were tested and retested, and those with special aptitudes in science or mathematics were "tracked" into special "advanced" classes and treated like little prize hogs who had to be stuffed with the finest corn the quickest and fattened up for college. The rest of our peers, who were perhaps not quite as good at taking aptitude tests, were sidetracked into ordinary pens and treated with far less attention than those in advanced classes. Though this was called "letting them work at their own pace."

Science. More science was crammed down us than anything else. Even when we got into English class, we couldn't avoid it. Instead of getting better literature to read, we received new "scientifically" prepared reading workbooks. The level of the trash contained in these was staggering, enough to convince you that reading was perhaps the most uninteresting and stupid thing on earth.

Then there were the language laboratories which we were dumped into like so much laundry. The teachers used these as if they were new household appliances to make their work easier. Just put the kids in the language lab for a couple of hours, come back and collect them. The truth was, however, that language laboratories only made the need for a good teacher even greater.

Finally, there was a course I took in junior high school which I will never forget. It was called "Citizenship" and was taught by a fat grandmotherly woman with bluish hair, who wore crepe-bodiced dresses which collected dark patches of perspiration down each side. Her name was Mrs. Barnes. She wanted to make us good Americans. Of course, we *were* good Americans. But she wanted us to *know* that we were.

We learned how terrible Russia was and how wonderful
America. In fact, said Mrs. Barnes, Russia was so terrible they even used brainwashing techniques on their school-
children. They actually gave their children *propaganda* in
school! She spat out *propaganda* as if it were the foulest
word she could possibly imagine. How illuminating this was
for all of us little prize pigs in the advanced section. Our
"tracked" brains caught the hypocrisy in Mrs. Barnes's
statement at once. I remember walking out of that classroom
and five or six of us breaking into hysterical laughter. Did
she really think we were so stupid that we didn't understand
the idiotic propaganda she was trying to feed us, based on
the enemy's use of *propaganda?*

Another of Mrs. Barnes's American activities was to
require each of us, twelve years old and in the seventh grade,
to write his autobiography. We were encouraged to make
it as intimate as possible, to include whatever we wanted
about our parents, our lives at home, our problems, and so
on. This kept us busy for several weeks. We were only allowed to work on it during actual class time and Mrs. Barnes
collected the work after each class section. It could never
leave the room.

Finally, Mrs. Barnes introduced us to our "permanent
record folders." She held up a dark brown folder and waved
it around in the air. "By the time you are seniors, this folder
may weigh four or five pounds. Into it goes everything we
know about you in school. Your grades. Your tests. Reports
on your behavior and your personality. Your autobiography
will go in here. And, perhaps most important, boys and
girls, your citizenship reports which I will write out."

For the next five or six years, this brown envelope will
haunt us, floating in gray metal cabinets behind lock and
key, full of information about us, never to be seen by us.
Only by the school officials, the teachers, and finally, The
Colleges.

Little Sputnik circling the globe, I curse you. You made

my life miserable. Like a strange moon, you washed America with a new tide. It never fell, only got higher and higher, threatening to push the junior high schools and high schools of the country right out of this world and into the darkest corners of Citizenship.

———————

Bloom and I are in the same section of gym. All Columbia undergraduates are required to take two years of gym. You choose different activities, changing in the middle of each term from handball to touch football to swimming to physical fitness to fencing to bowling. Bloom and I have chosen to begin with bowling.

We report to the alleys in the basement of Carman Hall. So this is Ivy League life? Bowling class. The instructor is a short, muscular man who has been teaching gym at Columbia for thirty years. He is not the same kind of gung-ho young coach you find in high school. Not the guy to give you long pep talks on a balanced diet, masturbation, and next year's defense at Hackensack High. Our college gym teacher, who can teach anything from bowling to basketball, seems to take us all in stride. He knows we are putting in time, fulfilling the requirement. But this year the class of '69 almost makes him lose his cool.

A good example of why is a guy in our bowling class. His name is Forad and he comes to bowling the first day with hair that hangs over his shoulders, thick and sticky and dark black, and a full beard that springs out of his face as if electrified. He wears sandals and ragged jeans and a thin Indian shirt. He is a freshman. A friend of Bloom's from high school. Forad likes to come to bowling class stoned.

The gym teacher stands behind the alley and watches Forad scamper with the ball toward the pins, a stalk of wild hair running to the foul line. He releases the ball. It rumbles smoothly down and connects right in the pocket between

first and second pins. They all fall down. Strike! Forad jumps
up and down giggling and screeching, stoned and over-
whelmed with happiness; he has made a strike.

The gym teacher shakes his head, grits his teeth, and
moves far down the line to a group of serious-faced engineer-
ing students who are having trouble keeping score.

Bloom and I quickly become best friends. Not only do we
have such similar backgrounds in the Jersey suburbs and the
prep schools of Riverdale, but we share a common angry
cynicism about most everything. One thing, though, we are
not cynical about. That is girls.

We drive up to Bronxville early on a fine afternoon of
fall breezes. It is Saturday. Tonight, the first Sarah Lawrence
mixer takes place.

Sarah Lawrence girls have much more glamour at-
tached to them than the girls of Barnard. Perhaps it is because Sarah Lawrence is outside the city. Barnard is right
across Broadway. But each school definitely has its own
image. Barnard girls are known as grinds, on their way to
graduate school, prone to sweatshirts and dirty sneakers
and gulping beers at the bar in the West End right alongside
Columbia men. Sarah Lawrence girls, on the other hand, are
a trifle exotic. They all paint, or dance, or write poetry.
They tend to be beautiful: dirty-blond hair and long, tanned
legs, Madras skirts, red shetland sweaters. They are rebel debutantes. Occasionally they marry Asian princes or
French viscounts.

Bloom knows some girls who went to Fieldston with
him who are now Sarah Lawrence freshmen. We spend the
afternoon talking to them, walking around the lawns underneath the fall trees, sipping a Coke in the school snack bar;
casing the joint.

One of Bloom's friends has a roommate who interests

me. Her name is Monique. She has the longest hair I have
ever seen. Monique has grown up in Peru. Her mother di-
vorced her real father and remarried a Peruvian millionaire. Monique has gone to an American high school in Lima.
How far away from Keaton can you get? She is intelligent
and quiet, seems very sophisticated.

Dinnertime. The girls have to eat in the dining hall.
Bloom and I get in the Triumph and drive down into Bronxville where we find a little bar that serves hamburgers.

"Good thing we came up here early," I say.

"Definitely. We've got a headstart."

"I feel like getting blasted."

"Me too." We order Scotch with beer chasers, keep
ordering until eight o'clock and time to head back to the
campus for the mixer.

The parking lot which was deserted this afternoon is
now dark but dancing with white headlights and crowded
with groups of excited boys walking from cars. Hundreds of
boys are coming to this mixer from all over the East. Sarah
Lawrence girls have reputations. Beautiful and smart, and
they like to make love as much as you do! So goes the image
line.

Inside an auditorium that is a series of terraces running
down to a pit where the dancing takes place, a band from
Columbia is warming up their electric equipment. The rack-
et is awful, and on purpose. They keep it up for half an hour,
so that when they finally begin to play real music it creates
an instant surge of climactic relief. Outside in the hall, at
long tables, they sell beer. Beer at a dance! This is definitely
not prep school where only the most daring would smuggle
in half-pints of Southern Comfort under their coats.

The girls are beginning to arrive. Already three hundred
boys here. Now the blonds and the redheads and the chest-
nut-haired young ladies move down over the terraces. Most
of them wear dresses. Not the "party dresses" of senior year
in high school. But the boutique creations they have bought

for college. Low-cut, no back, wild patterns, they cling to young breasts and thighs. And the crowd of gaping, sport-jacketed college men trembles with the sight. As soon as this band starts to play music, there is going to be an insane rush down the terraces to the most attractive girls. "Would you like to dance?" holler five boys at once in front of the same little girl with the large breasts and the golden hair.

The music begins. Bloom and I begin to mix. I dance with several girls. Then see our friends from this afternoon sitting in a circle up the terraces. I join them, pulling a seat up beside Monique. We talk about things. Mostly about what a drag this mixer is. Though, of course, it is exciting as hell. We are both enjoying it. But that is what you talk about at a mixer: How awful it is. Soon, I lead her down into the gyrating pit and we dance. For about thirty minutes we keep it up, then finally, covered with sweat, we climb back up to rest.

The point of a mixer is to mix and so, when a boy comes by and asks Monique to dance, she looks at me for a second and I say, "Sure," and she goes off with him. Monique definitely interests me. But I want to look around. There are just so many incredible girls in the room.

Bloom has found himself a lanky blond he is talking and laughing with. She is from Chicago and I sit and talk with them, my eyes combing the crowd. Then I see a young lady with what strikes me as *the* Sarah Lawrence face. Oval-shaped, classic features, framed by brown hair which is parted in the middle and which hangs to the middle of her back. Everything sleek and . . . I am on my feet, moving in her direction. For I have just seen her say "Thank you" to the guy she was dancing with and turn for the terraces.

Forad's apartment is in a building with a reputation as a local whorehouse. True, the halls are thick with garlic fumes and

Puerto Rican girls in red skirts and white shoes. We are going to a party at Forad's. Monique and I.

There are four bedrooms. Each occupied by a different Columbia guy while the kitchen is a communal mess and the bath is filled with cat crap. Forad is the only freshman living in the place. He has pulled the same trick I did and lied to Columbia, told them he would be living at home with his mother.

The door flies open two seconds after we buzz. There stands Forad in jeans and T-shirt, his hair exploding off his head, on top perched a wobbly blue beanie with a 69 on the front. "Hey, yes, come on in!" shouts Forad. We step inside. There are already about fifty people spread around the apartment. Four different stereos in each of the four bedrooms play four different records at top volume. "Come on and have some punch!"

There is an Orange Julius stand across Broadway. They have mixed the thick orange drink with quarts of cheap vodka and bottles of wine. I get Monique and myself each a paper cup of the dynamite. Forad is admiring her long hair. "Can I touch it?" he asks.

"Okay." He picks up a handful and runs his fingers through it.

"Oh, man, wow! Incredible hair you have!" It is down to the backs of her knees. Hangs like a brown cape all across her back. The longest hair anyone has ever seen on a girl before. Monique's face is small and round, not all that pretty, but the hair . . . that's her triumph.

The party becomes more crowded. Soon joints of grass are traveling up and down the hallway. Things get whacked out and foggy. The music is jumbled. More punch is made. Some dance beside the low mattress in Forad's room. I lie back on the bed and Monique leans against me. This is really our first "date" and tonight Monique will be staying in the city at my apartment. It is all arranged. In a way, I would like to get up and leave right now. But it is only 10:30. I watch Forad wander from conversation to conversation. He is getting belligerent and spraying a little saliva with his words. Forad features himself a great deal. He likes to lecture you on any subject that arises: drugs, women, rock and roll music, books, W. C. Fields movies. Especially rock and roll music, though. It's 1965. The Beatles are at their peak. The Stones, the Animals, the Kinks, the Bee Gees are invading from England. And right here in New York we can claim Dylan as a native son. He is electric now. Everyone at Columbia seems to want to be in a rock and roll band. There must be fifty groups around the campus. This fall the number one is called "The Walkers." When they play, huge crowds form under the apron of the stage. Available girls. And hungry musicians, looking for new techniques.

Forad plays the guitar and the harmonica. Both poorly. But he has compensations with his long hair and his image as a "stoned head." It will take most of the class of '69 six months to catch up and shed their Madras jackets, Weejun loafers, and neat haircuts.

Always plenty of pot around here. Forad is especially paranoid and passes out bust rumors like leaflets. Now he comes over and leans down in my face with his bad breath: "Your chick has groovy hair."

"Thanks. So do you."

"Thanks." He walks off crookedly. The apartment smells of a mixture of pot fumes, Japanese incense, mouthwash and cat shit. I nudge Monique. "You think maybe we should split?"

I lost my virginity one night when I was sixteen. She was a model, twenty-one years old, beautiful and alcoholic. It was a hot night in July. Steve was away visiting his mother on Fire Island. I had the plush apartment all to myself.

I had known her in Tenafly. Ellen was good friends with the older sister of one of my best friends. Thin and red-haired with vivid blue eyes and a thin screen of light freckles, Ellen was almost a Tenafly legend. Yet unlike most pretty girls in suburbia, she avoided the cheerleader bit. Instead, she was "one of the boys," hanging around with the "coolest" crowd, learning to drink as they did, to race cars through the deserted streets of dawn Tenafly, roaring back from New York State full of beer. We had known each other at my friend's house for years and become close, almost as if we were brother and sister. It was only natural that I should call her up since we were both living in the city that summer. She would invite me over for dinner. This night I had taken her up to see Steve's mother's apartment; we had stopped in a couple of the East Side "pubs" and gotten high.

In the living room, full of expensive knick-knacks and Oriental rugs, the two of us sat finishing a six-pack of Bud-weiser. I wanted her, had known her so long, had imagined her body so often in fantasies. She was drunk. I was too. The first soft taste of her beer-stinking lips. The softest kiss I could ever recall. She reached up and put her hands around my neck and drew me down. And when we moved through the dark hall into the bedroom, lay down onto a feathernest of a bed, she said, "Oh Spike!" Not with passion. But as if to say, "This was inevitable, wasn't it?"

When it is finished and I lie on my back looking up into the shadows which come off the city street and hover on the canopy of the bed, I think: "Now I am a man."

This thought sounds like a Ping-pong ball bouncing in an empty gym. It sputters for a few moments and then dies on the floor. I am not a man. Not yet. This time has been good but worked no magic.

The bare light bulb hangs directly over our heads in the kitchen. Unfortunately. It illuminates far too clearly the stove caked with grease, the stained sink, the crusty cupboards and dirty linoleum on the floor.

Forad is slicing peppers and onions and dropping them into a pan of sizzling pork chops. There are about four of us in Forad's place tonight. An ordinary school night in the fall. Getting together to cook a communal supper.

"That fucking bulb! I just changed it last week," he says. We have suddenly been stranded in darkness.

"Hey! All the lights in the apartment are out," shouts somebody down the hall.

"Must be a fuse," I say.

"Get the candles." There are plenty of candles in the apartment, usually lighted when everyone is stoned late at night and lying around listening to the stereo. We manage to fill up the rooms with candlelight in several minutes. The doorbell rings. Forad opens it and one of his roommates enters. "Hey you guys! Every light in the city is out! We're having a blackout."

"Christ! Maybe we're being attacked by Russia?" says Forad, his paranoia emerging.

"Wow. This is it. The end of the world!"

"Turn on the radio."

"There's no electricity."

"Tom has one in his room, a transistor."

Eight million of us in New York City are dropped into blackness. Across the Hudson, New Jersey sparkles with lights. Poor New Jersey has missed out on this catastrophe. "Let's take a walk up Broadway," suggests Forad. We take candles in our hands and lead a solemn procession through the halls of the building and outside onto the street. What's happening? It looks like a big party on Broadway. Happy crowds milling about with nowhere to go. No looting, not even any panhandlers around. Pretty Barnard girls walk down the street in groups holding glowing sticks of incense between their fingers. We cross the street and poke into the Gold Rail. With candles on every table, the usually depressing restaurant suddenly looks romantic and ancient. We run into some friends. "What's going on down at your place?" they ask Forad.

"A party. Come on over." We walk up to the West End, all along the way meeting people and inviting them to the party. Stop in the Drive Liquor Store for jugs of cheap wine. Then back to the apartment. Some girls are finishing the pork chops in the kitchen. They smilingly wipe the grease off their lips. Oh well, nobody is hungry any more. It is the best party of all. Guitars are played, pipes bob and weave like orange bugs in the shadow, the crowd enlarges and shrinks with a regular rhythm. Until about four in the morning. There are ten of us huddled in a dark room. A candle burns down near the aluminum foil of its base. A couple of high school girls from Brooklyn have wandered into the party. The subways aren't working so they have no way to get home. We have overheard their reassuring calls to nervous mothers. John Taylor is here. Bloom. Forad. Eventually, everyone finds a corner and falls into a heavy technicolor sleep under a lid of marijuana.

In the morning, I wander into the kitchen. The bare bulb is hanging there glowing stupidly.

Sometimes I talk to Forad about psychoanalysis. His father is a psychoanalyst and he has been going to one since the third grade. It seems, the way he talks about it, as if it were a natural part of his growing up. Just before he entered Columbia, he "finished" his analysis. Now he says he is thinking of going back.

Both my father and my mother have gone to analysts. Since my father took the job with the Congregational Church, they have been able to "go through analysis." The

Congregationalists carried a kind of health insurance which applied to both mental and physical health. My father was paying for it out of his salary anyway. My mother went to one in Tenafly. My father goes to one in New York City.

I do not understand "psychoanalysis." But both my parents claim it is a great thing. I understand it has something to do with talking about your childhood.

Several of my friends in Tenafly have been to analysts. Several were sent by the school and visited once a week for a couple of months. My friend Steve has visited one. He said it was stupid and he didn't care for it. One day when I was sixteen, home from Keaton on vacation and very down, I asked my mother if I could go to a psychoanalyst. She said she would ask a doctor if he would see me.

The day arrived. She drove me up to his Colonial house on East Hill. And said she would be back in an hour. I was nervous and asked, "What exactly do I do?"

"Just talk to him. It's okay," she said.

I leaf through magazines anxiously in the waiting room.

A tall man in a suit appears. He is very serious and says, "Come in." Inside his comfortable office, I spot the special couch right away. I move for this but he motions me to a chair beside his desk. "Your mother tells me you want to talk to me."

"I wanted to see what psychoanalysis was like. Both my parents have done it. I was curious."

"Do you have anything in particular that you would like to talk about?"

"Not really."

"How do you feel these days?"

"Not so hot."

"What seems to be the problem?"

"I'm not very happy."

"Why?"

"This school I go to. It's a prep school."

I wait for the next question. Wait and wait, but it never

comes. So I examine the walls, the ceiling, the rugs, the view of shrubbery out the picture window. What is going on here? This silence. So this is psychoanalysis. This long silence. I don't see why this costs $25 an hour. Not at all. My father has told me it helps you accept yourself the way you really are. I have thought about this often but cannot quite absorb the idea. Who am I? My parents talk about "traumas" and "insights" at home occasionally. How do these words fit with this rather ordinary-looking man who is staring at me right now and won't ask me any more questions?

"Is this it?" I ask.

"What?"

"Psychoanalysis?"

"Well, I guess you don't have much to talk about today. But if you ever want to talk to me again, I'll be happy to see you."

Why would I ever want to talk to this man? He is the most boring man I have ever met.

I sit in Forad's room. His kitten is purring on my chest. Forad is trying to explain psychoanalysis to me. I think it must be something. Perhaps one dose was not enough.

I am sitting on the couch in my father's office. We are talking about Columbia and about how I feel. "I'm really sick of school. I've been in school every year since I was five years old."

"Can you arrange a leave of absence at Columbia?" he asks.

"I could. But then there's the draft. I don't want to go to Vietnam."

"What would you like to do?"

"I don't know. Maybe travel around Europe. Write a novel." These are my two main dreams.

"What would you do for money?"

"Work, I guess."

"I guess so. I couldn't support you. You know, Paul, I think now you are eighteen, you should be on your own. I think one of the worst things *I* could do would be to give you too much help."

"Sure. I guess so." I'm not really listening to what he is saying. I'm thinking about being on my own. My dream of Paris, a romantic garret, typing away on a novel, maybe a Swedish girlfriend . . .

Columbia is one of the last Ivy League colleges to liberalize its rules concerning women visitors in the dormitories. This year several hours have been added to the amount of time women are allowed to go upstairs in the company of dorm students. Bringing the total number of hours to about ten.

For the students who have their own apartments, this regulation is meaningless. But for the thousands of boys living in the big gray elephants of dorms, with their long narrow corridors, the rooms the size of closets, bunkbeds, bare lightbulbs, no lounges, this rule about women is torture. The administration has agreed to negotiate. Slowly, painstakingly, the Dormitory Council tries to extract more liberal concessions from the Kirk administration.

Bloom and I have two friends who are roommates in Carman Hall: John Sagner and Paul Auster. Sagner wants to be a rock musician and Auster writes poetry and studies French.

One afternoon I am in their room. Just Sagner and I. He went to Putney School in Vermont. He still has a girlfriend up there, a senior, whom he is always talking about, calls several times a week, seems to have placed on top of a big pedestal in his life. He obviously worships this girl. Her name is Nora.

"You want to see a picture of Nora?" he asks me.

"Sure." I am curious. He goes to his dresser and opens the top drawer. Comes back with a medium-sized color photograph.

She is dancing across the grass, both feet off the ground, her blond hair flying in the air. Her face is indescribably lovely. A classic beauty. She seems like every Columbia guy's dream of a girl. Her eyes stare out of the picture with intelligence and, also, a kind of sadness. Her full lips are sexual. Her nose perfect. The color of her skin very white, so you can almost see the veins behind it, blue streaked marble. She is a moving statue.

"This photograph, John. I think I see why you are in love with this girl."

He nods his head and smiles. Takes the photo and re-places it in the drawer, shutting it tight.

About four in the afternoon, my father's office gets more relaxed. I have come to visit him as I often do. His door is closed, but June, his secretary, says I can go inside.

"Hi," he says. He is sitting at his desk with his legs up, thinking.

"Hi, Dad." I move to the couch and sit down. "How are you?"

"Very well. I've decided."

"Decided?"

"To take the Chicago offer."

"You're going to quit the Commission?"

"Yes. I've told the university I'll be able to start as of January first."

"You'll be moving to Chicago then?"

"Your mother wants to stay here and let John finish this year of high school in Tenafly. I'll go out there and rent an apartment. Commute back here on weekends. Meanwhile, I can look for a house in Chicago for the family. They'll move out in June."

"What about the Tenafly house?"

"We'll hang on to it. Rent it."

"I see."

"I'm very excited about this."

"You're really going to do it?"

"I told them this afternoon."

As 1965 unfolds, the civil rights movement has been drifting with a new current. Away from the Southern towns. North into the cities. The word "freedom" has gradually been over-

Listening to Rev. Andrew Young of SCLC speak to a tense crowd during the Savannah riots, 1963.

shadowed by the word "power." Demands for this "black power" from younger leaders like Stokely Carmichael and James Forman have upset and confused older civil rights leaders. And riots have replaced sit-ins on the nightly news, changing the tide of liberal white sympathies into suburban panic and "white backlash."

My father has told me that "black power" is an inevitable and desirable stage of the struggle. As a white man and a "church bureaucrat" he has not been able to have much to do with it, naturally. But he said, "I think it's time they had a black man as director of the Commission." He has grown increasingly frustrated, anyway, by the massive red tape that must be cut through in order to take action within the National Council of Churches. This huge institution is made up of all the major Protestant denominations in the United States, kind of a United Nations of Protestantdom. And equally as stalemated and conflicted as the real UN. Denominations run the gamut from liberal (Congregational) to middle-of-the-road (Episcopal) to conservative (Methodist).

The Chicago offer is from the University of Chicago's Divinity School, one of the leading seminaries in the country. There is a group of faculty there who have come to feel increasingly frustrated about the kind of training given to young ministers. They have been meeting and talking and have finally come up with something they call the Doctor of Ministry Program. This would offer a new degree, between the old Bachelor of Divinity and Doctor of Divinity degrees. It would require longer than the B.D. to fulfill. Involve many of the same elements: study of Bible, theology, psychology, preaching. But incorporate many new elements. What exactly these are to be, the Chicago people are not certain. In general, they want to turn out ministers capable of working with the rapidly changing society that has come about since World War II. New ministers alive to new social issues, new social patterns, new social problems. They must bring creativity to their work. How do you preach an anti-materialist,

social revolutionary Gospel in a society of staggering mate-
rialism and entrenched middle-class values? How does one
begin with a Puritan-based religion and adapt it to the sensa-
tionalism and technology of "post-industrial" America?

Ministers are naturally supposed to "minister" to people's problems. In the days when problems were roughly the
same, year to year, small town to small town, birth to marriage to death, it was not all that difficult to do this job of
"ministering": formulas gradually developed.

But what about today? How do you minister to families
in Watts? How do you minister to men working on Madison
Avenue? How do you minister to boys drafted for Vietnam?

The University of Chicago has asked my father to direct
this new Doctor of Ministry Program. His title will be Professor of Ministry. He has accepted. There was really little
alternative. The job seems made for him.

Bloom and I still don't study. Instead, each night is an
adventure.

He arrives with a pocket full of pot. I have a bottle of
bargain Scotch I bought that afternoon. "Let's make a pact.
For every joint we smoke, we'll have a drink."

"Sure. Good idea."

After four joints, we are lurching around the room,
getting up to change the records, dialing the telephone to
talk to friends. Bloom calls his girlfriend at Sarah Lawrence.
I thumb through the telephone book. Hey! Look at this listing: A. Ginsberg, East 10th Street. It must be Allan Ginsberg the poet. When Bloom finishes his call, I dial the
number.

"Hello?" says the unmistakable voice.

I introduce myself. Ginsberg is friendly. I tell him
Bloom and I are Columbia freshmen and stoned out of our

minds tonight. He begins to reminisce about his Columbia days. I mention that my father was minister of Judson to see if there is any reaction. "Oh, Reverend Spike? Sure I knew him." We talk for perhaps forty minutes. The famous poet is enjoying himself. I am very impressed by the fact that, just like that, I have been able to call up and talk to someone whose writing has inspired me for years. I read *Howl* when I was twelve. Probably it had a great deal to do with why I was so miserable in junior high school. You can't read *Howl* at home and then come into school the next morning and open up a reading "workbook" about the adventures of "Big Mike, dam builder on the Columbia River," not with a straight face. I tell this to Ginsberg. He laughs. "Call me any time," he says.

Bloom and I are yawning. Another adventure is drawing to a close. Time for him to wander back up Broadway. And I am ready to crash.

The jet of my freedom rises at such a steep angle that it is a relief when it gradually begins to level off. Boredom sets in to a certain degree. The same adventures are no longer adventurous but habits. Drinking in the West End, sharing joints of grass in Forad's, even the trek to Sarah Lawrence loses its glow of "newness." As the winter settles down on New York, I am not even running on a level plane any more. Without realizing it, I have begun to dive.

Saunders has dropped out of Columbia and enlisted in the army. Bloom tells me as we stand around the Lion's Den at noon, waiting for a table.

"I can't believe it."

"Apparently it was his first acid trip. He had a very bad time. This morning he disappeared and when he came back he showed his roommates the papers."

"Isn't there some way out of it?"

"No, you don't understand. He is serious. He *wants* to go to Vietnam, he says."

"What an incredible bad trip he must have had. This is the story they should use to discourage kids from dropping LSD. 'James Saunders, age eighteen, previously a typical freak, dropped acid for the first time, decided to leave Columbia, and signed up for Vietnam with the Army infantry.'"

"Nobody would believe it."

The headaches begin. It seems, at first, as if I must have some kind of sinus condition. The pain comes right behind my eyes. Then it seems that I have an allergy to alcohol. Every time I have a drink it brings on one of these pains. They get worse and worse. Until I am running home to lie down on my bed the moment I sense another headache is about to begin. So painful that tears squeeze out of my shut lids and even aspirin will not work.

Exam time. I suddenly sit down and for two weeks cram myself full of the term's work. I have no idea what Columbia's exams will be like. It turns out they are not too bad. I feel satisfied with the way I have been able to answer most of the questions. They are usually essay questions and I have developed my "bullshit style." Very rarely do I have an accident. "Thus we see," "on the contrary" and "as a result" grease each sentence so that a professor, two-thirds asleep anyway, glides easily over the surface of my essay without realizing that it is all surface, floating on no substance. I get a B or B+. Not outstanding work, but easy to read and it seems to make sense.

After exams, there is a short recess. I am suddenly

knocked off my feet by a wave of depression I have never felt before. Nothing seems worth doing. Even these exams have depressed me. This is what I will be doing for the next four years? It doesn't occur to me that I might get interested in a subject and spend four years really studying. That idea seems hopelessly . . . *corny.*

I stay home now. Bloom calls up and I say I don't feel like going out. I am having these headaches all the time. And now I suddenly have begun to feel sharp attacks of a panic which is based on apparently nothing. This increases. It occurs to me: am I losing my mind? Too much pot, or what? I get paranoid. I am now afraid of being nailed down with another one of these pains in my head. What is happening to me?

Recess ends, and second term begins. I have figured out my schedule, go through a day of lines and red tape registering, and go home. Next day, classes begin. I go to all my classes. In each one I sit with thoughts far away. This all seems so irrelevant to me. What I want is . . . what is it? I feel I am wasting my time studying these things. What I should be doing is living my life. Somehow, I don't connect this college life with "my life." Rather, it is still a preparation . . .

I really get the fear! Cold beams of fright running through my arms and legs. My stomach gags in nausea. All night sleepless on my bed until the queasy light of dawn. I feel so alone. My anxiety seems to grow more anxiety which it feeds upon, in turn, growing larger and larger. Pains stab in my forehead. I try hot and cold showers. The din of the water will not drown out the pain in my head. I am terrified of the terror: my pain is a set of Chinese boxes. My father, I would call him up but he's in Chicago now. I have no idea what this is about. Erik Erikson is not around Columbia to tell me. Suddenly, inexplicably, like a baby dropping free of the mother's womb, like a boulder tumbling into a canyon, I am falling into my identity crisis.

Typical. My story seems built out of the most typical bricks. My imagination yearns to intercede, to invent here a brand-new set of unheard-of characters, a new adventure, a behavior that would not end with this thud: identity crisis.

Perhaps this is what makes the nightmare so powerful. As catastrophe piles on top of catastrophe, each one becomes more "typical" than the last. We have our typical breakdowns. Our typical crises. The typical riots are begun by typical assassinations. We even have a generation of typical freaks.

My life is typical. Breaking the barrier of the typical, a frontier which has been crossed a billion times before, seems more difficult than jumping into an unknown wilderness. Typical panic and typical suffering: the bones of a modern life.

I call home and my mother answers. "How have you been?"

"To tell the truth, terrible."

"What's wrong?"

"I've been having a lot of anxiety. When you feel panic, and you don't know why, that's anxiety, right?"

"Yes. One kind of anxiety. Maybe you should go talk to an analyst?"

"Why?"

"He can help you figure out what you are anxious about."

"What good will that do?"

"Once you realize what it is that is causing your anxiety, you stop feeling so anxious. It's called an 'insight.'"

"Are you sure?"

"Of course."

"I don't feel like seeing that other guy."

"I'll give you the number of Dr. Shapiro, Daddy's analyst."

My father finished his treatment with Dr. Shapiro several years ago. I hesitate for several days before calling. Then give in and call Shapiro. I have met him once before. At a party given for the publication of my father's last book. "This is Dr. Shapiro," said my father. "He knows more about you than anyone in the world except your mother and me." A mild-mannered guy with a quiet voice. My father's introduction seemed lame to me. Why should I want this man, a stranger, to know anything about me? I stood there beside him. He asked me a question, a polite one, and I answered him. Then nothing. This seems to be the way these guys are. Completely dull, they never say anything. I got away from Dr. Shapiro as soon as I could and moved to a more lively section of the party.

Now on the phone I tell him I have been feeling extremely anxious. I would like him to recommend an analyst for me. "Fine. I'll call you back tomorrow with a name of someone who can see you."

The next day he calls with the name of a Dr. Steinberg. "He sees a lot of students," says Shapiro. I thank him, hang up and call Steinberg. A big voice answers the phone.

"Oh yes, Dr. Shapiro called me this morning. Let's see. Could you tell me about how you have been feeling?"

I describe my anxiety and the headaches. This is not pleasant work. Then he asks, "Have you been going to your classes?"

"No."

"How many have you been to?"

"About five in three weeks."

"Well! You *must* start going back to classes. We need to

know how you react both *in* and *out* of school." He makes an appointment to see me in a couple of days. I let him but have no intention of ever keeping it. After hanging up, I call Shapiro back. I explain that I already know the other doctor is not for me. Could he come up with another name?

"Have you considered seeing me?" asks Shapiro.

"Well . . . I thought about it. But since you were my father's analyst, I thought . . . "

"I don't think that is necessarily important. Would you like me to make an appointment for you to come and talk to me?"

"Yes. I guess so."

Shapiro makes an appointment for Tuesday.

His office is just off Riverside Drive on West 86th Street. A comfortable living room separates his and his wife's offices. She is also an analyst.

The first session is nothing. Except tension. His office feels gloomy to me. The air conditioner hums, not with cool air, but just mixing the stuffy atmosphere around. There is the couch. I sit on a chair beside the desk. The walls are covered with full bookshelves. I don't know what to say. I list symptoms. He asks a few questions. The long silence begins. At the end, he hands me two prescriptions: sleeping pills and tranquilizers. And an appointment for next week.

I have had this date with a girl from Vassar for some time. I decide to keep it. Her name is Alice Geller and she went to school with Bloom. I knew her one summer at Fire Island. She is down for the weekend, staying in her parent's brownstone in the Village.

I pick her up in my father's Triumph. We head uptown

along Fifth, then over on Park Avenue. Stop first for one drink. Then shoot up over the border at 96th Street which separates Manhattan from Harlem.

High-pitched scream of rubber tearing the asphalt. On my left, just before it hits, I see the grill of an old Dodge about to rip into us.

The sportscar's frame buckles. Alice is thrown right out onto the street. I fly up and collide with the metal frame of the convertible top. Lucky. For the narrow well where my legs sat on the pedals has disappeared, crushed with ugly jagged metal. The pedals are twisted around each other like spaghetti. My legs, had they not flown up, would have been cut off at the knee.

The shock of the street, blood pouring off my head, Puerto Ricans trying to get us to sit down on the curb, the first sirens and the arrival of three or four squad cars. The Dodge was stolen. It ran the light. None of this is my fault. But I cannot help feeling guilt. My father's car is beyond repair.

A police car takes us to the hospital. Into the Emergency Ward in our expensive clothes.

"How old are you?" asks the nurse.

"We're both eighteen."

"We can't touch you without parents' or guardian's permission. Or somebody over twenty-one."

"Look, what am I supposed to do? I'm bleeding."

"Call your parents. When they get here, we'll take you."

"They live in New Jersey."

"Sorry." She turns her back. Very busy tonight. It is Saturday night in Harlem. I see the phone booth against the cinderblock wall and begin to cross the room full of black emergencies. A man has just entered surrounded by police. He is holding a crumpled shirt to his bare stomach. Caked with reddish crust, the blood must still be pouring out. Was he knifed in the gut? The cop has an iron grip on his arm. I pass benches full of black mothers and sick children. Old woman holds an enormous white compress to her jaw. Distorted faces. The walls of the room are sickening green. I call home. It is the weekend and my father is there. He takes the information and thirty-five minutes later he is standing in the doorway. We are the only white people in the emergency room. "Are you okay?"

"Yeah. But I think I need stitches. And Alice should have an X-ray or something."

As soon as he tells the nurse his name ("Dr. Spike") she leads us behind the desk and into the treatment rooms. A maze of tables, each separated from the next by stained white sheets which hang from the ceiling. It is a kind of bazaar under fluorescent lights, green cinderblock walls, white-coated interns moving back and forth. They lie me down on a table and a nurse arrives with a bowl and razor to shave the hair around the cut on top of my skull. This hurts like hell. When she is finished my father says, "I passed the car."

"Bad."

"Unbelievable. I almost threw up. I don't know why you two aren't more hurt."

"Well . . ."

A girl begins to moan and cry out on the other side of the sheet. She is only inches from where I lie and the noise is terrifying. Then a doctor says loudly, "What happened to this one?"

"Fell down a stairwell. Four flights."

"Probably drunk! How old is she?"

"Seven."

"Well . . . let's see what we can do . . ."

This conversation sends me rifling into shock. "Probably drunk"? What must it do to work the Emergency Ward in the ghetto on Saturday night? And then see two punk suburban kids come in from a crash-up in their sportscar. I look at my father's face. It is white and the gristle of his beard stands out too clearly under the lighting. He looks ill.

I flash the front seat of the car, what I saw as I pulled loose, those crumpled pedals and what my legs would have looked like . . .

"Why am I still alive?"

The accident is the final boost up into a world of total panic. Monday night I am paralyzed by anxiety. I sit on the couch and try to focus on the tranquilizing television. It won't work. I have already taken one Librium. Now get up and take a second. The prescription says four times a day. But will two at once be an overdose? I panic about this. Get Shapiro's home number and call him. He assures me that two Librium will not be harmful. Do I want to see him earlier than our scheduled appointment? See him tomorrow? Yes.

I go into the bedroom and lie down in the dark. Dim music floats through the floor from the apartment underneath. People are living all around me. Cells of different lives suspended in the sky. Try to relax. Impossible. Try to think of something. What about my mother's words: ". . . it's called an 'insight.'"

When exactly did this feeling begin? When did I have the first of these headaches? Try to think back as far as I can. The last weeks seem like a solid wall of pain, but just beyond there are images to grasp at.

What about my feelings. Anxiety. But what exactly does this anxiety feel like? A bubble bouncing inside my mind, threatening to break. A pressure behind the eyes. Something threatening to . . . I'm afraid of "going crazy." What does this mean? Afraid of losing control?

When did this begin, dammit?

"I've decided." Who said that? "So I'll rent an apartment. Commute back here on weekends." My father. He's back in Chicago tonight. This makes me very frightened.

My mother . . .

What about my mother?

As long as I can remember, I have not had a good relationship with my mother. We have so many fights, always over the most trivial things. It is my father whom I always go to for support and for love. I have thought that I actually hate her. I am so very angry . . .

My mother. A wheel is spinning its way up through the darkness, and on this wheel are the faces of my father and my mother, glowing faces, and all order is suspended as the wheel spins like those in carnival booths, but this has significance, this is terrifying . . .

Inside my head, for the first time, I allow a piece of self to slip into the light of consciousness.

I want to fuck my mother.

These terrifying words! I think I will die now. This secret I have been concealing from myself all these years. It is true. But . . . of course, I already recognize the change. I feel better at once. I want my mother. Not realized before. I love my mother. How strange to recognize this fact for the first time at eighteen.

But at the same time, it dawns on me that I do not want that. I think of her. It inspires no lust. The true key lies in the four words: *I want my mother.*

I slowly explain the insight and its circumstances to Dr. Shapiro. I am nervous. Will he jump up and throw me out of his office? Get out, you awful person. I notice a tiny grin forming on his face. "What's wrong?" I ask.

"Excuse me. It's just that you seem so much better than the last time you came."

So begins the analysis. The insight is only an open window into a dark house. Why was I so angry all my childhood?

What spoiled my relationship with my mother? How did it grow so cold and distant?

I sit in the office and look at Dr. Shapiro. I assume that he already knows the answers to all these questions. It is my initial understanding, crude and optimistic, that one's analyst only has to hear you talk for two or three sessions before he can put together the total formula of your life. Then gradually, week by week, you pay him to reveal it to you in stages so you will be able to digest it properly.

Months later it comes as a great surprise when I realize Shapiro knows much less than I had assumed. We have been making the journey together. I had thought he had a secret map somewhere in his pocket.

I ask Shapiro, "What about being a writer?"

"What do you mean?"

"I'm not so sure I want to go through analysis. When you are a writer you deal with your neuroses by working them out with your imagination, in your fiction. If I go through analysis, then I'll just work them out in this office. What will I have left to write about? I sort of feel like my problems are the fuel that keeps my imagination running."

He sits back and thinks about this. I watch his face. It is impossible to read. But I trust this man. And, I think, if it is true that he already knows so much about me, as my father said at the book party, won't this help my treatment? I feel strange calling it "treatment." Like taking doses of radiation to get rid of a cancer. Somehow the word does not fit this office, this quiet man in his suit, me in this chair, the hum of the air conditioning and the books along the wall.

"I think . . . perhaps you should think of it another way," says Shapiro. "The problems you might have worked out in your imagination, with your art, you can begin to resolve here. Which will only mean that you will advance to a new stage of understanding, a new look at your problems. Psychoanalysis is a tool, perhaps, to get you to a more advanced point of understanding. I can assure you it will not somehow mysteriously dissolve your imagination. Or cure all your problems. Really, what it is, is a kind of educational process."

I think about this. It occurs to me that the world I live in is filled with psychoanalysis. Already other freshmen I have talked to at Columbia have admitted that they are beginning to see "shrinks." Bloom has told me that he went to one in high school. It seems that if I am to be a writer I must write of the world I live in, a world which now thrives on Freudian and Freudian-based therapy. It is a "tool" I cannot afford to ignore because of some Hemingway mysticism about the need to keep one's imagination "good and true," one's "juices flowing" like a Big Two-Hearted River.

"All right. I think I see your point. But I still don't think I really understand how psychoanalysis works."

Shapiro shakes his head. "Come on. I don't think you want to talk about that here. You can read books about that. When you come here you have more important things to do than listen to a lecture on Freud."

He's right. The reality of the situation is I'm paying (at least my parents are paying) a good deal of money for every hour I sit in this office.

"What should I talk about, then?"

"Talk about how you feel."

I fall out. What drifts to the ground after a large explosion? Fallout.

I was born in 1947. A member of the generation spawned under the residue of Hiroshima and Nagasaki. The thousands of soldiers returned from war to make love and as a result, in 1947, so many babies were born they called us "The Baby Boom."

I fall out of Columbia. Go to see a dean. I explain I have

been having "personal problems" and skipping all my classes.

"Are you seeing anyone, Paul?"

"Yes. I have an analyst."

"Good. You can take a medical leave of absence. First you have to go talk to one of our psychologists. Fill out a few forms. This is quite common. Lots of our boys do this."

I nod.

"What I usually tell boys, what I'm going to advise you, Paul, is quite simple. We at Columbia feel you shouldn't waste these months you are out of school. You shouldn't spend them as you would if you were still a student either. What I advise is to take a boring job, perhaps a clerical job. The kind where you have to get up every morning and ride the subway. Nine to five work. Learn what it's like out there in the world. And get yourself a sense of the self-discipline necessary. So when you come back you'll be ready to really study."

This is a little strange. First of all, I'd already done this when I was sixteen. The dean seems to feel the best way to prepare for a Columbia education is by working at a "boring job" filing thumbtacks somewhere, riding the rush-hour subways. Anything would seem good after that. Even Columbia.

The classified section of *The Times* is full of jobs. But none of them applies to me. They all want experience of five years in "refridgeration" or something.

I have to write my draft board a letter, too. Vietnam is being escalated month by month. Everyone is locked in college. The alternative is a splash of training and a flight directly to the jungles. Photographs of young men our age stare out of all the magazines: armless, bloody casualties — guys who dropped out of high school or college. I tell my draft board the truth. I am taking a medical leave from school. I am seeing a private psychoanalyst. In a few weeks,

I get their reply. It is a small Draft Classification Card with the magic "1-Y" typed on it. Unless a grave national emergency arises, I can skip the Vietnam nightmare. When I show this card to people at Columbia they shake their heads with envy. "Spike, you lucky bastard. There's no date on it!" Everyone I know wants to be crazy enough to beat the draft. The "leave of absence" is being taken by dozens of guys this winter. The phenomenon is called "freaking out." It is nothing to be ashamed of nor is it a joke. One by one, the class of '69 freaks out. Most leave Columbia for six months or a year. Some stay in school. There is no strict formula but it is definitely a bond which ties the class closer together. The first ecstasy of college freedom all too rapidly disintegrates into the panic and anxiety of turning inward, dropping one's image, and stopping to pick up the pieces. Guys sit around the Lion's Den, the formica-and-linoleum-cold snackbar provided by the university, and discuss the details of their freakouts:

"I was hallucinating like crazy. The walls were turning colors, orange and blue . . ."

"Good thing you weren't on acid."

"Well, I was. The acid started it. But I didn't come down for two weeks."

"Did you take Thorazine?"

"I was taking more Thorazine for breakfast than orange juice. What time is it?"

"Ten to three."

"Got to go. See my shrink at four. His office's down the Village."

I have freaked out. Now, Columbia recommends a boring job and psychoanalysis as healing agents. I take the subway down to Times Square and begin to search through the employment agencies. In a sixth-floor office on West 44th Street, a woman looks over my application and gives me a frank stare, up and down. I have on a tie and jacket, my

Wasp nose is polished with soap, and she has seen Columbia written under "Education" on the card. "Just a minute,"
she says, "I think I've got something for you."

The Four Seasons is supposed to be the most exclusive
restaurant in New York City. It's not. Perhaps the most
expensive. Far too many tourists (millionaires from Peoria
and Golden Anniversaries from Locust Flats) churn their
way through a butter-drenched dinner beside the pastel
bubbles of the fountain in the famous Pool Dining Room.
The really exclusive restaurants in New York, the ones
where the Kennedys rub elbows with the Paleys, are French
and relatively unknown to the mass of tourists.

I am a page. My duties are numerous but center around
one primary function: I guide the customers from the maître
d's desk to their assigned table in one of the Four Seasons'
dining rooms: Pool or Grill.

The chain of command in the restaurant runs like this:
Directors, chef, maître d', captains, waiters, kitchen workers, pages, dishwashers. The waiters have a very strong
union, they make a great deal of money, and nobody pushes
them around. The captains have fancier uniforms, often
make less than the waiters, but have more dignity. The
kitchen workers are bossed and protected by the chef. The
pages are a group of about eight boys, many of them trying
to make it as actors or dancers while working in the restaurant for a living. The dishwashers are Puerto Ricans. They
work in white-tiled rooms full of steaming garbage odor and
many of them look more than a little strung out.

Just what is my job? For the first week I am frozen out.
No pages talk to me. I do my "duties." Besides seating people, I bring cigars and cigarettes to the table, plug in tele-
phones, run special errands. All this for a pay check which

after taxes is less than $80. I slowly begin to understand that
the other pages are not working here solely for this meager
check. They are getting tipped. But I never seem to get any
tips. Why not?

Finally, I make friends with a guy from Canada who has
been working here for five months. He explains "hustling"
to me. This is the art of extracting tips.

When Mr. and Mrs. Longhorn from East Jesus, Texas,
come up to the desk, the maître d' snaps to attention, looks
at the chart and says, "Page! Take the Longhorns to table
number 54 in the Pool Dining Room." He then, if the Longhorns aren't too tacky, steps out from behind the desk and
grasps Mr. Longhorn's sleeve, starts to propel him in the
right direction, with a nauseating smile dripping off his
teeth: "Just follow the page boy, Mr. Longhorn. And enjoy
your dinner."

There is a long alley between the Grill and the Pool. A
marble alley. Full of plants, modern chairs, and the Four
Seasons' Picasso. This is a huge backdrop the artist did for
an opera or ballet years ago. It is not one of his finer works.
In fact, it is quite muddy.

But the "hustle" begins.

"Is this your first visit to the Four Seasons, Mr. Longhorn?"

"Yes," coos his wife. They are smashed.

"May I show you a few features of the restaurant?"

"Hell, why not?" says Mr. Longhorn.

"All this marble you see was quarried . . . and over here
are the famous Barcelona chairs designed by . . . and out
here is the most prized possession of the Four Seasons. The
Picasso!" They pause and stare at it. He rubs his jaw and
shakes his head. She just stares.

"What the hell *is* that?"

"The Four Seasons paid . . ." (I make up a different
figure for each party. It amuses me, passes the time) ". . .
two million British pounds sterling for this Picasso."

The joking stops. "How much is that in dollars, boy?"

"I'm not sure, sir. Roughly six hundred thousand dollars." The figures are all wrong but so what?

"I see." He's giving this tarp a second look.

"It is an impressive work of original art, honey," says his wife like an advertisement on the back page of *Life* Magazine.

"I reckon."

"This is rumored to be the most beautiful Picasso in America, sir."

"I reckon."

"Now if you'll follow me . . ." When we get to the table, I pull out the chairs and hover expectantly. Learning how to hover expectantly is something all pages, waiters, bellboys must do. Now Mr. Longhorn goes into his pocket. He withdraws his wallet and extracts a bill. Then comes the most mysterious part of the "tip" to me. These men invariably crumple up the money into a tiny wad that fits securely in the central pit of their palm. They push out what looks like a hand ready to shake, I go to shake with my right hand, and then find them quickly scraping this wadded bill off into my hand. They are afraid to show anyone how much they are giving. Yet, it is all done so dramatically everyone invariably looks to see what the big secret is all about.

After a few weeks, hustling becomes a bore. I begin to daydream on the job. Several new pages are hired so I am no longer the director's favorite target. After the lunch shift, I have three hours free. I take a notebook and pen over to a nearby library on Lexington Avenue. And in a nook on the second floor I begin to write again. Each day I make myself fill up five pages of the notebook. For after my insight, and after the collapse of my "image," I have suddenly been forced into looking around for an actual identity. Page at the Four Seasons is not quite satisfactory. I have not written anything since that story which got me in trouble at Keaton. Except for school themes.

I get my meals at the Four Seasons. Not the rich food, but a special menu prepared for the lower echelons of help. Often it is hotdogs and beans. If only the gourmets out front could see the trough of greasy wieners floating in the steam table beside their sweetbreads in *beurre noir*. Once I learn to hustle I begin to pull in about $150 a week.

The worst enemies of all of us who work on the floor of the restaurant are "stiffs." These are people who demand service but never tip. Sometimes you get people who try to hand you a dime. One responds with: "No thank you, sir. We never accept tips at the Four Seasons." This is such a blatant piece of surrealism that it completely throws the dime-tipper into a headspin. If there is one thing that is accepted at the Four Seasons, it's tips.

After six weeks, I have seated enough captains of industry, super-salesmen, and middle-aged actresses to be immune to just about any celebrity who is likely to show up. But one afternoon I am rocked out of my lethargy when a familiar bulldog face comes tromping up the stairs. Grayson Kirk, president of Columbia University, a grand toastmaster in the nineteenth-century tradition. Kirk has a university limousine with full-time chauffeur. A Rembrandt owned by the university which hangs on his office wall for the pleasure of him and his guests alone. And a university mansion on Morningside Heights, with a sweeping vista of some of the most wretched tenements in America. I have to grin at the thought of attempting a hustle: "Is this your first visit to the Four Seasons, President Kirk? . . . and over here is our most prized possession, our Rembrandt, I mean Picasso, which cost three billion Yugoslavian dinars . . ." As luck runs sweet, I am the only page at the desk. I escort him down the alley and to his table where several other overweight bulldogs are already seated. All my suspicions are confirmed. Kirk is a stiff.

Talk about my feelings? I am going to see the "shrink" twice a week.

Two kinds of feelings. Those which are current events. And those which are history. My sessions take the form of a tapestry woven from these. Last night's dream will remind me of sixteen years ago and a feeling I had then.

I begin to understand the value system of analysis. It is pain which is the standard by which you judge how significant your feelings may be. The more pain you feel about something, the more important it usually turns out to be. Thus, analysis becomes almost necessarily a kind of self-destructive means of self-construction. You comb your mind for areas which give off painful signals. When you encounter a memory or a fantasy, and want to drop it immediately, to move on to a discussion of this month's baseball schedule, anything, then this is the right track. You must talk of the things which cause the most agony. Somehow talking moves one through pain to the other side. The other side of what?

When this question can be answered in full, I suppose therapy can be considered a "success."

But this seems to be a rhythm, a dialectic, which occurs over and over again. The worst events spark the best events. The most pain precedes the greatest calm. Rip yourself apart, so you can pull yourself together. Up and down, life seems to move in waves of hot and cold, yes and no, suffering and relief.

Bloom and I are drunk on the East Side. On a dark street off Fifth Avenue, I have stopped to take a piss. Bloom keeps watch down the block. Suddenly I hear him shout: "John!" I look up and see Sagner and a girl standing with Bloom.

"Hey, Bloom. This is Nora," goes the introduction.

"Hi. Spike's over there. Taking a piss."

"What are you guys, drunk again?" laughs Sagner.

"Of course!" I shout. And turn to meet the eyes of Nora, a slightly overweight angel bundled in a purple winter coat. The first time I have ever seen her except for that photograph. What an impression I must be making. Standing here in the shadows with my bladder emptying like a patter of rain on the lids of two garbage cans.

"That's Spike," says John.

"Hello Spike," laughs Nora.

"Hello."

———————

Plenty of money bulging my pocket now, I leave the Four Seasons about eleven. Sometimes I ride the subways up to Morningside Heights: straight home to read and sleep. I am still having bursts of anxiety. But it is a different kind. Not the unknown challenge of my unconscious, but rather a gnawing insecurity. I am alone, working at a job to support myself, without the security of school to rebel against (and take comfort inside). My father is in Chicago. I see him much less than when he was working in the Interchurch Center. Sometimes he calls. He is still writing for the White House. He says they called him late one night and asked him to have a speech ready to be picked up the very next morning. He stayed up all night working on it. I gather they take these speeches from several people, then give them to speechwriters in the White House who rip out sections, build a composite, clothe it in presidential rhetoric.

Though I see him on nights off, most of the time Bloom is involved with new friends and activities around Columbia. I am on my own, without many close friends, for days in a row. Get up, go to the restaurant, home and go to bed. Sometimes I take the subway up the East Side instead and walk over to my old prep school haunt, Nick's.

One evening at the bar I feel an elbow nudging me in

the side so blatantly that it cannot be an accident. It is a woman, about thirty, well dressed and pretty. She sees I have finally left my daydreams to look at her, turns and asks me for a light. "Do you come here often?"

"I used to," I say.

"It's quite a place."

"I guess."

"There's always something going on, anyway."

"Yes."

"What do you do?"

"I work as a page at the Four Seasons."

"What?"

"Well, actually I go to Columbia. But I'm on a leave. So I have this amazing job at the Four Seasons restaurant taking people to their tables and trying to beat them out of a tip."

"Do you like it?"

"It's better than a boring job sitting in an office from nine to five."

"I'll bet. That's where I spend my time."

"Doing what?"

"Secretary. For an investment banker."

"That sounds like it could get a little dry."

"Oh, it does. How old are you?" she asks.

"Twenty-one," I lie. "How old are you?"

"You aren't supposed to ask me that."

"Why not?"

"It's not polite."

"I don't care. How old?"

"Take a guess."

Shit. I got myself into this one. "Ah . . . twenty-five?"

"You're a character, aren't you," she laughs.

"Too old? Are you twenty-three?"

"Look, I'm thirty-one. But I don't like it."

"Why not? Thirty-one is probably a great age."

"Not if you are a woman. Not in this city." She looks at me and seems to be studying my mouth. "You have thin lips."

"Yeah? What does that mean?"

"Oh . . . nothing. But you have blue eyes. Big ones."

"So do you."

"I know. My eyes are the best part of my face." She hoists her glass and finishes the last inch of whiskey and melted ice.

"Would you like another?" I ask.

"All right. Thank you."

"I think the best part of your face is your face." Her hair is dyed blond and there is a thin coating of flesh-colored make-up trying to hide stray lines on her forehead and around the corners of her mouth. But it is a pretty face, a little desperate tonight. Lonely and high, at the bar in Nick's. She looks at me and smiles.

"Thank you. Mind if I ask a question?"

"No."

"Why are you so nice?"

"I'm not."

"Are you engaged?"

"No."

"Married?"

"No," I say.

"I was."

"Ah . . . for how long?"

"Six years. He wasn't so nice."

The bar is practically empty. You can see the craters on the red rug: a thousand burns from the carelessly dropped cigarettes of the weekend mob. The jukebox bellows a Ray Charles song into the narrow gloom. A drunk is at the end of the bar, a young drunk only about twenty-four, his suit rumpled and his hair falling haphazardly now. She turns to me and says, "Do you want to come home with me tonight?"

"Yes."

"I'm drunk now," she says. "Or I wouldn't ask you that."

"That's all right. I'm drunk too."

"I suppose. But it's not polite for a lady to invite a gentleman home with her, I don't guess."

"It's not bad."

"Oh Jesus, I'm really drunk. Could we go now?"

"Sure." We stand up and she takes a last sip of her drink, then puts it back on the bar. We are the next to last people to leave. Only the young man remains, letting the music from the machine roar through his head. The bartender gives me a serious look, as if to say, "Nice going." But he's too used to this sort of thing and too cool to wink. Thank God. We move out the door and toward the street to find a roaming taxi.

Her entranceway is full of silver mailboxes and bright light. Inside, a dark corridor and then the elevator. She fumbles for the key. She *is* drunk. The door opens, she flips the light, and we enter her world. A sad world, New York world. Off to the left are a tiny kitchen and a plastic-tiled bathroom. Then her "studio" with the bed still sticking out of the couch, sheets tangled from this morning's rush, and the prints on the wall, a large closet open and jammed with clothes. "Sorry about the mess. Would you like a drink?"

"Yes please." I sit down on the edge of the bed as she wrestles with the ice tray in the kitchen. Glasses and ice collide, the whiskey bubbles out of the bottle, now here she is with one in each hand. I take it and taste, too strong. She takes a sip and says, "I'll be right back." She goes into the bathroom and shuts the door.

The walls are very thin and I can hear everything. The rustle of clothing, the thin music as her urine hits the water, a lot of indistinguishable sounds: a woman in her bathroom. Finally, she opens the door and says, "Would you reach over and snap off that light?"

"The one beside the phone?"

"Yes." I snap it off. She walks out. In the light flowing

out of the kitchen doorway she crosses toward me. She is undressed except for her panties, white panties with lace in the front. Straight across the room to where I sit like a baseball player on the dugout bench, elbows on knees, watching: she leans over and firmly puts one hand on the back of my neck, one to my cheek, and gives me a kiss that is hot and whiskey-sour.

"There. Now get undressed and get in bed," she says, stepping around me. I stand up. She begins to straighten the sheets. "Turn off the bathroom and kitchen lights too, please, like a dear." This "like a dear" is trying for something. It doesn't work. But it doesn't sound bad really. I unbutton my shirt as I move to the light switches.

At last, I pull my underpants off and scoop up the edge of the blankets. Under the covers fast. To meet her open arms. My head is full of the picture of her crossing the room. Her breasts slope low and end in very brown circles. Now they feel incredibly soft as they yield under my chest. Not like the rubbery young flesh of girls I have been with before. But flesh in which each cell seems to float separately, alive, reaching out for contact. My head moves down to search with my lips for one of those dark points . . .

Thrash and squeeze, I use my stock of techniques garnered from eighteen years of life to touch everything, to turn her on . . . "Wait," she says. "Lie still for a second." Her hands push me gently back.

"What?"

"No, just lie there. I want to show you how to touch. Slowly . . . you make love like this . . ." her hand skimming slowly with the words, down over my chest. The elevator is purring its mechanical growl through the paperthin walls. Outside, the sky over Queens is a curtain of blue. Already, hundreds of tiny birds twitter in the expectant moments before a city dawn. Where do these birds live? A feather on my loins. On my neck a spot of moist heat. The tip of her tongue writing my name. My hand moves back to her breast. Try to imitate her hand, not heavy, a thin scarf of touching. The tip hardens. She gives a cry. A city bird, her feather suddenly runs the length of me and I must moan.

When I am finally set and we begin to move, her rhythm is so much more confident than my own, it takes me out of myself to the top of its flow, like rapids shooting through a tricky gap in the forest, and I have no hope but to run as it runs: and run out of time and end my stream so soon, in surges, and satisfying, but she does not mind. Her hand presses firmly at the base of my spine and she is moving for herself. "Don't move," she says, but does it all and I stay there, only half strong, but this is enough as she adjusts herself to it and moves in staccato and then . . .

One night in the West End, Bloom says, "Look: Saunders!" I look through the crowd around us at the booth near the wall. Sitting with three other guys, all of whom we know, is a new Saunders. His head is practically shaved; he is dressed in a starched khaki army uniform.

"He sure looks different with that haircut." Saunders before had been a vaguely "preppy" guy with a large crop of brown hair that hung over his forehead. He had worn tweed sport jackets and bluejeans with loafers. Now he has this tight khaki shirt on. We watch him. He doesn't smile very much as they talk. Before he had seemed quite typical of a lot of guys in our class. Now he has done something that clearly sets him apart and gives him his own identity. I see that he looks far more confident than he ever did before. He has made up his mind . . .

When one of the guys at his table gets up and comes to the bar for more drinks, I lean over and ask him, "How long is he back for?"

"Just tonight. He's going to Vietnam in three days."

"How does he seem?"

The guy gives me a look, rolling his eyes briefly up and into his head. I nod.

Bloom and I spend a lot of our time together talking about other people. We work out elaborate descriptions of almost everyone we know, categorize them, put them in the right cubbyhole. It is usually done with extreme defensiveness on our part. We are not the only ones. It seems that most conversations around Columbia have similar themes. You are either talking about who has pot for sale, how many classes you cut this week, how many papers you have to write, or how you dislike so-and-so. And one more topic, the most prevalent, girls.

Saunders! I feel more than a little guilty. We had him pegged as a jerk trying to be hip, pretend he was cool, stay out of trouble. Basically, we had him pegged as someone sort of like ourselves. Which is just intolerable, of course. Now he is alone and almost a tragic hero. He is going to Vietnam. The thought is hard to accept. Nobody we know goes to Vietnam. The worst thing that can happen to somebody from Columbia is that he has to go to Canada to dodge the draft. But Vietnam? Saunders sits there looking quiet and "trained."

"I'd like to say something to him," I say to Bloom. "But what can I say?"

Spring arrives in New York and so does my friend Zeke. He has finally finished high school in the suburbs of Philadelphia. At the moment, he's not thinking of college. Eventually, he'd like to go to art school. But right now he wants to make money. He hopes to ship out with the Merchant Marine. But he has to get "papers" first. Every morning I get up and go to the Four Seasons and Zeke gets up off the couch where he is sleeping and goes off to find these elusive "papers." At night, we meet in either the West End or the Gold

Rail and talk over the day. The day is usually grim and neither of us is very happy. This spring is cold and rainy too. The depression of Keaton seems almost better than the depression of this season. Two years ago he was getting thrown out of an institution. Now he's trying to get into one. I was then cramming my head full of facts to get into a good college. Now I'm doing idiot work for a bunch of idiots.

Twice a week I go to sessions with the analyst. The phenomenon called "transference" begins almost immediately. It is perhaps inevitable that I transfer many of my feelings for my father to Dr. Shapiro. Here is another man, older than myself, whom I go to for support. To whom I confide myself totally.

But the support which Shapiro gives is largely an imaginary one. I have a fantasy in my head that Shapiro must think I am exceptional, that my analysis is going faster than others, that I am "smarter" or more "interesting." It is a shock when Shapiro turns out to be not just a quiet listener but a tough critic.

My father is in Chicago. My mother and brother are living out the end of the school term in Tenafly.

It would be a mistake to imply that after my Oedipal insight, everything suddenly cleared up and all my conflicts were resolved. On the contrary, all the insight did was bring out of the darkness anxieties which I now struggle with in the daylight. The first time I see my mother after the insight, I am very nervous. I enter the house in Tenafly. She is sitting in the living room, looks up and smiles. She is short, black hair, a kind of pixyish face with dark-rimmed glasses. This face which is so incredibly familiar. This woman is my mother.

"Hi!" she says.

"Hello." Do I want to lunge at this woman, ravish her, as in the flash of insight I felt the desire to do? My mother? Absolutely not. The thought is absurd, ridiculous, my mother has absolutely no attraction for me in this way. But suddenly I have to figure out, honestly, what my feelings toward her are. I know that I love her. This is clear now. I understand why for so many years I may have wanted to believe I hated her: to avoid the Oedipal curse. To reject it completely. Impossible. There is something very strong in me, a feeling which makes me want to go over and sit down beside my mother and have her stroke the top of my head with affection. This feeling aches with pain. I would certainly not be able to hold back tears if my mother were to do this. I can only accept such affection with extreme awkwardness. Is it all because of my Oedipal conflict?

There is more to it. My Oedipal feelings are basically the same feelings shared by every man and woman raised in this society. But they have been twisted and bottled up with anger and hurt. What is it I sense every time I feel anxiety about "losing control"? At first I think, when I am very anxious, that I may be "losing my mind." Translate this into "losing control." After the insight, I feel afraid of "losing control" over my Oedipal feelings. But gradually this passes away. This phrase "losing control" is like a silver coin tossed in the dark. It shimmies with a flashing panic and it has two sides. On one side, I am afraid of losing control over myself. On the other, I fear losing the control which others have over me.

Who has control over me? I'm free, even supporting myself. These are the facts. Underneath the facts runs the truth in a swift river. My mother and father both have fantastic control over my life. As I gradually begin to understand this, mostly because of the talking I am doing in Dr. Shapiro's office, for the first time in my life I realize what work it is, just to be a man.

Zeke leaves the Gold Rail early. Tomorrow morning he has an interview with an officer of the shipping union. They are starting a program for juvenile delinquents and retarded students to train them for service in the Merchant Marine. Zeke is trying to get into this and wants to get a good night's sleep so he can act as dumb as possible tomorrow. He needs all his wits about him for this, because Zeke is very smart.

Standing at the bar, I recognize a minister named Ted Walsch. He has just entered and comes over and offers to buy me a beer. I have always liked Ted. He worked with my father on several projects. His sense of humor is sharp and surrealistic and he is hardly what one expects of a minister.

Several years earlier I had a long talk in my father's office with Ted about colleges. I was looking around for "safety" schools in case Harvard rejected me. Ted had gone to Oberlin and he thought I might be interested in that. He knew I wanted to be a writer someday. And one of his best friends at Oberlin was an English professor who apparently had inspired him and was very good with young writers. Whatever that means. Ted offered to write to the professor, if I wished, and set up an interview. I thought about it but eventually realized I didn't want to go to a small isolated campus like Oberlin's but rather to a large place in a city, like Harvard or Columbia or the University of Chicago.

"What did you think of Johnson's latest speech?" Ted asks.

"'Ah've told Hanoi thet mah restraint is naht unlimited,'" I drawl.

Ted has a lot of contacts in Washington and he likes to tell inside stories. Which is probably one of the reasons I like him. I have a large curiosity, and "inside stories" never fail to grab my attention. We stand around drinking beer and talking about the truth behind all the current headlines. Raised in Citizenship classes, I am always surprised when I find out that behind the images presented to us there are starker images, real flesh and real blood.

At the time, the U.S. is pouring napalm into the villages of South Vietnam at a rate quickly increasing day by day.

The campus is full of atrocity pictures as a result and the logic of the war seems insane. We are burning the Vietnamese alive, roasting them in napalm, to save them from communism.

"You know," I say, "I don't believe that President Johnson has any conception of *pain.* Of death. Look, his family is intact and thriving. His daughters aren't going to have to go into battle. Neither is he. If only there were some way to *hurt* him a little bit, just as an illustration. 'Look, LBJ, see? Pain *hurts!'*"

"Drop some napalm on Luci, maybe," says Ted. This is not the first time I have heard somebody make such a suggestion.

"Maybe. But just enough to show LBJ that, indeed, napalm really *hurts!* I think there ought to be a special demonstration for all politicians about this. They don't seem to realize."

"No, they don't." I look up at the clock. It is almost four in the morning. Closing time.

"Well, better drink up."

"What a shame. You feel like coming over to my place for a nightcap?" asks Ted.

"Ah . . . maybe. I don't have to work tomorrow. Sure, okay." He lives only a few blocks north of the Gold Rail on West 120th Street. In the bright lights of Ted's living room, I notice he is drunker than it seemed in the bar. Something about the way he falls into his chair like a rag, too reckless. After mixing a couple more drinks. The room is long and white, with only a few decorations on the wall, and bright lights. I sit down on the couch.

"Talked to your father recently?" he asks. Not for a couple of weeks. Then he goes on to say how much he thinks they will miss him in the Movement. Ted admires my father more than just about anyone, he says. The way he combines toughness with understanding, without being after headlines either. I enjoy listening to people build up my father. I feel exactly the same about him and I want everyone else to feel that way. For my father is still an extension of myself. Ted must sense this as I say, "Yeah. My father is a kind of genius, I guess."

"He's one of the most important ministers in the country. In the history of the country. Who knows what he's going to accomplish in the next ten years?" Building up my father builds *me,* because it means this genius, this great man, is the same one who loves me. Me, the preacher's bad boy, the prep school rebel, the freak-out page in the Four Seasons.

Ted begins to talk about women. About getting laid. "Do you get laid a lot, Paul?"

"Not enough," I boast. He laughs. Then he starts to talk, suddenly, without a blink, about his days in seminary. They used to be so horny all the time. They used to sleep with each other, the men did. He is at once in the middle of a discourse on homosexuality. I groggily begin to get the point. Ted must be a homosexual! He's making a play for me.

I'm not interested. But something keeps me hanging around listening to him talk. I realize slowly what it is: he has still not stopped talking about my father. He is weaving the conversation out of two very different strands of material: homosexuality and my father.

"If I told you all the people in Washington that are homosexual, you'd be amazed," he says.

"Who? Tell me," I insist.

He names some famous people. I have heard some of them in rumors before. Others are surprises. I am drunk now. And I feel as if I am already over some invisible ledge: tumbling down an incline into . . . Ted sits across the room staring at me with, I guess, lust. There is a question which I have barely formed in my mind. It is no accident. Ted has done everything but write the question down and hand it to me. He sits there staring, waiting for the question. I suppose he is trying to decide how to answer.

"Ted, wait a second. Are you implying something?"

"What?"

"You know what!"

"Do I?" The ice in his voice makes me shiver.

"Is my father homosexual?"

"What do you want to hear, Paul?" he says, and looks in his hand.

"The truth, you . . ." I don't finish.

"Yes."

"He is?"

"Yes. He is, if you mean does he have sex with men."

"Did he have sex with you?"

"No. But . . ." This seems to bother Ted. "He'd probably like to though."

"How do you know . . . that he is?"

"You can tell."

"Did you ever discuss it with him?"

"No. We don't talk like that."

My first thought is a memory. About six months before. I was helping my father clean out his desk. I came across a letter and it was marked "Personal." I could not resist taking it out of its envelope and reading it. The letter was from a distinguished Protestant layman. It said something like: "Dear Bob, I have been invited to talk before the Mattachine Society. I am not sure what I should do. But I would appreciate your guidance and thoughts on this. Love,——."

Sitting there in the office I pieced together a partial understanding. I had heard of the "Mattachine Society." It was a homosexual organization, respectable but outspokenly homosexual. This man must then be a homosexual? Not necessarily. But it seems likely. What stopped me was the "Love" at the end of the message.

Was my father a homosexual? This was the first time this weird thought had ever entered my head: my freshman year at Columbia, going through his "personal" mail. I got a strange feeling. There was something in this notion of my father's "homosexuality" that seemed to work.

As well as I knew him — and that was better than almost anyone in the world, for he confided many of his anxieties and secret thoughts to me as I did all of mine to him — there was a part of my father that was hidden. I sensed this as I got to be around sixteen. By the time I was eighteen I was sure of it.

For one thing, my father was very unhappy a great deal of the time. He suffered tremendous anxiety and worked so hard, I think, often as a way of filling up the pain with constructive activity. My father had this incredible ability that led him no matter who he was with, even pompous or nasty people, to see the good in them.

Was it possible that he had difficulty seeing the good in himself?

His father had taken away all love at such an early age. For no reason. What could a boy of two years old do to deserve his father's total rejection? Nothing, unless . . . The way a two-year-old mind works it is clear that nothing could be found as a proper excuse. The rejection of a father's love is the rejection of a god. If your father stops loving you, it is because you are not worth loving.

The nights I found my father tossing on the living room couch, obviously suffering — sometimes he had difficulty talking his throat was so dry — I would be confused and scared. What was bothering him? There was something. He had his private demons and he was not going to talk about them with me.

"There is a difference between being homosexual and bisexual, Paul," says Ted. I can tell he is explaining this as part of the seduction. "Your father is obviously bisexual. I mean, you're sitting over there as proof of that."

"I don't know." I shake my head.

"What did you just think?"

"That my father was a 'queer.'"

"Sure. I'm a queer. He's a queer. And so are you. We're all queers."

"I don't think I'm a queer."

"You are, though. Your father's one. You've got to be one too. I've studied psychology. You mean you have never had a homosexual experience?"

"Sure. When I was twelve years old. My friend and I were curious what a blow-job felt like. We each did it to the other guy for about three seconds."

"How did it feel?" asks Ted. I just look at him. I am beginning to hate his guts. "You're queer, Paul. You ought to start the right way."

"Huh?" Is Ted right? About the psychology. The coin is tossed flickering with its sharp panic edges in the darkness.

"You ought to go to bed with someone who loves you. I love you, Paul."

What can I say? I don't love Ted. I hate him. I want to get out of his apartment and never see him again. My father? The truth, the truth . . . what is it? My head is ringing with the word "queer." How many times have I mocked or talked about "queers" or "faggots" in front of my father? Did it hurt him? It never seemed to. I can remember him laughing at such remarks. But . . . there is something about what Ted has told me which I cannot simply push away. I stand up and say, "Ted, I'm getting out of here."

"Why?"

"I may be queer. I don't care. I don't want to go to bed with you." Oh Jesus, Oh Jesus I am praying to you. Help me with this. Outside as I leave the stoop of Ted's building and enter a flooded city, flooded with a nauseating dawn, I pray almost aloud. My lips move. I never pray. I am asking for strength now.

———————————

Back to the apartment and wake up Zeke in the living room. He sits up without his glasses, his eyes popping wide and glazed with dreams slipping away. "Listen, I'm sorry to wake you up but I have to talk."

"Of course. What is it, buddy?"

I tell him the whole story of the evening, from meeting Ted in the Gold Rail to my leaving his apartment moments ago. Zeke gradually wakes up as I tell him the details of this conversation. He is looking at me, I can tell, to see if he can read in my face just how I am reacting. And I am curious, more than curious, desperate to know how this will affect me. As if there is a kind of delayed reaction time whenever a crisis springs up, moments of anxious fever between the time the gun fires and the time the bullet hits.

"What do you think?" I ask Zeke when I have finished.

"I don't know . . . one thing . . ."

"Yeah?"

"One thing is pretty clear. This guy Ted is a strange guy. I mean . . . he sounds like a complete fucking lunatic to me."

"Yeah. He was trying to get me into bed."

"He's got quite a line, doesn't he."

"My father is a queer so therefore I am one too. But . . . what do you think?"

"About your father." Zeke nods. Then looks left out the windows. The grays of early morning over the West Side flat and grainy. No depth, no shadow. A mask of dismal morning. "What do *you* think?"

"I think it might be true. Part of it."

"I think it could be true, too."

"What's this going to do to me, do you think?" There is panic in my voice.

"I don't know. Why should it do anything to you?"

"It's such a surprise. And it makes me feel as if . . . maybe my whole childhood was a fraud?"

"How can you say that?"

"I don't know. I'm sorry. I appreciate your talking, listening to this."

"Come on. What are you talking about? What are friends for?" He tries to joke, but it doesn't matter.

"I got this incredible bad feeling that perhaps if my father is homosexual he didn't want to have me. You know, to have a child, because that is heterosexual . . ."

"That's pretty ridiculous, really. Listen, if part of this is true, what difference does it really make? So your father makes it with both men and women? So what? So what does that mean to you?"

"Nothing. Except that I never knew that about him before."

"So know it now. If it's true."

"How can I tell if it's true?"

"Ask him."

"I don't think I can."

Eventually, Zeke gets dressed and leaves the apartment. He's on his way downtown to the union hall in the Village to be interviewed. I strip and lie down on my bed. I am coming out of the alcohol now. The depression is increasing. I cannot sleep.

At nine o'clock, I get up and go into the other room. Look at the phone, pick it up and dial. My mother answers. In brief, I tell her what has happened.

"This person Ted sounds like he's going crazy. He sounds like he's out of his mind. Don't worry about this. I've been married to your father for twenty years. I've never seen anything homosexual about him. Have you been to sleep?"

"No."

"I think you should go to sleep now, Paul."

"I think so too. All right, I'm sorry to call you with this.

I just felt so . . . horrible. I just felt like I had to talk to
somebody."
"That's all right."

I manage to fall asleep and wake up around four in the
afternoon. It is still a gloomy day. More gloomy now than
this morning. But I feel better. Sleep has these incredible
healing powers, without which we would surely die. The new
information has somehow been made slightly more accessi-
ble. Is it true? Or false? Whichever, it doesn't matter, for
now I must go looking for the truth. The phone rings. I
climb out of bed and answer it.
My father's voice sounds quiet but tense. "Your mother
called. She told me about this. I guess I don't think we
should talk about it over the telephone. But I want to talk to
you about it. How are you feeling?"
"I'm feeling all right."
"Good. A lot of what this guy told you, at least what
your mother told me, is just rubbish. Completely untrue.
I'm going to be in New York in three days. Let's talk then,
okay?"
"Fine."
"I'm going to call Ted and tell him exactly what I think
of him," says my father.
"He was just trying to get me into bed with him."
"What an insane way to try. He could have jeopardized
our relationship, Paul. That's what makes me so furious.
Our relationship." His voice is full of anger. I want to say to
him:
"Yes. But don't worry. It's all right. Whatever happens,
it's all right. Nothing can ruin *our* relationship, Dad." Talking to him has made that fact clear to me. The sound of his
voice moving through me with such warmth. There really is
so much love in my father. Perhaps that is part of it.

A double-barreled shotgun could not have had much more of an explosive effect had it gone off in my face. Except that a shotgun would have killed me. While these two pieces of radical information will not extinguish my life. Rather, they will shape it, change it irrevocably. My sudden awareness of my feelings toward my mother. And the news about my father. Both fly at me in the space of three months.

The fact that I called my mother this morning could be seen as a classically Oedipal thing to do. Find out my father may be bisexual. Call up my mother and inform her. In certain ways, I am sure this was part of my motivation.

But really more crucial was the fact that I was able to turn to my mother for support at a critical time. Something I would never have been able to do in the years before my insight. This seems more significant to me. And another irony; another example of how well "prepared" I have been. Each crisis prepares me to forge through the next. So you almost look back with gratitude at your worst moments for, without them, you know you probably never would have made it. Life seems like a ladder in which each rung may be a success. But the two side rails are a connection of painful moments worked through, locked together, the real support.

Crossing the bridge to New Jersey, my father steers the car through afternoon traffic. I look at his face. He is thinking, staring ahead.

"I called Ted."

"You did?" I ask.

"He claims he told you nothing you didn't already know." Perhaps, on a very basic level, this is true. I think otherwise I would not have believed a word of what he said. But in a literal way, it is a lie.

"That's not true."

"I told him I was angry enough to punch him in the nose." My father never talks like this. "I told him he was risking the possibility of destroying our relationship just so he could get you into bed."

"That's true. But it doesn't matter to me."

He looks at me. "These things are very difficult for me to talk about, Paul. Especially with you. I don't want to lie to you, though. And I don't want you to get the wrong impression from what Ted said."

"I won't."

"There was . . . an element of truth in what he told you. The rest of it was lies. Like his saying I wanted to go to bed with him. I mean, stuff like that really makes me wonder if Ted isn't having some kind of breakdown or something. Though I don't think there is anything I could do now to help him. But that's a complete fantasy."

It doesn't matter to me. All that matters is that I can see the future now. There are going to be some awkward moments. There is going to be a process of getting to know my father again. My *real* father, all of him, not just the perfect image which he has just acknowledged, without saying anything, is dead.

In the next weeks, I do a great deal of reading about bisexuality and homosexuality. And I walk around New York City and, of course, there are obvious "queers" and "queens" in abundance. And at each paragraph and each time I see one of these people, I say to myself, "Is my father like *that?*" Each time I get a negative feeling. Until finally it dawns on me that these people and these descriptions are just images too. My father is a man and he has his own sex life. I am his son. Thinking about the sexual life of one's father is an outstandingly dull pastime after a while. It is his private life. I have no business in it. I can remember standing naked in the bathroom with my father at some friend's house when we were changing out of our bathing suits. I was perhaps nine. Surely almost all men have had a similar experience. I looked at that roll of muscle hanging down: my father's penis. And found a combination of fascination and shame in the sight. That was the instrument which planted me in this world. That was my father's penis and it was much larger than mine. Fascinating, and embarrassing.

If my father is bisexual, this has no importance for me. What matters is that I have not been betrayed. He still loves me. Yet this is not the crucial danger either. Even more important is that *I* do not betray *him*.

My grandfather betrayed his son. He whipped him and turned away, refusing to acknowledge any of his successes. Perhaps each reminded him only more clearly of his own failures. Yet that had no importance to the young boy. He grew up in a world without male affection.

Now riding up over the Palisades, I realize that this man sitting beside me, my father, is frightened. He is afraid I will reject him. He lost his father's love. He does not want to lose his son's.

And I am frightened as well. Frightened that all this rich substance of his affection was perhaps an illusion. For when I think of my father's sex I can only think of it as the tool which planted me in my mother's womb. The notion that it might be used for something else, this threatens me. But not so much I cannot see this is all contained in a moment of steel and glass moving down the highway toward an exit, a rolling hill into the valley and home. Home still exists. It's changed, that's all.

My father wrote a book called *To Be a Man.*
    One of the chapters is entitled "To Be a Man in Love."

I imagine this must have been a difficult chapter for him, for his feelings were probably extremely complex. He had to fit them into a context that would be used as a study book in hundreds of churches around America. But just the same, I have read this chapter over and over and think it is one of the best pieces of his writing that remains. So many of his speeches were hastily written on yellow legal pads and then tossed away. Let me quote several passages from his book:

Love in one context is a word for the purest and most ethereal of feelings. It is an exaggerated form of casual liking when we sign it to a letter. It is also sometimes a synonym for sexual intercourse whatever the quality of the relationship, just another four-letter word. It is no wonder that we are confused about male and female and about what it means to be man and woman in our culture.

There are at least four factors that contribute to our confusion, and they are so interrelated that it is almost impossible to assess cause and effect. There is the greatly changed role of women in our society and the consequent upheaval in what normative masculine and feminine behavior is thought to be. There is the cult of worship of youth and adolescence in our society. There is the preoccupation with public sex symbols and the conscious commercial manipulation of these symbols. And underneath there is the residue of guilt and shame that post-Calvinist Protestantism and Irish Catholicism fastened upon us.

The Christian man thanks God for his sexuality, teaches his children the same thankfulness, and shows mercy and forgiveness to those around him who are caught in the bondage of sex fascination.

Now for us, the degree to which we worship the Hollywood variety of sexual romantic love is a measure of our own loss of overriding religious and ideological purpose. All else having failed us, cynical of the purposes of history, with God as an irrelevant superstition, we cling to romantic love as the one magic talisman.

The last point is that, for the Christian, love is the gift of response. Isn't it interesting how the Bible is always using the marriage relationship as an analogy of God's relationship to His people? This analogy can work both ways. God's relationship to mankind, his love for us, tells us something about what earthly love is like. In the Biblical view, God takes a terrific chance, a daring step into the midst of his creation and makes a covenant with his people, and though men break the trust and betray the confidence, God never leaves. He is long-suffering. He is beyond the darts of contempt and the weapon of hatred. He is Christ on the cross.

To be human is not to be natural. To be a man in the fullest sense is to be disturbed and intrigued by what we see in Christ.

A janitor found my father in a pool of blood. The back of his head had been bludgeoned and was gaping open. He was dead.

His body was discovered in a guest room in Columbus, Ohio. It was October 17, 1966. My father had preached the dedication sermon for a new Christian Center at Ohio State University.

No clues were found. No murder weapon. There were signs of a violent struggle. But no traces of the murderer, not even a fingerprint.

The Protestant Establishment reacted immediately with statements of sympathy and tributes to my father's life and character. He had a great many friends across America.

He also had enemies. He had been savagely murdered. In the rush to praise his life, certain questions were shunted aside. Who killed him? Why was he killed?

It seemed, incredibly, as if nobody wanted to ask fundamental questions. The churches were running scared. The

police were acting strangely. The murder had been vicious.
But no clues were found.

Who killed my father? Or was he guilty of his own
murder?

He wrote in *To Be a Man:*

We pray also for the raising up of men who shudder less at
death and who, by the hard unconventionality of their martyr-
dom, will illuminate the path that the rest of us travel.

After the spring of 1966 with its double-barreled anxieties
and the Four Seasons job and my parents' eventual move to
Chicago, I was offered the chance to take a "vacation." My
parents, I guess, felt sorry for me. And my father was making a lot more money at the University of Chicago. He and
my mother seemed very happy. Happier than I could ever
remember. This job would mean considerably less travel for
him, and they were both glad. They found a two-bedroom
apartment off Harper Square in Chicago's Hyde Park dis-
trict. I left aboard a charter flight before I had a chance to
visit. Bloom was also on the plane. We were headed for
Paris.

We split up in Paris after three days. I went south to
Spain. Bloom had a Eurail Pass and wanted to ride the Orient Express all the way to Istanbul.

After two weeks sitting in a miserable little tourist joint
on the Costa Brava, I headed for Pamplona in a battered
Volkswagen with some other American guys. I was looking
forward to the running of the bulls. Instead, the festival had
become a running of the California freaks. By noon on the
first afternoon, the gutters were pink with spewed-up 10-

peseta wine and doorways were sagging with young bums passed out cold in their University of San Diego windbreakers. It began to rain. We were all staying in a huge tent city erected on the Pamplona municipal football field. The rain turned the field into six inches of muddy frosting. The tents all leaked. The drunks staggered and tripped over tent pegs, pulling everything down into the mess. After two days, including a look at the runners (how do you get past this mob and in there with the bulls?) and a lousy bullfight, I met a girl who wanted to share expenses south. She had a car and was driving through Madrid to Torremolinos.

We arrived five days later, stiff from Spanish roads and sick of each other, and I jumped out in the central square and stopped two long-haired boys. "Where's everybody hang out around here?" A foolish question since there were, I soon found out, at least four hundred bars in this monstrosity of high-risers and bad plumbing, once a quiet fishing village.

"There's a place called the Fat Black Pussycat," said one.

"Is that owned by a guy named John Mitchell?"

"Sounds like the guy's name. A real nasty guy?"

"That's him," I said. Mitchell had come to the Village in the late forties. My father answered an ad Mitchell had put in the local newspaper for odd jobs. He hired Mitchell and a man named George Dennison (who later wrote *The Lives of Children*), both from Pittsburgh, to paint a room in Judson. It was their first job in the big city and they muffed it, didn't know how to paint, got themselves covered with the stuff, but became friends with my father anyway. They were all around the same age.

Mitchell went from odd jobs to working as a waiter in the San Remo bar, hanging around with Maxwell Bodenheim in his last years, and earning a reputation as one of the toughest fighters and biggest ladies' men in the Village. Eventually, he hit on the idea of opening up a coffeehouse, like the coffeehouses which already abounded in lower Manhattan, for the Italian immigrants. But this would be a coffeehouse strictly for his friends, local artists, bohemians, and runaways from uptown life. Mitchell built the Figaro Cafe, sold it and built the Gaslight Cafe. This became the most famous coffeehouse in the country, featuring poetry readings with Ginsberg, Kerouac and Corso; then folk songs with Dylan, Peter, Paul and Mary, Dave van Ronk, Phil Ochs. My father and he stayed good friends during these years, though they saw each other rarely.

Eventually, Mitchell went on a campaign to stop the graft which all the coffeehouses were having to pay to the New York City Police Department. This created the much-publicized "coffeehouse scandal" which raged on the front pages of the city papers for weeks. Mitchell's life was repeatedly threatened. He was beaten up several times. Arrested and fined hundreds of times. Finally, John took to carrying a shotgun through the streets of the Village for his own protection, à la Huey Newton of the Black Panthers, but years earlier.

He had to sell the Gaslight. Built a new place on Minetta Lane called the Fat Black Pussycat, but eventually fled from New York completely. Over the years, he had changed from a carefree young bohemian into a bitter and suspicious businessman, and he knew it. He wanted to stay alive, too, and there were still threats on his life. So he went to London, then opened a restaurant in Tangiers, and finally crossed over the Gibraltar Straits and into Spain. He found a tiny village just outside Torremolinos which was called La Carihuela. Here he decided to build a new bar and called it the Fat Black Pussycat.

I found my way there and in the gloom, underneath fishnets and rusty lanterns for "atmosphere," was John, whom I had met several times before and who was a kind of idol to me (one of the original "beatniks" and all that). He was talking to a thin English girl with straw hair called Pamela. I told him who I was. He said, hello, let me buy you a drink. In a few minutes I had met Andy and Jules, the two English guys who were working behind the bar for Mitchell this summer. John said I could sleep on a couch in the back of the Pussycat. And I was set. For the next two months we lived a wild series of non-events, hundreds of girls coming and going, parties and chess matches, the life of the Carihuela. You found yourself after a sangria lunch rolling out to the beach and falling asleep under the shade of a little fishing boat. Being awakened two hours later by the gutteral cries of Swedish tourists. Back to the bar for a beer. See what new chicks have arrived, and so on and so forth for the summer.

My father came to Europe in July. He had led one section of a conference in Geneva held by the World Council of Churches. He was to come down and visit with me, and see his old friend Mitchell, for four days near the end of the month.

I reserved a room for him in a good hotel down by the beach. He arrived looking tired, but said he was exhilarated by what had gone on in Geneva. Especially, he said, by the strong voices of the church leaders from the smaller African countries. They had really lashed into the American clergy present and, said my father, had "opened a lot of eyes."

We spent four of the happiest days we ever spent together then. The hotel was big and expensive and not at all what I was used to, sleeping on the couch in the Pussycat. But this was a good time for us to talk. And we did. About everything, as we lay around the pool during the daytime and as we ate our meals in the restaurants of the Carihuela at night.

My father told me he had been working hard on settling some housing disputes between the black community in Chicago and the Daley Democratic machine. He also said he enjoyed the University of Chicago, though more the students than the faculty. He said it was difficult for him to adjust to a "reflective" life and to professors after three years of action in Washington and the Deep South. Anyway, he was still active in various parts of the movement and anything might happen.

At night, we went to the bars together. And we drank and talked with my friends. There were a lot of crazy Europeans around the Fat Black Pussycat. Both Andy and Jules were from extremely upper-class families in Britain. They had both been thrown out of Eton. Then served commissions in the British army. Now they were down here goofing around. Andy had a beautiful red Marcos sportscar and a pretty French bird named Babette. Julian was drunk a good deal of the summer, staggering around the Carihuela looking like a young Lawrence of Arabia with his blond hair and sunken cheeks. Eventually, he hooked up with a Greek bombshell from Brooklyn.

Then there was Billy, the Belfast Protestant kid who liked to split doors in half with his forehead. And Jaime, who lost his girlfriend to Mitchell in a game of chess. And Mick, the plodding Yorkshire kitchen boy, who eventually ran off with Mitchell's till in his pocket. And Danny, who brought the crabs into town and . . .

My father enjoyed it a great deal. He hadn't taken a vacation in close to a year. And he hadn't hung out and talked with people like this since he left Judson and the Village bars.

He and Mitchell had several long talks and vowed to keep in better touch in the future. The morning he left, I rode with him in a taxi to the airport. He turned to me and I realized how fast he had lost his tired face. Tan and young, he looked ready for anything. He said, "This has been a terrific trip, Paul. I've really enjoyed it and I've learned something, too, I think. All these last years that I have been running in and out of airports, trying to help run the world, I sort of forgot about all the people who live in the Carihuela. People who live a life full of sensations. Both ways are pretty important, I guess."

My father was obviously formulating something in his mind.

"Somehow there has to be a way to bridge the gap between the people in Geneva at that conference, who are so busy working to run the world, and the Carihuela people, who are so busy trying to live. They are trying to pack as much experience into each moment as possible. And that's good. But somebody has to run the world, too. Somehow, we have to bridge this. Get these people together, if that's possible. Though I doubt it. They hate each other."

I said that was probably true. And then we arrived at the Malaga airport. My father had to rush to catch his plane back to New York.

I left Europe in September and arrived back in New York in time to re-apply for Columbia. It was not so easy to get back in. I had to talk to several deans and see the school psychoanalyst and then wait a week before they agreed to re-admit me.

Bloom and I went hunting up and down the West Side for an apartment. Eventually we found one in a renovated building on the corner of West 84th Street and Columbus Avenue. It was a raunchy neighborhood and a poor job of "renovation" but there wasn't much choice. It was too late in the fall to find a better apartment.

Bloom and I had by now discovered that not only did our similar backgrounds and temperaments make us friends. They also made us fight with each other. We had constant arguments, always over trivial issues, kept alive because of our stubborn natures and our rather oversensitive feelings. We could argue about which LP to put on the stereo. We could feud over where to eat dinner, this luncheonette or that delicatessen. Consequently, the apartment had a temporary atmosphere, sort of like a three-room sleeping bag. The sink was piled high with dishes which neither of us would wash. Occasionally we would cook dubious feasts of watery hot dogs or prepackaged casseroles. We were best friends. But it was very stormy on the high seas of brotherhood this fall.

Sometimes, though, we could talk without fighting. And when we could it was always worth it. I was glad to be back in school but still feeling restless and panicky. Bloom was drifting downward into anxiety as I was trying to pull myself upward. He was due for a leave of absence soon. We talked about our lives and our parents a lot. We had no furniture in the living room which separated the two bedrooms. Only a small table and a stereo on the floor. Lying on the floor, we would sip beer and share a joint, soaking in the imagery which ran off Dylan's latest album, *Blonde on Blonde*. Behind us, the sink was gradually growing a thick psychedelic hide of green, blue, yellow and red treacle. This mass of mold titillated our stoned eyes but sent us hurrying out to the local greasy spoons. We were both taking a class called "Projects in Imaginative and Critical Writing" with a poet-professor at Columbia named Kenneth Koch.

We took several excursions up to Sarah Lawrence together. Met some girls. They came down to visit us in the city several times. Nothing serious developed.

Some afternoons I arrive home to find a blond, blue-eyed girl in a school uniform waiting outside the apartment door. She sits on the filthy floor and does her homework. Her name is Sophie. She lives on the East Side and she has a crush on me. She's sixteen and I am three years older. Sophie comes inside and we spend forty-five minutes or so "making out" on the bed in my room before she has to run for the bus in time to arrive home before her mother's curfew at six. Sophie is a virgin, of course. But one afternoon she asks me not to stop but to make love to her please, only hurry up because it's almost five o'clock. I shake my head and kiss her instead. Sophie is nice as a surprise. In the tenement hallway after a day at school, all washed and schoolgirlish, straight from a fancy academy on the other side of town. But I don't want to get involved. And I think Sophie deserves better than a quick screw before running to catch the bus.

After she leaves, I often sit down at the typewriter and begin to fool around with one of Koch's assignments. I am enjoying his class very much. It is definitely for people who like to use words in new ways and who can get high off language. Koch loves words, just for their own sake, and the class is kind of a circus of them. He is the ringmaster. Watch him make the ferocious nouns jump through his hoop! His verbs slither around the ring! The adverbs howl brazenly and the dangerous adjectives suddenly lie down like lambs under his control. Unlike most creative writing teachers, Koch gives *detailed* assignments. Not just "write a poem." But what assignments! Often minor works of art all by themselves. "Write a story about a sport. Use the members of your family as the team players," is a typical Koch assignment.

Some days Koch likes to ramble on for a while about the life of a writer. At least, how he sees it. "You must have all seen these interviews with writers. Those guys who make these statements about how tough it is to write. 'Sweating blood,' the 'agony' of sitting down at the typewriter. Grueling, terrible, etc. Well I think that's all a bunch of crap. If you don't have *fun* when you write, then for God's sake why bother? There are a lot of easier things to do."

The paradox of Kenneth Koch. He makes writing "fun." But the more you write, the more critical you become of your own writing. You have to work harder and harder to get the same satisfaction or "fun" from your words.

Bloom doesn't like Koch. I tend to disagree and find

myself rapidly coming under his influence. A good many of us in the class become Koch disciples for a while. Our Koch plays and Koch stories and Koch poems pour out. And the relationship with "Professor Koch" changes into friendship with "Kenneth." Eventually, you find yourself drifting off on your own, to find your "voice," and Kenneth appreciates this. He's smart enough not to go around urging students to "find their own voice" but lets that take care of itself. Finally, there comes a time when you look at the words on the page and they are an instrument you have carved out of your own substance, which only you can play in tune, to make a new music which is yours, yours alone. That's fun.

The first time my father visits New York this fall he comes to the apartment and takes a chain lock out of his briefcase. Then a hammer and a screwdriver. He has promised my mother, who does not like the sound of my address, that he will not leave without installing it himself. I can just see her as he is hurrying out the door to catch his plane, handing him the lock and tools. She has a very thorough mind and does not overlook details. After putting up the lock, my father takes Bloom and me out to dinner. We have a bottle of wine and several drinks and everybody enjoys himself.

President Johnson has appointed my father to the National Council on the Humanities. This group has several million dollars of federal money to give away to "advance" the "humanities" in the country. As usual, my father is concerned over the conservative lack of imagination displayed by some of his fellow Council members. "They just want to give more money for grants to do the same old things: Shakespeare dissertations. Dig up another pyramid. Write a biography of Ben Franklin.

"I have to go to Mississippi in a week or so. I think I'll be in New York the weekend after that. We can get together then, if you want," he says. We leave him at the restaurant door. He is flying back to Chicago on the last jet. Bloom and I head up to Morningside Heights to take a look in the West End and see who's around.

This fall, I'm taking a course on Chaucer. All future English majors are required to take this course. My section is taught by Professor Lyle, the shrimpboat aristocrat of the department.

I sit in the back of the Hamilton Hall classroom. Lyle is standing at the podium, clearing his throat over and over again, shuffling the papers in front of him. Next to me is a sophomore from New Jersey with an angular nose and slightly bulging, fierce eyes named Mark Rudd. We are sort of friends. Usually we talk about girls.

Lyle begins the lecture with a loud cough. The door bangs open and three latecomers barge inside. One heads down the aisle toward Mark and me, drops into the seat directly in front of me, and exudes a labored sigh. He is a member of Columbia's most exclusive fraternity, which has a large mansion down on Riverside Drive: St. Anthony's Hall. A large rotund boy with expensive clothes: pink-tinted shirt, brown paisley bow tie, a tweed jacket. Shades of Dink Stover!

Lyle resumes the lecture on "The Miller's Tale." One everybody seems to have enjoyed. I feel Rudd's elbow knock mine. He leans over to whisper, his finger pointing at the Waspish late arrival in the next seat. "After the Revolution, this guy is going to burn!"

Shades of Mark Rudd!

My father calls from Jackson, Mississippi. "What about dinner on Saturday night?"

"I have a date but . . ."

"That's fine. Bring her along too."

"Okay." I have promised to take Sophie out to dinner. She has continued to visit me several afternoons a week after school. I don't think she will mind having supper with my father. And, I think, it will save me a little money, too.

My father is standing under the gold clock in the Biltmore Hotel. We are ten minutes late. He smiles. But that doesn't help. In just two weeks, he looks four or five years older. His tan from Spain has gone. And around his eyes the veins are visible: dark, troubled purple. "Let's have a drink in here." He directs us back into the Biltmore cocktail lounge. Palms around the sides. Small marble-topped tables. A violinist wanders through the deserted area. Only about four tables are filled.

"What were you doing in Mississippi?" I ask after we order.

"Did I mention to you about the Child Development Group of Mississippi?"

"I don't remember."

"Part of Johnson's Office of Economic Opportunity program. Actually, comes under the heading of the Head Start programs. It's been the most successful single part of Johnson's poverty thing. They are doing incredible work with the local people in Mississippi. The CDGM, as they call it, is all local run. For some reason, the administration decided to get rid of it this fall."

"Why?" asks Sophie.

"It's complicated. Nobody is sure why. But I have my own hunch. The official reason is that the OEO office in

Washington is accusing them of misusing government funds. They have a room of accountants in Washington who do nothing but go over every scrap of paper that comes out of the CDGM. And the charges are ludicrous. For example, a local Mississippi leader uses his government car to stop for groceries on the way home from work. This makes him guilty of misusing government funds and property. The administration is just nitpicking. They want to ax it."

"Sounds weird. What do you have to do with it?"

"I am part of a new group called the Citizens Crusade Against Poverty. It's nothing full-time. Just a group of people. Walter Reuther is the chairman. I am the co-chairman. Roy Wilkins is in on it. Robert Coles of Harvard. We decided to look into the administration's charges ourselves after the CDGM people called for help. So some of us spent this last week doing our own fact-finding in Mississippi."

"I didn't know you knew Walter Reuther," I say.

"Yes, I know him. Actually I've worked more closely with his brother Victor. But I went up to visit Reuther at his house in Michigan last year. What a fortress, by the way. Remote and protected by all sorts of electronic devices and a bodyguard. Anyway, he didn't go to Mississippi with us."

"What did you find out?"

"The administration's case is based on nonsense. We, or rather, they—the CDGM staff—are being railroaded. People are upstairs right now writing the report. We all met at the end of the trip and agreed to meet in Washington after this weekend and release this. I had a meeting with Shriver. Christ! That was unbelievable," he looks at Sophie. "Shriver is Johnson's hatchet man in this. He's head of the OEO."

"Why are they getting rid of their best program?" I ask.

"Vietnam, I think. Johnson is a great deal-maker. He is escalating this war. And it's not a 'declared war.' He needs the cooperation of the Senate Armed Services Committee to send those troops over there. On that committee is Senator Stennis. Stennis is also on the Senate Appropriations Committee. That controls the funds for the OEO."

I have heard his name before. He is the senator from Mississippi whom they had so much trouble with in past years on civil rights bills. "You think Johnson made a deal with Senator Stennis?"

"I think so. The CDGM has really shaken them up down in Mississippi. I think Stennis would like to see it run out of his state damn fast."

"That's terrible," says Sophie. My father looks at her and nods his head in agreement. Then smiles.

"There are a lot of terrible things going on in this country these days which people don't know about," he says. "This one in particular is the dirtiest fight I have ever been involved in, I think."

"Would you excuse me?" asks Sophie, standing up and then leaving for the ladies' room. My father turns to me.

"The dirtiest fight of my life. I feel like taking three showers a day, it's so dirty."

"You look tired again," I tell him.

He nods. "By the way, she's really very sweet. And very pretty."

"She's very young, too."

"I don't know. How old is she?"

"Only sixteen."

"Oh." But I can tell he's thinking about Washington again.

"What was Sargent Shriver like?" I have always thought of him as one of the glamorous Kennedy clan, a dapper man. The idealistic young head of the Peace Corps under JFK.

"One of the nastiest men I have ever met. He kept shouting at me, 'Are you calling me a liar? Are you calling me a liar?' I had just seen for myself that these CDGM charges were not based on the truth. He insisted they were. I could only say, 'I'm not calling you a liar. I am saying that this is not true.'"

"What did he say then?"

"This is why I feel so furious, I guess. He threatened me."

"Threatened you?"

"He said, 'The FBI knows about you, Reverend Spike.'"

"Really?"

"Yes."

"Knows what?" I ask.

"Who knows? They are tapping everybody's phone in this country. They have files on everyone. I don't give a damn what they know about me. But it frightens me that this kind of crap is going on in the government."

Sophie arrives at the table. We finish our drinks. "Do you mind if we eat just around the corner? I know this Italian restaurant. It's not bad. I have to get back upstairs and help with the report soon."

"Not at all."

During supper we talk about lighter subjects. But I feel nervous about what he has told me. President Johnson is trading the black children of Mississippi for Vietnam troops? The FBI knows about my father? It sounds slightly fantastic. But I know my father would not invent such a story. There is just no reason for that. And his face, how worn it looks, I know that is not an invention either.

I suppose Shriver means about the bisexuality. This gives me a funny feeling in my stomach. I have gradually over the months since my encounter with Ted come to adjust to this fact. The more I think about it, the more I realize it changes nothing in my life. What bothers me is that I think this must be a source of great unhappiness for my father. I remember his words to me about psychoanalysis: "It helps you to accept yourself as you really are." I can accept my father. So can millions of other people who know him as a minister, a writer, a civil rights leader. But he has this image which, I suppose, he must worry about maintaining. Though he does not let it interfere with his life. "I don't give a damn what they know." There is no question that my father does not. He is the kind of man blackmail would not work with; the kind of man with unshakable commitment to what he believes is justice.

The Italian food turns out to be mediocre. But I am glad to be with my father. And it is fun to be out with Sophie too. I am secretly a little proud: my father obviously thinks she is an attractive girl.

We walk back to the Biltmore. He is leaving tomorrow, Sunday, to fly back to Washington to meet with the rest of the Citizens Crusade group. "Would you like to come upstairs for a minute? I'd like to introduce you to these people from CDGM who are helping us write the report."

"All right."

Upstairs in his suite, four or five young men and women are working around one portable typewriter. Books and papers are scattered on tables and chairs. My father introduces them to Sophie and me. We shake hands. I see again how proud my father is of me. And I am so proud of him. Even at this moment when in sessions with my analyst I am talking about problems which my father has helped create. The problems of rebelling against so much unconditional love. The impossibility of it. And the success and wisdom of my father such a difficult barrier to my own ambitions. For there are voices in me which say, "Why try to compete? Why struggle and then fail to equal him? He will love you no matter what you do." These are problems which should create a good deal of hostility toward him. Yet I cannot feel it. Not watching him glow with pride as he goes out of his way to introduce his son Paul, who is just an ordinary sophomore at Columbia, to a group of dedicated young people who have been working in the danger zone called Mississippi. He is showing me off. *He* thinks *I* am special. I don't know why. All I know is that this love from my father is richer, more addictive, than any tonic or nectar or drug.

He takes the elevator back downstairs with us. And escorts us through the brass door to the top of the steps.

A warm breeze launches me up the street on Monday afternoon. My mind is clear. One of those days when a session with Dr. Shapiro leaves me feeling buzzed with a peculiar warmth, as if things are going to be all right with me, I walk down past the Puerto Rican groceries on Columbus Avenue, nod at my Haitian-refugee super who is picking his teeth on the front steps, and enter the building which might be called "home." Will Sophie be waiting there, sitting lackadaisically doing her French assignment outside my apartment? The elevator door slides open. No, she's not here today. I unlock the door. Lock it behind me once I'm inside. And go lie down on top of my bed to read the newspaper I bought on Broadway a few minutes ago.

The downstairs bell cries out like an angry locust. Not ringing, but an electronic scratching noise. Who could this be? I let the person in with the remote control. And then wait behind the apartment door, leaning against the wall, reading the news.

Elevator opens. I look through the peephole. Can't recognize this person. He rings my doorbell.

"Who is it?"

"Paul Spike?"

"Yes . . ."

"I'm Chaplain Cannon. From Columbia." I open the door. Yes, I recognize his face seen briefly at two or three formal university functions. Short, cropped black hair. A fleshy set of jowls. Clerical collar and black shirt under his gray tweed jacket.

"What's up?"

"May I come in?"

"Sure," I step back and he enters. Then quickly turns and blurts:

"I'm afraid I have some very bad news, Paul."

Each word falls out of his mouth like a shadow, dissolving into the dark glaze which eclipses all light in this apartment. I think I may puke. Step back. The sun has just crashed behind the Palisades over in Jersey. Eerie universe. The chaplain and I are hovering above the skyscrapers, talking in an isolation booth. There is a halo of white starch around his beefy, raw neck. "Who is it?" I ask. "My mother or my father?"

"Your father. He died early this morning."

"How?"

The chaplain places his fingers on my shoulder. I flinch. Something is ringing through my head, like a telephone in a distant apartment.

"I'm not sure how he died, Paul. It could have been a heart attack."

Shock. I can think of very little. Must call home, says the chaplain. I want to call Dr. Shapiro, my father-in-transference.

I dial in the phone booth near the front of the drugstore on Columbus Avenue. The chaplain wanders just outside. That last night at the Biltmore my father said, "Our phone is tapped again." During all the years he was at the Commission, the phone made a symphony of strange noises. Then it stopped. He moved to Chicago. The phone there was normal. Until a few weeks ago, when he began to work on this CDGM problem. "We do all our talking over pay phones. They call up and give me the number of a phone booth. Then I go out and call them there from another phone booth. Very weird," said my father.

I tell the operator I want this collect. In a few seconds, there is the click of connection. Then the familiar bleep of the busy signal. I hang up. The chaplain has his face glued to the door. "It's busy."

"Why don't you come over to my apartment and call from there?"

"I want to call my analyst."

"Oh?"

I nod and turn back, find the number in my wallet, and dial Shapiro. He is probably with a patient. I will make it quick.

"I'm sorry to disturb you. But I just found out my father is dead."

"My God! That's terrible. How?"

"I am not sure." My father respected Shapiro enormously. And I believe Shapiro felt the same toward him. During the final stages of his analysis, my father felt uncomfortable because up to that point it had been such a one-sided exchange. My father did all the talking, intimate revelations, to a man he knew little about. So, to a certain degree, Shapiro and my father switched roles and my father began to listen as the analyst talked about his life. A brilliant minister and a brilliant analyst struggling with their lives in that rather gloomy office, with the hum of the air conditioning in the background, the books on the walls, the rugs soundproofing the floors. After his analysis was finished, he and Shapiro continued to meet occasionally for lunch and talk. They became friends. Shapiro's friend is dead. But he is still my analyst.

"Is it possible I could have an appointment tonight?"

"Let's see . . . well, you could come at nine o'clock."

"Thank you."

Outside in the pink neon glare of the drugstore, the chaplain hooks my arm in his hand. "I want you to know, Paul," he says, "if I died, that's just how I would want my own son to act. Call his analyst if he feels like it. I don't want you to think twice about it."

Riverside Drive building. One of the best Columbia addresses. An antique elevator lifts us through the floors. Only two apartments on each floor here.

His young wife looks at me with frightened eyes. As if I might spoil supper. A couple of children are chased out of the front room. His wife retires into the kitchen. The chaplain offers me a brandy. I refuse.

I call Chicago again. No busy signal this time, but my mother's voice, tired but strong.

"How are you, honey?" she says.

"I don't know. How are you? And John?"

"Your aunt and uncle are here with us. They flew this afternoon. When are you going to come?"

"I don't know. Tonight. Tomorrow morning."

"Where are you right now?"

"At the Columbia chaplain's apartment. I'm going to call Newman."

"Good."

"Daddy had a heart attack?" I ask her.

"Who told you that?"

"The chaplain . . ."

"Daddy was murdered."

My father is dead. I am looking for new fathers. Frantic. Immediately, I search for his support. It has always been there before. Now I must look for it in others. In the analyst we shared. In my father's best friend.

Robert Newman met my father at Judson Church around 1950. Newman was studying at New York University and came to live in the Judson "Student House," a red brick building on Thompson Street with a group of between ten and twenty students. This was something of a "campus religious community" in the midst of New York City. Actually, it was more a "community" than anything else. People usually chose to live in the Student House because it had a terrific location in the heart of Greenwich Village, was dirt cheap, and interesting people lived there.

Newman was from Paterson, New Jersey. He had left home very young. Was now working his way through NYU, was brilliant, and had what must have been the funniest sense of humor in the world. His jokes were like a string of firecrackers, surrealistic, pop pop pop. And he knew how to talk to kids. Never talked down. He could make any occasion special for us just because "Newman was there" and that meant jokes, games, wrestling, adventures. To a large degree, he had the same effect on adults.

It was impossible to be bored with Newman in the room. Along with the Spikes, there were the Wrights. Dean was a minister and he and his wife Margaret had come from Ohio to Judson Church a year after my parents. Dean took over half the ministry. He was director of the Student House program and Newman and he also became very close friends. Around this nucleus of the Spikes and Wrights and the Newmans (Bob married Rhoda in the early fifties), there was a loyal group of friends who included the Potters, the Murphys, the Hendersons, and other names barely remembered fifteen years later.

Newman was my father's closest friend for years. And he was another bridge between us. For Newman was also my best friend. Though I was only a child, and Newman was a young man, we both enjoyed each other's company and talked to each other as only best friends can. Newman used to go across Thompson Street on hot summer afternoons to a bar. It was a strip club at night. Cool and dark during these days. Newman would order a beer after lifting me up to the top of a stool. The bartender would ask me: "What are you having?"

"Beer!"

"Coming right up," he laughed as he poured me a mug of ginger ale. I was about four. Newman was twenty.

Fifteen years later and I am almost twenty. Newman has two children and he and his family live in the suburbs. As I dial his number, I cannot help remembering all the crazy Christmas presents, all the wonderful times. Rhoda answers and my voice is thick. "Hello. Is Bob there?"

I have not been able to cry yet. I am too busy looking for fathers.

"Hello?" says Newman. It sounds like he knows.

"This is Paul."

"Paul! Where are you, buddy?"

"Will you come take care of me?"

"Dean is over here. We're going to drive in to Judson. Can you meet us down there in forty-five minutes?"

"Yes."

Chaplain Cannon stops the car outside the church. I thank him and shut the door. Mount the worn marble steps off West Fourth Street and turn left into the office. I grew up on these steps, in this office. The lights are burning in every room. It is after seven. A small crowd of people sits in the waiting room. They look at me strangely. I don't recognize any of them. "Is Newman or Dean Wright here?"

"Paul's here," shouts someone to the back. Suddenly, there are Newman and Dean and Howard Moody. Each one hugs me and then we go back into Howard's office, my father's old office. Howard took over the ministry of Judson when my father left to go to the Congregational Church. They were good friends in Ohio and my father urged the church to invite Howard to New York City. Now he is famous as the crusading minister of Judson, has written many articles for national publications, worked hard in the civil rights and anti-war movements, been perhaps the key man in reforming the abortion law in New York State. Howard sits down behind his desk and I see that he has been crying. "We were afraid you'd find out from the television, Paul. It was on the networks."

"The radio is full of the story," says Newman. "I just got home tonight. The phone rang with the news. Then five minutes later, the phone rang and it was you. I turned around and drove right back to the city."

"Apparently the Commission people are putting together a statement. They've got Gene Blake. The United Church is putting one out. A lot of other denominations," says Howard.

I detect a nervous tone under this talk of "statements."

My father has been bludgeoned to death. My mother has just told me an hour ago. I am reeling but I get set for more bad news. What more could possibly exist? "Is there something you haven't told me?"

They look at me.

"Please tell me everything. Otherwise I'll find out later."

Newman looks at me. "There are certain things the Columbus police are saying to the newspapers. They found certain pieces of evidence in your father's room."

"And the way he was dressed," says Dean.

"How was he dressed?"

"He had on his raincoat but nothing else."

"So what? He always used his raincoat as a bathrobe when he traveled. I've taken hundreds of trips with him. He always did it."

"What's important is the way the newspapers are playing this."

"What else did they find?"

"They found some magazines which they are calling 'pornographic magazines.' Nobody is sure what exactly they found. But this is the way the Columbus police are handling the thing. Also, they found a list. A list of supposedly 'suspect' bars in Columbus."

"Your father went to Denison in Granville right near Columbus. And he has been back to visit there dozens of times. He probably knew Columbus as well as he knew New York City. I don't believe he needed a list if he wanted to go out to any bars," says Dean.

"The list doesn't sound like him," says Howard.

"What's going on?" I ask.

"Somebody is trying to smear your father's reputation. And it is working. Already the Deep South is full of this news tonight."

"What about New York?"

"I don't think so."

"The National Council of Churches is putting out a statement. And they have hired a lawyer in Columbus to look out for your family's interests and to try and get the police to cool this," says Dean. He is the head of the Baptist Pension Board, one of the most important men in that denomination.

"You can stay with us in Montclair tonight," says Newman. "Then we'll fly with you, Dean and I, to Chicago tomorrow. Do you know what your mother is planning for funeral arrangements?"

"No."

"She probably could use some help," says Dean.

"What's Columbus like?" I ask.

"It's a right-wing city. There was a branch of the Klan there for years."

In Columbus, a group of Ohio ministers urges that the building in which my father was murdered on Monday morning, the building he had dedicated on Sunday afternoon, be "re-dedicated."

Newman drives me uptown to keep my appointment with Shapiro. Passing through the city streets, the car is filled with radio. Newman is turning through the channels looking for news. One station seems about ready. The rock and roll deejay finishes his amphetamine screech and then the calmer voice of the newscaster fills the breech of silence.

I am feeling hollow. My father is one sure way out of any crisis. I would call him right this moment. He would talk to me, console me, he would be strong and yet not overbearing. The crisis has come! Where is my father? Dead. In less than four years, he went from an "outsider's" position in America, where the news is what you are fed on network television, to the heart of darkness. Into the dirtiest political battles. Into the realm where every struggle is interlocked, reality held together by straining fingers of men who have awesome power and ambitions. In less than four years he went from our living room reality in Tenafly to the back offices of the White House. It was too quick. Perhaps. He never had time to stop and sense the danger. He did not fight his way into the offices of power. It happened in a fluke of circumstances: events, his talents, history. He was still an innocent. "Three showers a day," he said. Not the sentiments of a hardened political infighter. Now he is dead. Who killed him? Why?

The radio crackles: "In Columbus, Ohio, early this morning, civil rights leader Rev. Dr. Robert W. Spike was slain in a guest room . . ."

Paralyzed, I listen to the newsman recite the wire-service mass for my dead father.

On the same news program:

"In Washington, Sargent Shriver, director of the Office of Economic Opportunity, has criticized clergymen who want to interfere in the domestic programs of the federal government. Shriver said, 'I am shocked to find some clergymen resorting to character assassination tactics to protest an administrative decision.'"

October 18, 1966. These two stories run back to back on the news! Only a handful of people in the country must see any connection. What grotesque timing. *"Character assassination tactics"?* What is happening? I will never understand. "This is the dirtiest fight I've ever been involved in," he said. Did this have something to do with it, the murder? That's too impossible to believe. But what is this Sargent Shriver statement doing here beside the news of my father's murder? What a "coincidence." I am too hollow to even care to understand. I only lay my head down on the sticky plastic of Newman's automobile and let myself sob. Inside the darkness of my shell, I can see his face. I say to myself, "Study this now. Press this down into your memory like type on a page." But already it is starting to fade.

When we arrive late that evening in Newman's Montclair, New Jersey, house, Rhoda has food ready. We sit around the table in the kitchen. I tell Newman the story which my father told me that night in the Biltmore. Newman listens and says, "I don't have any idea what this is about or what happened. We'll have to wait and see what the Columbus police find. In any case, these next weeks are going to be hell. One thing you should remember. There aren't any rules. Act as you feel. Don't play roles for other people. And don't feel guilty."

"Why would I feel guilty?"

"Death makes a lot of people feel guilty."

There is a radio in my room.

Twenty minutes past the hour of one in the morning as Earl Williams your guide through this wild and wooly October morning is still sitting here sending out the sounds to you and how are you? let the good times roll, all those of you out there motorizing over the hill: watch your mirrors carefully and if you're sitting around your local saloon and you just had one for the road, why tempt fate? take a taxi home. So easy to DRIVE CAREFULLY now let's hear from the Beatles . . . that was the Beatles now let's hear from Otis, take it Otis, take it . . . now thank you Otis and here are the headlines on this cool morning, October 18th:

In Columbus, Ohio, civil rights leader Rev. Dr. Robert
W. Spike was slain in the guest room . . .

I cannot force myself to get up from the bed and turn
this off. I lie until dawn, helpless, the radio splashing news
all over me like blood. His news. The room fills with dismal
light like dirty water in a glass. Finally, the radio still trum-
peting, I fall asleep and swirl through dreams of murder and
radio and dark sirens passing through streets . . . Newman
is standing there: "Time to get up. We have to catch an
airplane."

In the terminal at O'Hare International Airport, a seminary
student stands at the gate. He has come to drive us into
Chicago. In his arms he holds a stack of newspapers.
"You're Paul?" he asks.
"Yes."
"I've got the morning papers all here. Here's the . . ."
He hands it to me. On the front page is a huge photograph of
my father's corpse being wheeled out of the guest room in
Columbus under a sheet.
"Oh no!" I drop the paper on the ground. I am gagging.
This photograph is a sledgehammer in the face. Newman
grabs my arm.
"What is it?"
"Tell this guy to take these papers away from me."
"What?" He reaches out and grabs the paper off the
floor. "Oh fuck it!" He takes the rest of the newspapers
from the seminary student's hands and quickly dumps them
in a nearby litter bin. The student looks confused.
Riding the concrete river into the city under black skies,
I stare at the bumpers of other cars. The student chats ner-
vously. Finally, Newman says, "We're all kind of tired. Maybe we should just not talk for a while."

The rest of my family is waiting in the living room. There are three of us today where there were always four in the past. It feels like a wagon with only three wheels. Stuck in the dust, one spoke deep into the ground. Three wheels sit foolishly at standstill.

We embrace. My aunt and uncle are there. Tears begin again. I hear my father's secretary on the telephone in the kitchen: "The other boy has just arrived. It's awful."

Columbus police remove my father's body.

Newman and Dean sit down with my mother and go over the funeral. She wants it back East. A small funeral. There are large memorial services planned already. The funeral itself for family and closest friends. Then bury him in a cemetery in New Jersey. It does not take long to decide. Newman and Dean Wright go into the bedroom and get on the telephone. In two hours, they have everything arranged.

Once my mother gets up and opens the bedroom door.

"Careful what you say on that. It's tapped," she says. But what could we possibly say today?

My mother is in shock. Her life has been split apart like lightning cracking down the center of a tree. The exposed wood stands bright and gruesome. Her face is white and her eyes glazed. She is different. She is a widow. This is awful to see. She moves softly around the apartment as if she did not want to disturb the people downstairs. "Are you hungry, Paulie? Are you tired?" she asks. She has not called me "Paulie" since I was a baby.

My brother sits on the sofa and looks lost and nervous. He is in shock too. Perhaps more so than anyone else in the room. His feelings are walled off, he can't get to them. His father has been murdered. He is fifteen years old. I do not understand the relationship which my father and brother had between them. But I know that it was strong and as deep as the one which I had with my father. John is four years younger than I am. We have never been too close. We are different people. My father has loved us both differently.

I do not feel as if I am in shock. I feel in severe pain. And extreme anger. I feel like hitting someone. I feel like murdering someone, whoever it was did this to him. To us. To so many people who loved him. Even to all the people who needed him but did not know him. I am furious.

"Here," says my mother. She hands me a stack of thin yellow paper. Fresh telegrams arrived this morning:

DEEPLY SADDENED TO LEARN OF THE DEATH OF OUR DEAR FRIEND BOB SPIKE. HIS DEATH COMES AS A GREAT LOSS TO THE NATION AND TO THE FELLOWSHIP OF THE COMMITTED. HE WAS ONE OF THOSE RARE INDIVID- UALS WHO SOUGHT AT EVERY POINT TO MAKE RELIGION RELEVANT TO THE SOCIAL ISSUES OF OUR TIME. HE LIFTED RELIGION FROM THE STAG- NANT ARENA OF PIOUS IRRELEVANCIES AND SANCTIMONIOUS TRIVIALI- TIES. HIS BRILLIANT AND DEDICATED WORK IN THE NATIONAL COUNCIL OF CHURCHES WILL BE AN INSPIRATION TO GENERALS YET UNBORN. WE WILL ALWAYS REMEMBER HIS UNSWERVING DEVOTION TO THE LEGITI-

MATE ASPIRATIONS OF OPPRESSED PEOPLE FOR FREEDOM AND HUMAN
DIGNITY. IT WAS MY PERSONAL PLEASURE AND SACRED PRIVILEGE TO
WORK CLOSELY WITH HIM IN VARIOUS UNDERTAKINGS. AS WE CONTIN-
UE TO GRAPPLE WITH THE ANCIENT EVILS OF MAN'S INHUMANITY TO
MAN, WE WILL BE SUSTAINED AND CONSOLED BY BOB'S DEDICATED
SPIRIT. PLEASE KNOW THAT WE SHARE YOUR GRIEF AT THIS MOMENT
AND YOU HAVE OUR DEEPEST SYMPATHY AND MOST PASSIONATE PRAY-
ERS FOR STRENGTH AND GUIDANCE IN THESE TRYING MOMENTS

MARTIN LUTHER KING JR

Talking to James Forman of SNCC in my father's
office at the Interchurch Center.

I WAS DEEPLY GRIEVED AND SHOCKED BY THE NEWS OF THE DEATH OF
DR ROBERT SPIKE. I KNEW HIM FROM ASSOCIATION IN THE CIVIL RIGHTS
STRUGGLE. THE CIVIL RIGHTS MOVEMENT HAS LOST ONE OF ITS MOST
VALIANT WARRIORS. THE COUNTRY HAS LOST A GREAT AMERICAN; A
GREAT MORAL STATESMAN AND A GREAT MAN. I JOIN YOU IN SORROW
OVER THIS GREAT LOSS

A PHILIP RANDOLPH PRESIDENT BROTHERHOOD OF
SLEEPING CAR PORTERS

MAY I EXPRESS ON BEHALF OF THE NATIONAL ASSOCIATION FOR THE
ADVANCEMENT OF COLORED PEOPLE AND ON MY OWN PERSONAL BE-
HALF ESPECIALLY OUR PROFOUND SHOCK AND GRIEF AT THE TRAGEDY
WHICH HAS STRUCK YOU. AS A COLLEAGUE FRIEND AND DEVOTED CO-
WORKER BOB SPIKE HAD A PLACE IN OUR HEARTS SHARED BY ONLY A
TREASURED FEW. WE SHALL MISS HIM GREATLY

ROY WILKINS

OUR HEARTFELT SYMPATHY IN YOUR LOSS WHICH IS A LOSS FOR ALL OF
US

STOKELY CARMICHAEL

With Vice President Humphrey.

MRS HUMPHREY AND I WANT YOU TO KNOW HOW MUCH OUR THOUGHTS
ARE WITH YOU AND YOUR SONS. BOB WAS A GOOD AND DEAR COUNSEL-
OR TO SO VERY MANY. HIS HELP STRENGTH AND FIRM CONVICTIONS
WILL CONTINUE IN THOUSANDS OF LIVES. WE WISH THERE WERE MORE
MEANINGFUL AND HELPFUL WAYS TO EXPRESS OUR SORROW. THE PEO-
PLE OF THIS COUNTRY FIND THEIR GUIDANCE AND THEIR LEADERSHIP

IN THE STRONG DEDICATION OF SELFLESS MEN OF BOB SPIKE'S STATURE. THIS IS THE LOSS THAT WE CAN ILL AFFORD. OUR PRAYERS ARE WITH YOU AND YOUR FAMILY

VICE PRESIDENT HUBERT H HUMPHREY

THE TRAGIC AND UNTIMELY DEATH OF YOUR HUSBAND ROBERT SPIKE HAS CUT SHORT A BRILLIANT CAREER AND DEPRIVED THE NATION OF AN INDEFATIGABLE CHAMPION OF INTERRACIAL JUSTICE. THE CIVIL RIGHTS MOVEMENT HAS LOST A NOBLE SOUL

WHITNEY M YOUNG JR

I AM DEEPLY SHOCKED TO LEARN OF THE TRAGIC AND INEXPLICABLE AND SENSELESS DEATH OF YOUR DEVOTED HUSBAND AND MY DEAR FRIEND. NO ONE EVER WORKED HARDER OR MORE COURAGEOUSLY AND MORE IN HARMONY WITH THE PRINCIPLES OF CHRISTIAN BROTHER-HOOD AND JUSTICE THAN HE. YOUR SENSE OF BEREAVEMENT AND LOSS IS SHARED BY ALL WHO KNEW AND ADMIRED HIM. MY DEEPEST SYMPA-THIES GO OUT TO YOU AT THIS MOMENT. PLEASE TELL ME IF THERE IS ANY WAY I CAN BE OF ASSISTANCE

VICTOR G. REUTHER

THOUSANDS OF POOR PEOPLE IN MISSISSIPPI MANY OF WHOM WOULD NOT EVEN RECOGNIZE HIS NAME OWE DR. SPIKE A DEEP DEBT OF GRATI-TUDE FOR HIS WORK IN HELPING BREAK THEIR BONDS OF DEGRADATION AND FEAR. THOSE OF US WHO KNEW HIM PERSONALLY WERE FILLED WITH BOUNDLESS ADMIRATION FOR HIS COURAGE AND DEDICATION TO FREEDOM IN THE DEEPEST SENSE OF THE WORD. AT THE TIME OF HIS TRAGIC DEATH HE WAS THROWING HIMSELF INTO THE STRUGGLE TO SAVE THE CHILD DEVELOPMENT GROUP OF MISSISSIPPI FROM DESTRUC-TION BY THE FORCES WHICH HE HAD SPENT HIS LIFE FIGHTING AGAINST. MEN OF DR SPIKES STATURE ARE NOT REPLACEABLE AND AMERICA WILL NOT EASILY RECOVER FROM HIS LOSS. WE WEEP WITH YOU

THE BOARD, STAFF, PARENTS AND CHILDREN OF THE
CHILD DEVELOPMENT GROUP OF MISSISSIPPI

Mississippi.

For a second, these are satisfying. But what a desperate satisfaction. What the hell are these telegrams? Good reviews for a Broadway drama? For a man's life?

"There are about sixty more in the kitchen. On top of the refrigerator, I think," says my mother.

I have a nightmare. I am in the room in Columbus. I am lying on the floor beside my father's bed. He is sleeping. There is a noise at the door. Someone opens it and enters. I see a hammer in his hand. He is going to try to kill my father. I leap up and he raises his weapon. I grab him by the throat and feel the flesh in his neck as my fingers dig . . .

Morning. Wake up on the couch in my brother's room. It is very early. I can hear voices in the kitchen. My mother and my aunt. I wonder what they know of the "evidence" which the papers are writing about. I wonder just what my mother understands of my father's bisexuality. What do I understand of it, for that matter? Nothing, really. Could he possibly have carried a few of these magazines and a list? Yes, I believe it is possible. But very unlikely. It does not sound like him. Is that just my wishful thinking? No, my father was not a dirty book reader. I don't think he needed a list of bars in Columbus. He was only going to be there one night anyway. He knew the city. He had gone to college in Ohio and certainly knew that the bars in Columbus were closed on Sunday nights. Could someone have planted this in his briefcase?

Could someone have murdered him? Could someone have beaten his head in and gone off without leaving a trace of evidence? It sounds unlikely. But it happened.

Could he have been murdered in the middle of the "dirtiest fight" of his life?

Television has made murder a vaudeville joke. Suddenly, I have the real taste of murder. Not the bang, bang, fall down dead on the silver tube. But the *taste*. Dirt between teeth. Murder in America? That's what you watch eating frozen peas off an aluminum tray.

We are all dressed in our overcoats, suitcases packed and ready to go to the airport. We'll arrive in New York about dinnertime. To stay with my parents' friends, out in New Jersey.

I am standing in the master bedroom. I look down at my father's bed. I lean over, peel back the edge of the spread and press my nose to the pillow. I can smell him. I can smell him faintly.

The telephone is on the table between the two beds. Lift the receiver to my mouth. "You fucking bastards. I hope this is still tapped. I hope you are listening. You killed him.

Please, please let me know who you are. Please, you fucking bastards. I'll kill you if I ever find out."

I could kill another man. If I knew which man it was who took my father's life.

What if he were a maniac? A sick man? A lone man acting completely on his own who stumbled by accident onto my father and bludgeoned him to death at the peak of his career?

It happens frequently during the sixties. Murder is our new Medal of Honor. All our heroes get it now.

The police in Columbus say he was killed with an object like a hammer.

Could this be a monster's idea of a joke? Our name is Spike. Was my father "hammered" to death as a kind of pun?

James Toller is the lawyer retained by the National Council of Churches to act "on our behalf" in Columbus. He talks to my mother on the telephone frequently. No, there are no new leads. No clues yet.

Meanwhile, he has apparently stemmed any more "evidence" from leaking out of the Columbus police headquarters like the "evidence" which has already frightened the Protestant church nearly out of its wits.

In the American moral code, murder ranks below pornography and bars as a "shocker." Why have the police been so ready to hand this out to the press? But that aside, why has this been so devastating? My father is dead. Yet everyone is more concerned with his reputation. *He* is dead. *He* was a man of action and wisdom. His *reputation* is nothing. It is an image to be pasted over one's life like thin paper. He is dead now and his reputation will soon disappear as well. What is important is that he is not able to act any more, to lead, to console us and find our strength when we have misplaced it.

The police investigation begins at once. A few days after the funeral, Newman gets a visit from a New York City detective acting on behalf of the Columbus Police Department. They have retained a copy of my father's personal address book and now are interviewing every name in it. Newman sits down with the detective. After a few questions, he asks Newman, "Did you know that Rev. Spike was a homosexual?"

"What?"

"Did you know that Rev. Spike was a homosexual?" repeats the policeman. A bizarre way to conduct an investigation. Or is it a way to spread rumors?

"No," says Newman. "I didn't know that."

Later in the day, a mutual friend of my father's and Newman's calls up. "Hey, there was just a cop in my office. He said Spike was a homosexual. What's this all about?"

The police continue their "investigation" in this fashion. My father devoted much of his life to a fight for American justice. It is odd, the way things work.

Several days pass. The lawyer, Mr. Toller, phones my mother. He tells her for the first time about the "evidence." Then he says, "The police have told me that they had your husband under observation in New York and Washington. They have evidence that he had homosexual experiences." This staggers my mother. In fact, it comes close to shattering her.

But what were the police doing collecting "observations" of my father's behavior? Which police? Was this the FBI? What were they doing collecting evidence about him? My father was not a Communist, had never joined a more radical political group than the Americans for Democratic

Action. He was a Congregationalist minister working for justice in America.

The implications which the police and the newspapers in certain cities wanted to make were clear enough. My father was "homosexual" and he had been murdered as a consequence of this.

What is it that lives in the police imagination which equates homosexual behavior with murder?

Perhaps the implications are all true. Perhaps my father met a maniac and was physically attracted to him. They went back to the guest room, made love and suddenly the maniac turned on my father and bludgeoned him to death. In any case, this must have been a brilliant maniac. For he left not one clue behind him. Not a trace of evidence.

It seems possible. But not altogether likely. When viewed in the context of my father's last weeks and how he felt about them, the coincidence of the perfect crime meshing with the moment of greatest possible motive (my father was functioning at the top of his strength; to many right-wing Americans his functioning was viewed with alarm and disgust) seems altogether too "coincidental" for me to believe.

It is like the coincidence of Bobby Kennedy, or the coincidence of Martin Luther King, or the coincidence of Malcolm X: these "coincidences" are fatal yet so readily swallowed by so many Americans. They have no other choice. For not to swallow one of these "coincidences" is to begin to doubt that reality in America is what the little box says it is.

Who killed my father? Was it a maniac? Still loose and roaming the streets of Columbus today after six years? Or was it someone else? Was it a professional killer? Do we have those in America?

Sargent Shriver. Senator Stennis. Lyndon Baines Johnson. Are these the kind of men who could plot a murder? I do not for a moment believe they are. When they deal in murder, it is with a pen or a phone call. It is signing a bill which puts bombers over peasant villages and napalm over jungles. Making a decision which stunts the growth of black children in Mississippi in order to save the Asian children of South Vietnam from "communism."

But the facts are there as plain as the knobs on the side of the little box. So many of the leaders of the country died violently in "mysterious tragedies" during the sixties. Who launched these bloody murders? Texas billionaires? Fundamentalist Bible commandos? The Central Intelligence Agency?

Who knows, who knows? Perhaps all we can do is reach back and find our culprit in the years when our forefathers were settling New England. Perhaps these bullets which pierced the heads of Kennedys and King, perhaps these assassinations can only be understood in fundamentalist terms. Perhaps the name of the conspiracy is Satan. Perhaps these were all the work of the Devil. Perhaps we should leave it there. And be done with it all. The darkness is cold and full of jeopardy in this land. Better not push this frontier too far. But stay here around the electric campfire, watching the programs and eating our frozen suppers.

———————————

The casket showroom is in the attic of the funeral home. We are escorted inside by the funeral director. He is kempt but dour, in his late thirties.

The lights are very bright. No gloom is allowed, even in the far corners of the showroom. Spots beam down on a dozen metal and wood boxes. They are set on biers, at waist height. Some have the lids open to reveal fancy silk linings. Others are completely shut. Long, reddish mahogany cas-

kets. Burnished bronze caskets. Polished blond caskets. Caskets for the whole family. Bargain caskets. Luxury boxes. A
complete range of available models.

My father's body has arrived this morning. It is downstairs in an empty parlor, lying in what the director called a
"travel container."

My mother walks slowly down the aisle, her fingers
sliding noiselessly over the slick wood lids. This must be her
decision.

"To start off," says the funeral director in his best sales
voice, "we've got three medium-range models. Hardwood,
domestic, the linings are very . . ."

In two seconds I am at his side, my hand on his arm. His
eyes meet mine and lock. "Not one more word, please," I
tell him. "Leave us alone."

He bows his head a notch. And moves away from this
relative of the loved one. Back to the stairs.

Riding behind the hearse in the hired black Cadillac, we are
silent. John and I sit on the two jump seats. There is a good
deal of traffic on Route 4. Children driving with their
mommies out to the colossal shopping centers in Paramus
stare at me through the back windows, their gooey fingers
stuck in their mouths, their eyes full of wonder. The passing
display beside the road salutes our procession to the grave-
yard: Midas Mufflers, Texaco, Allied, McDonalds, Belling-
er's Buick, Foam Rubber City.

How he would have hated this! The spanking new
hearse which carries the casket so pompously. This Cadillac
which contains the family. He would have yearned for it to
be over so we could get back to living. But he would have
carried on with it. And nobody could have told from looking
at him that inside he was miserable. Outside, he was young,
boyish, strong. Both old people and babies were drawn to

his thin, angular face with the blue eyes and the almost blond eyebrows above a sharp nose. I remember the last funeral I went to: my grandfather Spike. It was in Rochester. My father buried his father. Without a trace of either weakness or coldness, he guided the ritual from beginning to end in the country cemetery where his mother had been buried less than ten years before. She had died of cancer of the brain. His father of a heart attack. Now *he* was dead.

The cemetery is a new one. They do not allow gravestones, so it is really a large, uncluttered meadow stretching up a gradual slope toward the east. New York City, invisible beyond the Palisades, haunts the suburban graves.

When the final prayer is finished, Truman Douglas, my father's boss and close friend at the Congregational Church, scatters dirt on the polish of the casket. One handful and we walk back to the hired cars.

Truman Douglas's eulogy was quiet and true, without pyrotechnics or emotional pitches, but not without emotion in his voice. In many ways, Truman was burying a son. My father had often looked up to Truman as he would have wished to look at his own father.

> How can we ever isolate the effect of a single individual on an endeavor in which he has deliberately joined his efforts with all the efforts of thousands and hundreds of thousands of others? But when the Civil Rights Bill was passed, and the Voting Rights Bill was passed, and when in some parts of the nation, at least, we began to take them seriously, the hand of Robert Spike was unmistakably in them. We cannot mark off any single segment of these actions and label it as a monument to Bob. But we know that his blood and marrow, his toil and tears, his prayers and dreams are in them all.

His sympathies and understandings were as comprehensive as all life.

Bob was sternly self-disciplined in his sense of the efficient use of time. Without this quality he could not have accomplished all he did—traveling, speaking, writing, planning, consulting, spending the innumerable hours necessary for making the rounds of key people in public life. Yet with all the pressures upon him, I have seen Bob engage in the most prodigal waste of time—stopping to talk, as one human being to another, with a panhandler on Fourth Avenue; listening patiently while a bore gets off some wild idea about missions—not because Bob was ever undiscriminating, but because he respected the essential humanity that was underneath all the boredom and banality.

Is there anyone here who cannot recall acts of undeserved courtesy, of uncalled-for kindness and consideration, of surprising grace, which we received at his hands?

But I must stop speaking words which you know as well as I. I want to let Robert speak to us. These words come from his book, *To Be a Man*. I think these words might be taken, at least in a fragmentary way, as Bob's confession of faith.

"If one were to pick a virtue for the Christian life, endurance would be a good one. To stand in the face of the storm, with courage and without panic, is perhaps a more needed ingredient of Christian love than the flash of sympathy. This is not an endurance appropriate to the Stoic. It is not cold and gray, built of despair. It is an endurance that is warmed by the mysterious love of God, even in the worst of human situations. More than that, this endurance is taken as a token of a final crazy hope that God shall fully reign over his creation.'"

My father's words pierce my memory like shards of irony. Indeed, as Truman Douglas thought, these words seem to present the central core of my father's set of Christian beliefs. "Endurance" was the crucial quality of a good, a

"Christian," life in this age. And when the time came that one of "the worst of human situations" arose around his own death, so few had the "endurance" necessary to cope with the situation. Instead, my mother was flooded for a few weeks with "flashes of sympathy." Hundreds of letters saying "You have our profound sympathy and all our prayers" collected on the counters of our temporary home. All these people really writing "good-bye," for they would never be heard from again.

The church's endurance was expressed as a rush to shut off all news of his death. A race to the fountain of cleansing forgetfulness. For the church was glad to "celebrate his life" in a scattering of memorial services, resolutions passed at conferences that fall, and a special issue of *Christianity and Crisis* which printed excerpts from Truman Douglas's and Howard Moody's eulogies.

But the church was not ready to face his death. Not even in a tentative way. The church sensed that there was an element of truth in all the confusion about the "evidence" found in that guest room. Few people had known my father might actually be bisexual. Very few people. But thanks to the Columbus police, now few people thought of him as anything but some kind of sexual deviate. And the panicked reaction of the National Council of Churches was obvious. So that this impression was blasted into the forefront of the crime.

But what of the crime? Was not murder a crime? Was the church not possessed of even enough "endurance" to wait a while longer, to launch its own investigation, to "stand in the face of the storm, with courage and without panic" for a few weeks?

A sufficient number of people in the church knew my father well enough to know that there was something obviously wrong with the swirl, the whole smokescreen of innuendo and dirt, which surrounded his killing. He had lived an exceptionally straightforward life. His death was as crooked as an old stream about to break up in a thousand muddy puddles.

Enough people knew my father was involved in dangerous work. Enough knew that he had received dozens and dozens of hate letters, threatening letters, over the years since he went to work for the National Council of Churches. Carl McIntire, the right-wing fundamentalist radio preacher, had singled out my father on his program numerous times. Enough people knew about the tapped phone. Enough knew about so many "inside" things to make them want to look further.

But the sad truth is that these people, most of them in some way connected with the church, the Protestant Establishment in America, lacked the "endurance" to do more than issue a statement "praising the life of Robert Spike."

All this "praising of his life" began to eat away at my credulity in the church's guts. For by continually restricting itself to this praise for his life, it became glaringly obvious that the church was not willing to confront his death. And his death was as real as his life. More terrible. Threatening to many, perhaps. But it was a brutal fact. And he had written:

> We pray also for the raising up of men who shudder less at death and who, by the hard unconventionality of their martyrdom, will illuminate the path that the rest of us travel.

"The hard unconventionality" of my father's death would illuminate few paths. For the church was not going to "endure" the risky business of confronting this. Rather, it was much simpler, easier, and "kinder" to praise his life and ignore its conclusion.

My father was certainly a prophet. I cannot help believing that if we knew more about his murder it would illuminate for all of us more about this "path" in which we seem to move as helplessly as twigs in a torrent down over these last years of American history. Certainly, if the church had not been so panicked by the Columbus police revelations and instead had demanded a continual, thorough, and *reputable* investigation into the death and the circumstances of his last days, certainly the chance for illumination would have been doubled or tripled.

But the church was frightened. And the church was silent. My father's life was praised with "flashes of sympathy" and his death was swept out of the light.

What a devastating view this gives me of the church which my father gave his life to from childhood onwards. This church has not the "endurance" to stand and confront a difficult death among one of its clergy. How can this church preach on the Crucifixion?

―――――――――――

Here is the letter we received from the ministerial staff at the United Christian Center in Columbus, the building in which my father was bludgeoned to death.

Dear Mrs. Spike:

We, the staff, students and faculty of the United Christian Center of The Ohio State University express our deepest sympathy and concern at this time. Our prayers are with you and your sons.

We are ever grateful for the meaningful contribution that Dr. Spike has made to the churches, and to us in the dedication of our new building.

May God draw us close to Himself and one another with strong ties of understanding love that can never be broken.

Sincerely,
Robert M. Russell,
Convener of the Pastoral Staff.

This is the only communication I ever saw from these people.

Of all the letters we received, the one which most moved me was from Birmingham, Alabama. It came under the letter-head of the Salvation Army.

Dear Mrs. Spike:

We were all saddened by the untimely death of your husband as we read of the event in our papers. We wish to express our sincere sympathy to you and the rest of your family.

One never knows all of the good that one does in this world for other people and I am certain that when Dr. Spike joined in matrimony Mr. and Mrs. A. Tyler Griffin in New York, he could not have known that his influence would extend all the way down to Birmingham, Alabama, and that his good influence on their lives would cause them to wish to give a gift to the Salvation Army Home and Hospital in his name. But that influence was that extensive and long enduring. Mr. and Mrs. Griffin have given a lovely rocking chair which has been placed in our nursery. The plaque on the chair reads: A MEMORIAL TO THE LIFE LIVED BY REVEREND DR. ROBERT W. SPIKE.

May God continue to support and bless you in the coming years, as I am sure He has in the past.

The donation from the Griffins will be used by approximately two hundred girls each year as they feed and rock their babies and many more will see the plaque in Dr. Spike's memory, and so his influence will continue, not only in the areas where he was known so well, but even in the deep south in Birmingham.

Yours for "others,"
William K. Matthews
Captain
Superintendent

A few weeks after the funeral, I drive my mother and brother back to New York City. In Ohio, it begins to snow. By the middle of Pennsylvania, we are in a blizzard. But there is no point in stopping. Not until dark. So we drive through the thick white catastrophe of the highway, the ridges of the snow tires grinding away beneath us, going back East . . .

The people who have rented my parents' house in Tenafly are turning out to be difficult. A doctor and his wife and their two children, they react to my mother's first call as if she were an ogre threatening to push them out in the gutter. She had simply told them the facts. Not necessary, anyway, since the local newspapers were full of the news of the murder. She wanted to come back to Tenafly. Was there any chance these people might begin to look around for another house to rent? Of course, she understood they had a two-year lease.

The tenants reacted strongly. How could my mother make such a suggestion! There was no feeling for her circumstances. Only that they had "their rights" and would not be pushed around. Nobody had mentioned pushing them around. Just asked them if they would like to help.

The doctor and his family had a good thing going, and they knew it. The rent they were paying for this three-bedroom house in Tenafly, modern, in excellent condition, was minimal.

Late on the same day as the funeral, I went over to talk to them. My aunt came along. The doctor offered us sherry. Then his wife began to screech at me: "Your mother just doesn't understand that we have a lease. We can't be forced to break it and . . ."

"Dear," said the doctor, trying to quiet her a little.

"Well, it's true." She turned back to me. "Your mother has got to face reality!"

"Please don't talk to me about reality," I said.

My mother needs a job. She goes into New York City and asks around at denominational offices in the Interchurch Center. She is a very smart lady. Graduated from Northwestern. Has worked at different jobs. Taught school, science and math.

She is hired as a payroll clerk by the Presbyterian Church. An office job, sitting at a gray steel desk in an ocean of them, with a supervisor, forty minutes for lunch, a clock ticking off the seconds till five o'clock.

I used to come over to talk to my father in the Interchurch Center around lunchtime. He would be sitting at a table with five or six other people. They would be eating the day's menu off trays, talking strategy for the Commission, about Mississippi, or the morning *Times*'s story on the latest congressional hassle. It seemed as if they were always occupying the center of the large basement cafeteria. All eyes were on them. They were the "Commission people" and the whole building was proud of what they were doing. The church was getting "relevant" at last. They were really involved in this civil rights movement. My father was almost a kind of star around that building. Surely, with all that attention, many people who had trod in the rather gray underbelly of the Protestant Establishment for years envied him, were resentful.

Now I find my mother in a far corner of the big room. Eating a sandwich out of her paper bag, alone at the end of a long table.

When we get on the elevator, people stare at us. I hear someone whisper to his companion, "Those are Spike's wife and son, you know."

I wish my mother wouldn't work here. She feels people staring at her all the time. "The wages of sin," it seems to say in their eyes. They are perversely gratified, many of them, to see this. The young prophet's wife suddenly a widow, moving tentatively around these frigid corridors, alone and lost, looking suddenly five years older than she should.

These people look like zombies to me. Months have passed. Nobody is praising his "life" any more. Now all they are doing is thinking about his death. A death they were afraid to confront at the time. A death which nobody understands, a still-unsolved murder, yet in these zombies' eyes you can see where the guilt lies.

I'd like to pick up a cross and smash them in the face with it.

Riverside Park is tucked between the West Side Highway and the Drive. A stretch of grass and black boulders, trees arc beside bicycle paths, a mounted policeman watches six kids toss a football, the Hudson a mile wide and pushing out to sea. Sunday afternoons are a good time to walk in the park in the fall. A few lovers scattered among the piles of fallen leaves; men walk ferocious-looking Great Danes, Puerto Ricans picnic under the weak sun, a red plastic saucer skims over the dying grass.

I meet Art Thomas and his little boy Howard. Art worked for the Commission. He was the first director of the Delta Ministry in Mississippi. Originally a white minister in the South, Art joined the civil rights movement very early. He has few illusions. Has lived in both worlds in the Deep South: white and black. His life has been in constant danger. Now he has come North to "organize communities" and lives with his wife Joyce, also a veteran civil rights worker, and Howard on West 106th Street.

"It's good to see you, Art." It really is. I never got to know him very well in the days when my father was with the Commission. Art was always in Mississippi. Rarely did he come North to New York. But he seemed like an easygoing person with hidden reserves of toughness. A gentle man who was not afraid of the truth.

We walk for a hundred yards. Howard runs back and forth like a puppy. From one popsicle stick to another. Art and I sit down on top of a stone wall. "How is your mother?" he asks.

"Not so great," I say. "Being a widow is a rotten deal."

"I want to call her up. Good that I ran into you. Have you heard anything new out of Columbus?"

"Not a word. The police don't ever communicate with us."

"What about that guy they arrested?"

The Columbus police have picked up a suspect. He had been breaking into local churches and robbing them. The next thing we heard, through intermediaries, was that this man was being charged with the murder of my father. He had confessed!

For about two weeks, everyone believed the murder was solved. This man had a history of mental illness. We began to get set for a trial. Court-appointed lawyers took the defense.

Suddenly, murder charges were hastily dropped. The defense lawyers had discovered that this man who had "confessed" to the killing had been a patient in a mental hospital during the month of October, the month of the murder. The mental hospital was in Washington, D.C.

"That's strange enough, isn't it?" says Art.

"Strange and a little scary."

Art turns and stares down the long arcade. "Howard, please don't put that rock in your mouth." Howard looks at him and drops it. Art turns back to me. "I've wanted to talk to you for some time. There's some stuff. Stories I haven't talked about with anyone, really. But I wanted to tell you."

"Like what?"

"What do you think happened?" he asks.

"I honestly am not sure, Art." I tell him my doubts about the evidence found by the Columbus police, about my last meeting with my father in the Biltmore Hotel, about my father calling the CDGM struggle the "dirtiest fight" of his life, and his meeting with Sargent Shriver. But none of this adds up in my mind to any solid conclusion.

"Did you ever hear of Steven Currier?" asks Art.

"Sounds familiar."

"Steven Currier was head of the Taconic Foundation. He had married a girl who was a Mellon. One of Andrew Mellon's heirs. Steven Currier and his wife were completely behind the civil rights movement. And they used the Taconic Foundation, which was all Mellon money, to support the movement. Millions of Mellon dollars were poured into the South during the early sixties to support voter registration projects, education projects, all sorts of movement activities. Without the Taconic Foundation, the movement would have been in a great deal of financial trouble. Probably not nearly as successful.

"Your father and Currier were friends. In fact, at the time of your father's murder, they were talking about initiating a new organization. One of the names they were considering was 'Urban America.' This would combine your father's leadership and Mellon money. Some of the old Commission staff were considering coming in on it."

"That sounds like it would have been quite an organization," I say.

"It would have been. For a start, they wouldn't have been dependent on the conservative money of the National Council of Churches. That always irritated your father."

"I know."

"This new organization would have gotten into the trickier problems of the North. Suburban housing and schools, the job problem, especially with certain unions. All sorts of economic issues that hadn't really been touched on in the early struggles in the South. Anyway, your father was killed before this could get organized."

"It's too bad." What an understatement, I think.

"Do you know what happened to Currier?"

"No."

"He and his wife were in the Bahamas on vacation. They got on an airplane to fly to another island. It never arrived. The Mellon family spent a fortune hiring a Navy minesweeper plane to locate the wreckage. They wanted to bury the bodies. But they couldn't locate a scrap."

"I don't get it."

"I don't know if there is any connection. Or what this really means. But it certainly seems as if Steven Currier and his wife were blown up in that airplane. Soon after your father died."

"This is so scary. I'm getting more terrified every day in this country. Paranoid." The escalation of the war in Vietnam has gradually been overshadowed by the civil war at home. The government and President Johnson versus the war critics, the students and the black poor. Paranoia in America is an epidemic, sweeps through all classes, conquers all political ideologies, from right to left.

"You mentioned what your father told you about the CDGM fight. That fits with what I've been told," says Art. "Apparently, before he died, your father actually told people he was willing to stake his life on the CDGM struggle."

"Yes?"

"They took a fact-finding trip to Mississippi and then were supposed to meet in Washington and release their report, right?"

"That's how I understood it."

"Well," says Art, "I don't know how much you know about the CDGM investigation. But from what I have been told, they all left for the weekend agreeing that the OEO was out to destroy CDGM without good reason. They agreed to meet in Washington. Your father went off to write the actual report. When they met back in Washington, they got in this room together and one by one most of them backed down. Your father told people he believed somehow each of these guys, with several exceptions, had been compromised over the weekend. Some kind of pressure had been put on them."

"Who told you?"

"I've heard this from several sources. Apparently your father was furious. He saw these men back out, chicken out, and he said he was going to stake everything on this fight."

"And that was a couple of days *after* I saw him, I guess. After he had already called it a dirty fight. What do you think, Art?"

"Paul, who knows? Really? What can we do? What can we think? We just have to keep our cool, that's most important."

"It's so frightening, though."

Art just looks at Howard, about forty yards away, petting someone's dog. "Okay, I've got one more story, Paul. This is the weirdest one. I don't understand this either. But it scares the shit out of me."

"Let's have it." Listening to these stories is punishment. But Art is not a liar. Not generally even much of a talker. Art likes to listen, to ask questions, to bring people together around him by the sheer force of his openness.

"You know I left Mississippi and was living in Washington in 1966. One night a few weeks after your father's murder, a friend of mine came over to our apartment. He was shook up.

"He had friends who were the leaders of the National Student Association. The NSA office was only a few blocks from where we lived. Anyway, this guy had been over in the outer offices of the NSA. And there had been a lot of activity that night. Apparently, a couple of men from the CIA were with the national leaders. Putting the screws on them. Because the next day was when the NSA revealed it had been getting funds from the CIA for years. Now these CIA people were trying to persuade them not to make the announcement.

"My friend was outside and there were some reporters there from the United Press International. There was a lot of panic in the room. One of these UPI men said to my friend, 'If those guys in there are friends of yours, you ought to warn them to be careful. Damn careful. You saw what happened to Robert Spike.'

"He asked them what they meant but they shrugged him off. He freaked out and left the office. He knew your father and I were close friends and what the killing had done to us. He came over and told me this story.

"I thought it was pretty strange. Then the next day the NSA controversy broke in the papers. You remember how big it was? So I called up Eric and told him. He called some friends at UPI." (Eric Blanchard was a newspaperman and writer who joined the Commission staff to handle all its press relations.)

"Eric called back a few hours later," says Art. "He had talked to the UPI people. They told him there were two reporters who had been working on your father's murder. Apparently, they claimed to have found information which gave the murder an entirely new context. They were working on the story and, Eric was told, it was going to break in about a week."

"Who were the two reporters?" I ask.

"I don't know. I don't think Eric knew their names either."

"What happened?"

"We, Joyce and I, sat around waiting for this story to come out. We waited and it never broke. What *did* happen was that I got several strange telephone calls."

"How?"

"People, there was a woman and a man, people that I knew only casually. They were on the fringes of the movement. I didn't trust them that much. Two people called me up suddenly for no apparent reason. And like in the middle of their 'friendly' conversation, they asked suddenly, 'What's this rumor going around about Spike being killed by the CIA?' That really scared me. Scared the hell out of me."

"What did you tell them?"

"Are you kidding? I said I hadn't heard any such rumor."

"I don't get the connection between my father and the CIA."

"Neither do I."

"But I sure as hell don't understand the CIA either. Nobody has any idea if there is one CIA, or two hundred of them. It's all divided up into separate, secret parts. Anything could be going on down there."

"It could," says Art.

"What can we do? What can we do, Art?"

"I don't know."

This is what makes the murder so tragic. For if anyone would have had the strategic sense and the guts to know what to do, it would have been my father. I remember him on the telephone to the Justice Department the morning of the Birmingham bombing. I can just see him looking around the room at the faces of his fellow "Citizens Crusade" colleagues who had suddenly "changed their minds" after a week of agreement in Mississippi. I can feel the anger which he must have felt at that moment. Suddenly alone, his reaction would not have been panic but to redouble his efforts. Was there any way to scare my father out of pursuing goals he believed were necessary and just? I cannot imagine one. With all of his realism, he was an idealist in his heart.

If anyone would have known what to do, it would have been my father. But he is dead. That's probably why.

Paul Moore, Jr., was Suffragan Bishop of the Episcopal Church in Washington, D.C., for much of the sixties. He and my father were friends. They were roughly the same age, shared the same social beliefs, even if their styles were slightly different. My father was brought up in the Baptist Church and changed to the Congregationalists. Bishop Moore was a liberal Episcopalian.

I meet him at a party on Central Park West. He is tall and graying, a sharp nose; the backs of his hands are gnarled with veins much as my father's were. There is a slight resemblance between them.

I went to grade school for several years with one of his sons. It was long, long ago, in the first grade, and I don't really remember.

Bishop Moore asks me about the murder. "Have you heard anything new from Columbus?" This is a question I am often asked.

"No, nothing." It is always difficult to talk to people about this subject. They don't know what *I* know and they try to feel me out. But subtly. I wonder what kind of conversations they would have if I were not present. I know everything they know. And more. And I try, if I trust them, to make this clear without being too explicit. This is a party, after all. Even if it seems like a scene from an Agatha Christie book. Sitting here in a comfortable library in a private apartment overlooking Central Park. Then Bishop Moore says something which stops me.

"Your father heard about the CIA connection with the NSA weeks before his murder. He was going around Washington trying to get someone to act on this information. Nobody would touch it."

"How did you hear that?"

"I don't remember exactly. But I am sure of it. I was in Washington then."

"It sounds like he was trying to put pressure on the government," I say.

"I don't know what he was doing. But I know he had this information and everybody was scared to do anything with it."

Perhaps he got this information from some of those young people I met in the Biltmore suite that night. Perhaps some of them had worked for the NSA. Now they were working for the Child Development Group of Mississippi. Who knows what my father was doing with this information? Perhaps, being blackmailed by the government to abandon the CDGM fight, he was trying to re-blackmail them.

"It makes sense, perhaps," I say to Bishop Moore. He looks at me as if I am going to say more.

My father's best friend in the movement was Rev. Andrew Young, Jr., of the Southern Christian Leadership Conference. Andy was a Congregationalist minister and had known my father in the 1950's before they both went to work full-time in the civil rights movement. Today, he is a U.S. Congressman from Georgia.

Andy is quiet. When he talks, he measures his words carefully. "At first, I didn't know what to believe," he tells me one night when we happen to run into each other uptown, about a year after the murder. "But now I believe your father was assassinated. There have been too many of these. Some *person* . . . or some *thing* . . . is behind all these murders in the movement."

Andy was, next to Ralph Abernathy, Martin Luther King's closest associate. At this moment, King has switched his attention from racial justice toward a broader goal of economic justice, into which the racial questions seem to fit easily. Economic justice, and the war in Vietnam.

There are massive student demonstrations on the horizon in the fall of 1967. Andy is glad, but a little pessimistic: "For a lot of these kids, this is just a lark. Something to do in college. In a few years they'll be right back in Macon, Georgia, working for their daddies and sitting on the Junior Chamber of Commerce. Paul, I hope you're going to be involved in this for the rest of your life."

I have no choice. But I wonder if Andy is right about "these kids." There is such incredible alienation everywhere I turn. On our left, Harlem squats in misery. On our right, they are building a new School for International Affairs at Columbia, to train "statesmen" and "intelligence agents." On every front page: Vietnam. Right out on Broadway: a tattered army of heroin addicts. In the Columbia dorms: a growing battalion of addicts, even there. A "good" college. Several Ivy Leaguers will die of overdoses this year.

I don't agree with Andy. Far fewer of us will be counted among the ranks of the Junior Chamber of Commerce than in the old days when college was a four-year flirtation with radical ideas and wild stunts. A civil war seems to have begun in America between black and white, rich and poor, young and old. A "revolution" rolling through each moment of the present like an invisible wave. I don't think these kids are joking. They are angry. They are desperate for a change.

And the changes keep coming, and coming and coming. . .

I look for fathers, for him, in the midst of this. But it becomes clear that neither Newman nor my analyst nor Art Thomas nor a dozen other friends whom I admire and respect, none of them can work to replace him.

My father is a memory. But he is also a feeling. I never have to question, "What would he have thought of this?" I feel his thought running through my blood.

Inside stories are dangerous. These things which my father told me, which Art Thomas spoke of, which I heard from various people after the murder, in certain ways I wish I did not know them. It would be far easier to live without them.

What of my own inside story? What of the work begun with that insight about my Oedipal feelings?

The analyst's office never changes. One leaves the newspapers outside in the waiting room. The windows are thick and keep out the noise of the street. Does it all come down to this? Modern man wrestling with his genesis at $25 an hour? The missile-designers and the crisis-managers, and the sons of the bomb, the fallouts, sitting in these sound-proof offices with listening doctors and discussing . . . what? One afternoon on the toilet seat at age four and a half.

Shapiro's office. I had a dream last night. I am avoiding it. There is a feeling I do not like. I cannot avoid it any more. I tell him and he asks, routinely, "What does this dream remind you of?"

One summer. We had a cottage near a lake in northern New Jersey. My father was in the city at Judson most of the week. Came out on weekends. I was four years old.

I was in the bathroom, on the toilet. Constipated. I reached down and worked the shit free with my fingers. Relief. Then a game. Instead of wiping them on the roll of paper, I drew long lines over the white wall beside the tissue. A child's exotic fingerpainting.

Later that afternoon, I am out in the yard. It is very sunny, late July, and the screen door bangs and rapid steps come down the porch. I turn. I see my mother's face red with anger. She is coming after me. I panic. Just before she reaches me, she stops and breaks off the branch of a bush. She strips the smaller branches to make an evil switch. Green and elastic, this moves through the sunshine and I scream. She grabs me by the arm. I am wearing shorts. The switch cuts again and again across my bare legs. Thin red welts spring up where it bites my flesh. Screaming, panicked, I am paying for the bathroom wall.

I expect a load of sympathy when I finish this. Expect my analyst to shake his head and sigh—what an unhappy childhood I must have had.

"Why did you wipe your fingers on the wall?" asks Shapiro.

"I don't know." That seems like a stupid question. I was just a little kid.

"It sounds to me as if you were very angry. You deliberately did something you knew would get you punished."

"Perhaps." I shrug.

"Why?"

"Why?" I shake my head.

"What were you angry about?" He sits back. I am annoyed. Then gradually, I feel that panic begin to inch up my throat. A foundation is crumbling. I don't like this. This is not the usual session: two laps around the past and a couple of exercises with last night's dream.

Shapiro looks at his index cards. He looks at me. He stares at me for a long time. Then looks away and says gently, "How old was your brother when this happened?"

I was four years old when my brother was born. For forty-eight months, I had basked in the perfect bliss of being an only child. Thick syrup of baby love, I thrived on it. Then my mother went off to the hospital, I was put under the guidance of my grandmother for a week, and when she returned it was not alone, but with *it*. My poor brother John, how I hated him.

What determines how we react to classic situations? Especially when we are four years old?

I was utterly betrayed yet reacted not with grief, but fury. Cold fury. Four years and they were bored with me? I would show them. Show them nothing. Especially my mother! I would turn my back on her forever.

Jealousy is the most self-destructive of all emotions. It is a knife with two blades and no handle. The more you use it, the more of your own arm you chop off.

I built rooms in my life as I grew older. My behavior changed, depending on which room I happened to enter.

My brother's room, I hardly ever went there. Nothing interested me in there. I ignored him. He didn't really exist, did he? At times, I would break down and actually have a good time with him. John had a sparkling wit, was very smart, and looked up to me as his glorious older brother. He had a hell of a lot of guts. I remember afternoons on the front lawn when I would "teach" him how to play football. Tackling and blocking. I outweighed him by thirty pounds at least. He took it. A rotten pounding into the ground. Coming up with dirt on his face, ready for the next lesson. John had remarkable guts. But it wasn't really until I was twenty years old that I woke up and realized I loved him. Somehow, the last sixteen years had been a "mistake." Now we could be friends.

My mother's room I could not avoid. For she administered our lives. My father was working and traveling. My mother was sending us off to school, picking us up at the dentist, driving us down to football practice, cooking supper, darning gym socks in the early hours of the morning so we would not get in trouble. She ran the house. She fed us. She went down to school and tried to bridge the gap between our house and our teachers, who often didn't know quite what to do with these smartalecky Spike boys.

But from the age of four, our relationship was one of incredible tension. I did not, could not, bring myself to trust her fully. I was angry (and felt so guilty about it) and quite horrible. Nasty. She punished me. We fought.

Even though at times we could sit down and talk. Talk with a kind of honesty and understanding between us that none of my other friends had with their mothers. She was intelligent and undogmatic, practical and strong. What a sense of humor she had, too. Her imagination moved in hilarious flashes. Just like that, she would suddenly be off on a string of adlibs and imitations which would leave the rest of us breathless from laughing so hard. And then she would get serious and practical again. "Finish your carrots. You've got geometry homework, too." My brother and I both learned how to laugh from her. She had a satirical side which could be very sharp and dry. And both of us picked up on this and imitated it. Sometimes the three of us would get going and my father would be the audience. We would sit there around the dinner table cracking jokes, going on and on, while my father laughed so hard tears appeared between his eyelashes.

But far too often these good times would end with a terrible fight between my mother and me. I felt vulnerable whenever I began to feel close. I had to maintain that distance from her, avoid that pain and possible rejection.

Finally, my father's room. In this room, I kept my heart.

When Lyndon Johnson announces he will not seek re-election in a televised address to the nation, the West End explodes with joy. The bartenders, all four of them, cannot keep up with the happy demands for more beer, more booze, "Another two pitchers please, Don!"

It would have been a distasteful campaign. He could not move around the country without provoking violent demonstrations. His Vietnam war has destroyed his political career. The President of the United States would have had to campaign for re-election behind barbed wire and loaded machine guns, his schedule a military secret.

The rumor goes that the night JFK was shot in Dallas, there were celebration barbecues blazing in backyards all over Texas. Tonight, in the student quarters of the East, the downfall of LBJ provokes a massive fiesta. "Hey-hey-LBJ— How many kids did you kill today?" goes the chant. The West End is loud and drunken. But hollow in the center. There is too much poison in the place to be washed away in one night, with one announcement, a dozen drinks, and a deep sleep.

April 4, 1968. King's last speech is running on the tube:

> But it really doesn't matter with me now . . . because I've been to the mountaintop . . . and I've looked over . . . and I've seen the promised land.

> I may not get there with you, but I want you to know tonight that we as a people will get to the promised land . . . So I'm happy tonight.

> I'm not worried about anything . . . I'm not fearing any man! . . . Mine eyes have seen the glory of the coming of the Lord!

The black audience goes wild. King looks straight into the darkness, his face running with perspiration, a yellow cross riding the air above his head. Across the bottom of the screen, in letters of superimposed light, it says: "Last Night in Memphis."

Columbia holds a memorial service for Martin Luther King. President Kirk and Vice-President David B. Truman officiate in the university chapel.

In the middle of the service, a group of scruffy students,

led by Mark Rudd, stand up and loudly berate Kirk and the university as racists and hypocrites.

Across the street in Morningside Park, Columbia has bulldozers digging up the public ground for the eventual construction of a private gymnasium for its students. Morningside Park is one of very few parks in Harlem. Yet through some complicated behind-the-scenes dealings, Columbia has managed to lease this land, about a third of the park. Many city officials, including Parks Commissioner Thomas P. Hoving, have decried this deal worked out during the Wagner administration.

The Columbia gym is at this stage a huge muddy pit filled with machines. Around it rises a shiny hurricane fence. Signs warn people to "Keep Out!"

The SDS students shout their protests, shock the chapel audience ("But this is Martin Luther King's memorial service. Don't they respect his memory?") and march out.

Crossing South Lawn a few days later, I bump into Rudd. Clouds hang low over the green metal roofs of the dormitories. The sun is gathering its forces behind this low blockade. Soon it will bring us out of winter and into the New York spring.

In front of Low Library, a half dozen political tables are in a line. People buzz around them, turn the pages of the pamphlets on display, listen to the arguments, perhaps try to catch the eye of the pretty Barnard girl who sits on a chair and collects a dime for each pamphlet entitled "Socialism Will Work!" and drops it into a jelly jar. These tables are the real sign that spring is coming.

Rudd and I are talking about an article in this afternoon's *Spectator*. I start to say something but he barges ahead and then closes with that phrase again: " . . . after the Revolution!"

I have been talking seriously. So I say, "Mark, you know there isn't going to be *that* kind of a revolution in this country."

He just smiles at me. "Sure there is."

Rudd jumps on top of a ledge. The crowd is below him, outside Low Library. The sun rivets us. It is April 23. We have just tried to force our way into Low Library to present a petition to President Kirk. All the doors were locked and the security police fought off several students who tried to push their way inside.

"Quiet! Listen everybody!" shouts Rudd. People are confused. If something is not done in an instant, the whole demonstration is going to be a flop. "Listen! We've been locked out of here. Now we have to decide what to do next."

A rumble of confusion.

"We have two things we can do," Mark shouts. I see he is frantic. His mind is racing. "And those two things are . . . " (he had better come up with at least one) "these! We can either go down to the park and . . . RIP DOWN THAT FUCKING GYM FENCE . . . or . . . or that's it! WE CAN GO DOWN TO THE PARK AND RIP DOWN THAT FUCKING GYM FENCE!"

A magnificent sense of timing. His top field marshal, a guy named J.J., is already clearing a path in the direction of the park. I have no idea where the gym is being built. But I run, along with two friends, Brian Flanagan and David Wade, across the campus and out onto Amsterdam Avenue. Behind us comes the crowd. We are among the first dozen students to break into the streets. There is an eerie howl as certain students make a noise with their mouths copied from the revolutionaries in the movie *Battle of Algiers.* We are running down Morningside Drive now, J.J. is in front, and then we leap over a low stone wall. Down through

Brian (striped pants) and I (back to camera) attack
the gym fence at Columbia, 1968.

shrubs and scrub trees, into the park. Above us, a siren. Two
more sirens. The police.

We stream down the hill until we are caught like fish
against the webs of the fence. On the other side, below us,
the obscene excavation. The construction workers look up
at us astonished. There is a moment of hesitation. Then a
few people begin to shake the fence. It is solidly anchored
in the ground. But more grab and begin to push and shove.
Brian kicks and pulls furiously. I feel the steel cut into my
fingers painfully as I use every bit of strength I can collect to
pull this fence out of the park ground. "RIP IT DOWN!" shouts

somebody. "RIP IT DOWN!" The hardhats are backing away from us to the far side of the hole. This must look like the end of the world to them. Students attacking their own gymnasium! Behind us, someone snaps a photograph.

When the fence goes down, everything begins. The demonstration has become the Columbia Revolution. This first action will stretch into weeks, into five campus buildings, a thousand people arrested, a wave of similar "revolutions" on American campuses this spring.

We were born dreamers in the shadow of the bomb. Our dream was bound to break, explode, letting reality flood our sleeping heads with stark news. Vietnam was enough to puncture our American dream, our "good college" goals, the optimistic visions handed to us by our prosperous parents.

Add to Vietnam the violent confusion of black power. Then consider all the other ingredients: revolutionary technology, sexual revolution, population explosion, ecological crisis, drugs, assassination of leadership, on and on. When you reach the brim and the ingredients for chaos keep coming, and the mixture spills and the explosive fluid runs over the linoleum and under the doors, sit back. Light a fat American cigar. Consider what you have created. The sixties!

Perhaps God meant the sixties as a kind of purgatory for America. A decade of testing. All these crises adding up to a giant question for the American people. And what was our answer? To go to the moon.

Do you remember the girl in the photograph? Dancing across the lawn in Vermont?

We are standing beside the window looking down on Broadway. This is her small apartment on West 106th Street. The paddy wagons are endless. It is six in the morning. The green NYC Police Department trucks full of our brothers and sisters on their way to jail. Tonight was the night of the bust. It began before I could get in a building. But I was chased back and forth on the campus by the detectives in their Banlon shirts and khaki pants, with the saps like black figs in their hands, driving us into the mounted police who tried to herd us down Broadway. Two thousand students driven off their own campus. A litter basket explodes in the plate glass front of a dry cleaning store. The police get closer. We scatter into the side streets.

Now we are watching the people from the buildings being carted down the gray boulevard, down to The Tombs and their arraignments.

I lie down on the low bed underneath the window. Nora and I are in love. I pull her down beside me. I bury my face in her blond hair where it meets her neck and I wrap my arms around her. I will never let go. I do not want to die. Paranoia attack. The CIA, where are they? What about tonight? Students lying in pools of blood outside the Mathematics Building. I press my lips to Nora's skin, warm and white, the blue veins as clear as currents in the sky. Nora holds me but does not realize. Inside I am terrorized. I press my face into her. I do not want to die. "The FBI knows about you . . ." Angel of mercy, hold me tight as you can and do not let go.

We have been together for almost a year. Our relationship is "serious." This summer I am writing articles for *The Village Voice*. Also an interview with Mark Rudd for *Evergreen Review* and a short story which they publish in September. Nora spends her days studying dance with Merce Cunningham's studio. I am working on a novel called SPECKS, about how everything is just blown to bits. I use a small room in my friend John Taylor's apartment as an office. It is hot and stinking but I manage about four pages a day. In the next room, Gregory Corso, the Beat poet, and a friend of John's, is staying for the summer.

This afternoon we go to visit Nora's father and step-mother. They live in a penthouse on Fifth Avenue. The uni-formed "boy" from the Caribbean who drives the paneled elevator is very black and about thirty years old. I can hear the television.

Nora's parents are watching Robert Kennedy's funeral. Shots of the train passing through New Jersey. Then an inter-view with an SCLC leader named Hosea Williams from Resurrection City, the SCLC demonstration in Washington. Hosea is very angry. "We don't believe these assassinations are an accident. We believe there is a conspiracy. Too many of our most important leaders have been assassinated: John F. Kennedy, his brother Robert, Dr. King, Robert Spike . . . "

Murder.

_____

When I was a child, I had a recurrent nightmare. Something was chasing me toward the end of a pier in the dark. At the end, I looked into a black abyss. Then turned back to con-front whatever was pursuing me. Suddenly, I tripped and fell. Backwards, tumbling down and down into panic. I usu-ally woke from this dream loudly, screaming. My father would come from his bed to comfort me, to stay there until I was fast asleep again, my head on his chest, his arm around me strong and warm.

Now when I am anxious, I can feel this panic surround-ing me and I struggle not to fall. To tumble backwards off a nightmare pier from a child's dream into an adult abyss.

I have no father to put his arm around me. I have an "analyst." But comforting me is not part of his "treatment." I have a mother. But there are sixteen years of uncomfort-ableness between us. Finally, I have Nora. But with both her arms locked around me as tight as she can make them, both of us hidden in a private apartment far above the streets, when this panic begins there is only one rescue possible. The secret is that there is no mystery, no last "insight" to be scraped off the ground-zero of my unconscious mind. When I panic, when this anxiety attacks, it is with a jolt. Like a screamer sitting up in bed and letting out his yell into a dark void. The panic is a call for help. "Daddy, come here and let me know I am not alone in this world!" This is my own private panic. It may strike at any moment, in any situation: on a subway, eating ice cream in a shop on Central Park South, in the middle of a street.

The remedy is not a tranquilizer popped immediately. Nor is it to run home and lie down on my bed until I feel it pass. Nor is it to head for a bar and gulp three bourbons. There is only one way to dispel this. Look straight into the panic and say: "You *are* all alone. You want somebody to take care of you. There is nobody. You are alone but you can survive because . . . you *know* you can."

When I was in high school, as I have said, I read *The Myth of Sisyphus* by Albert Camus and nothing hit me harder or made more of an impression on me. I was fifteen. It was read outside of school, naturally, as "independent reading." Though I was not happy in the world of suburbia, I was certainly not thinking of suicide. Camus's book opens with the astounding statement that the most important philosophical question in the world is: Why not kill oneself?

In the next pages, he does not waste time or words. He doesn't bob and weave, box with the old religious or ethical reasons. Camus rips into life with fists, knees, elbows, streetfighting with every bit of gristle and bone in his body. He attacks the question: Why bother to live? Life is shit. Life hurts. Suffering is far more common than joy. Life is, at best, an "absurd" experience. Perhaps his existentialism is crude compared to Sartre or Kierkegaard. It is a fighter's philosophy, not a boxer's. Camus wants the answer if there is one and he will get it out of Life if he has to tear it out with his teeth. He wants to know why he has been born into this life.

In school I have been reading and listening, in social studies, in Citizenship, at assemblies, when the coach talks about life to his young athletes, and I have been getting nothing. I have been hearing excuses for life, but not reasons for living. Descriptions of various life styles and reasons to do this or that and why America is great and why I must go to a good university and it all rings hollow. Nobody believes these things they are telling me.

My father has struggled with the question as Camus has done. Once my mother told me about my father's first attack of severe anxiety. He was on a bus. His heart began to speed, careening out of control. Palpitations: a familiar anxiety symptom, of course. My father thought he was having a heart attack and about to die. It wasn't until fifteen years later that he could afford an analyst. He had, in the meantime, to face life without a Freudian guidebook. But he had his Christian beliefs. And in the end, it was to "God" that he turned. As he told me, "I rest in this feeling I call God."

What amazes me is that my father could have resisted the enormous temptation to instil "this feeling I call God" in me, his son. He had his answer to the question: Why bother to live this life of suffering? He could work it into life and he could even give it a name that others would recognize, and respect. But he had enough restraint to refrain from forcing this "God" onto me. He had complete faith in God. God was the foundation of his strength. Without his God, he would have been lost. Yet he would not do what so many other fathers have tried to do: give their son a "break." He would not force me full of religion, whether it be organized or his private visions. Instead, he told me to read books.

Camus found an answer. But he would not give it a name. It is given in the last line of *The Myth of Sisyphus:* "The point is to live."

This "point" assumes so much. It rests on no proof or empirical evidence. It is, it seems to me, the same kind of answer as my father found. It is a "feeling" which a man must finally rest within. Perhaps this is the same feeling which my father called "God." And I recognize this feeling inside myself. In the middle of a crowd, when I realize that I am all alone, when I think of the events which surround my existence, when there is a possibility of falling, falling through the floor and into an abyss . . . I get this feeling that I can finally rest within. As with Camus, it arrives without a label. "I will live . . . because I know I can."

What is this feeling? I suppose a psychologist would want to call it ego. Yet ego includes so many more pieces of equipment than this. Likely, this feeling is the tiny nucleus around which the ego was spun in the first place. But what is the feeling's name? Why give it one? Soldiers on the battlefield, mothers on the delivery table, athletes and ministers and salesmen, all men and all women: this feeling threads us together like paper dolls on a silver wire. This feeling from which the Will springs. This feeling that is unnamable.

But, see, father? See how you made your Conversion. I cannot resist. I must give this feeling a name. I call this "God." Once, I might have called this feeling "Father." But you died. And the irony of your murder: I learned how to be a man. As your life was taken from you.

The point is to obey the law of each moment. When caught in the gaps, stepping from one island in Time to another, anxiety flashes. Panic wants to send a scream crackling up the dry passage of my throat. I lean back into myself and search for this feeling.

"God will take care of the centuries," you wrote. I have never worried about a Century. It is the moments which heat or chill as they drop through my blood like crystals of possibility. This is called "living."

Father, I do not understand your death.

A NOTE ON THE TYPE

The text of this book was set in a face called
ENGLISH which is the film version of TIMES
ROMAN, designed by Stanley Morison for *The
Times* (London) and first introduced by that
newspaper in 1932.

Among typographers and designers of the
twentieth century, Stanley Morison has been a
strong forming influence, as typographical adviser to the English Monotype Corporation, as
a director of two distinguished English publish-
ing houses, and as a writer of sensibility, erudi-
tion, and keen practical sense.

Composed by University Graphics, Inc.
Printed by Halliday Lithograph Corporation
Bound by The Book Press, Inc.
Typography and binding design by
Christine Aulicino